John Locke's Two
Treatises of Government

John Locke's Two Treatises of Government

New Interpretations

EDITED BY EDWARD J. HARPHAM

 UNIVERSITY PRESS OF KANSAS

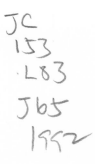

Published by the University Press of Kansas (Lawrence, Kansas 66049), which was organized by the Kansas Board of Regents and is operated and funded by Emporia State University, Fort Hays State University, Kansas State University, Pittsburg State University, the University of Kansas, and Wichita State University

Library of Congress Cataloging-in-Publication Data

John Locke's Two treatises of government : new interpretations /
    edited by Edward J. Harpham.
        p.   cm.
    Includes bibliographical references (p.   ) and index.
    ISBN 0-7006-0506-1 (hardcover : alk. paper)
    1. Locke, John, 1632–1704. Two treatises of government.
    2. Locke, John, 1632–1704—Contributions in political science.
    I. Harpham, Edward J.
    JC153.L83J65 1992
    320'.01'–dc20   91–27641

British Library Cataloguing in Publication Data is available.

Printed in the United States of America

10 9 8 7 6 5 4 3 2 1

The paper used in this publication meets the minimum requirements of the American National Standard for Permanence of Paper for Printed Library Materials Z39.48-1984.

To Wendy

Contents

Acknowledgments

A book like this has many friends who nurtured it from an idea to a working draft to a bound manuscript. Among this book's best friends are William Dennis and his associates of the Liberty Fund, who sponsored a 1988 symposium on Locke's *Two Treatises* in Dallas, Texas, for which these essays were originally commissioned. Participants at the symposium furnished valuable input on each of the essays. Sheryl Young helped make the symposium, and ultimately the conversation about the papers, work.

Other friends include Donald Dixon, Marilyn Herrick, and Peggy Ellis, who spent long hours proofing the text and researching the bibliography. Few political economists have been forced to read about Locke's *Two Treatises* as closely as these three. The book benefited greatly from their work and suggestions.

Ronald Terchek and Ruth Grant read the text in its entirety and furnished insightful comments on how to tighten up arguments both within and across the essays.

Gizelle Nunez, Donna Lamarita, Elvie Newbern, Cynthia Keheley, and Evelyn Stutts provided technical assistance in converting the essays into a common word-processing format. Retyping six lengthy essays on John Locke with extensive quotes from seventeenth-century English is a trying task at best. Their accuracy and good spirits through the entire project were deeply appreciated.

Michael Briggs of the University Press of Kansas was a good friend of the book from the outset. His support, patience, and understanding were deeply appreciated.

Perhaps the best friends of this book were three who were willing to obey the rules of justice and leave Daddy alone when he was in the study working on his book. But while Rebecca, Jessica, and William Harpham may be the book's best friends, Wendy Harpham remains the editor's. The book is dedicated to her.

Abbreviations for Works by John Locke

Correspondence	*The Correspondence of John Locke.* Ed. E. S. De Beer. 8 vols. Oxford: Clarendon Press, 1976–85.
ECHU	*Essay Concerning Human Understanding.* Ed. Peter Nidditch. Oxford: Clarendon Press, 1975.
ELN	*Essays on the Law of Nature.* Ed. W. von Leyden. Oxford: Clarendon Press, 1954.
FT or *ST*	Respectively *First Treatise* or *Second Treatise* in *Two Treatises of Government.* Rev. ed. Introduction and notes by Peter Laslett. New York: Mentor Books, 1965. Citations refer to paragraph numbers (no.). The 1965 Mentor edition of the Laslett text is a reprint of an edition of the *Two Treatises* originally published by Cambridge University Press in 1960 and reprinted with amendments in 1963. A second reprint with amendments was published in 1964. A second edition published in 1967 was reprinted with amendments in 1970. A student edition, published for the Cambridge Texts in the History of Political Thought series in 1988, contains some important updating in the introduction, the text, and the accompanying footnotes.
MS	Locke MS. Bodleian Library, Oxford University.
RC	*The Reasonableness of Christianity.* In *The Works of John Locke in Ten Volumes.* Vol. 7. London: T. Tegg, 1823.
1667 Essay	*An Essay Concerning Toleration.* In H. R. Fox Bourne's *The Life of John Locke.* Vol. 1. London: H. S. King, 1876.

SC   *Some Considerations of the Consequences of Lower-
                     ing of Interest and Raising the Value of Money.* Lon-
                     don: 1692. Reprinted in *Several Papers Relating to
                     Money, Interest and Trade (1696).* New York: Au-
                     gustus M. Kelly, 1968.

STCE   *Some Thoughts Concerning Education.* In *The Edu-
                     cational Writings of John Locke.* Ed. James L. Axtell.
                     Cambridge: Cambridge University Press, 1968.

TT   *Two Tracts on Government.* Ed. Philip Abrams.
                     Cambridge: Cambridge University Press, 1967.

Works 1823   *The Works of John Locke in Ten Volumes.* London: T.
                     Tegg, 1823.

Works 1824   *The Works of John Locke.* 12th ed., 9 vols. London: C.
                     and J. Rivington, 1824.

1 / *Locke's* Two Treatises in Perspective

EDWARD J. HARPHAM

The figure of John Locke looms large in the history of Western thought. Originally published in 1689, his *Two Treatises of Government* has long been recognized as one of the "great books" of political philosophy. Students and scholars have returned to it time and again, seeking out the intellectual origins of the modern world and the meaning of such fundamental political concepts as natural rights, social contract, limited government, and rule of law.

Given the large number of books and articles written on selected themes in the *Two Treatises* as well as the countless class hours spent by faculty and students alike scrutinizing the meaning of particular paragraphs in the text, one might think that it would be impossible to say anything new or different about the work. Surely a point must come in the interpretation of the work of any political theorist when diminishing returns set in and what is learned is hardly worth the energy committed to a particular intellectual inquiry.

Such is not the case with the *Two Treatises*. Far from working at the margins, Lockean scholarship has undergone a renaissance over the last thirty years that has recast our most basic understanding of Locke as a historical actor and political theorist, the *Two Treatises* as a document, and liberalism as a coherent tradition of political discourse. The Locke taught in the classroom of the early 1960s is a far cry from the Locke of the 1990s. Opening new avenues of inquiry, contemporary scholarship has raised fresh questions about the *Two Treatises* and its place in the history of Western political thought that are only beginning to be investigated. Scholars today can no longer simply read the work "on its own terms," as if its full meaning can be gleaned by a careful reading of the text alone. They must master a complex secondary literature that places the book in historical context and explains what particular arguments meant to Locke and to those who have read the *Two Treatises* at different times.

The secondary literature on the *Two Treatises* is almost as old as the work itself.[1] Interpretations and criticisms of it percolate throughout the eighteenth and nineteenth centuries in the works of such individuals as Bolingbroke, Mandeville, Rousseau, Hume, Smith, and the two Mills. For these individuals, the *Two Treatises* remained a point of reference against which their own political ideas could be developed. Their concerns were not so much to understand what Locke meant on his own terms but to use Lockean ideas, often critically, to highlight a particular problem that they were grappling with in their own thought.

Modern secondary scholarship on the *Two Treatises* has its genesis in the late nineteenth-century attempts to define and bring coherence to a history of ideas. Writers such as Leslie Stephen were particularly interested in reading Locke in terms of the history of liberal thought as it developed in Great Britain in the seventeenth, eighteenth, and nineteenth centuries. For early students of the history of ideas, the *Two Treatises* was part of a larger movement of thought that on the one hand sought to legitimate the revolutionary settlement of 1688 and on the other to lay the foundations for important philosophical approaches to be developed by later Enlightenment thinkers, including rationalism, hedonism, utilitarianism, and empiricism.

Such an approach dominated Lockean studies for the first half of the twentieth century as well. To be sure, there were differences in emphasis and orientation in these studies. While Sterling Lamprecht (1962) and Harold Laski (1920, 1936/1971) might agree that Locke presented a rationalistic approach to politics, they saw tensions in his work. For Lamprecht, it was a tension between rationalism and hedonism; for Laski, it was a series of "loose ends" in his philosophy and metaphysics that culminated in an "illogic" that was its "very strength" (1936/1971:78). Others were less favorable. George Sabine (1961), for example, saw an irreconcilable conflict in Locke's work between his political rationalism and his scientific empiricism that raised serious questions about his entire enterprise. W. Paschal Larkin, meanwhile, sought to uncover the role played by Lockean ideas in shaping eighteenth-century notions of property and concluded that his political and social theory "was neither remarkably deductive nor strikingly original" (1930/1969: 55).[2]

This early secondary literature tended to be based upon three working assumptions. First, it was accepted that we had a good understanding, or at least a good enough understanding, of who John Locke was and of why he wrote the *Two Treatises*. Locke was, in this regard, a conservative revolutionary who wrote the *Two Treatises* to justify in philosophical terms the Revolution of 1688. In the process he articulated the worldview of an emerging commercial society in England and its triumphant Whig oligarchy. Second, it was generally assumed that the best method for reading the *Two Treatises* was a detailed textual criticism of the work in light of Locke's other published works, particularly his philosophical and religious writings. Commentators thus assumed that the real meaning and significance of the text could be recovered through a careful reading and analysis of the text on its own. Finally, the *Two Treatises* was generally seen as part of a great "liberal" tradition whose origins lay in the seventeenth-century struggles against the Stuart monarchy and whose development was tied to the triumph of commercial and industrial capitalism in the eighteenth, nineteenth, and twentieth centuries. The *Two Treatises* thus was seen as one of the defining canons of the liberal tradition that stretched back in time to Thomas Hobbes and forward to Adam Smith and the two Mills in Britain and to the *Federalist Papers* and Thomas Jefferson in the United States.

A series of books written in the 1950s and early 1960s challenged many of the conclusions of these earlier interpretations of the *Two Treatises*. In *Natural Right and History* (1953), Leo Strauss located Locke's *Two Treatises* in a modern tradition of natural right.[3] Rejecting the idea that Locke was either confused or inconsistent, Strauss argued that the "prudent" and "cautious" Locke was a closet Hobbesian who sought to hide his radical philosophical claims behind what appeared to be a traditional natural-law argument. Locke's whole political philosophy was revolutionary in that it transformed the tradition of philosophical (and biblical) reasoning that had dominated Western thought since the ancient Greeks. "Through the shift of emphasis from natural duties or obligations to natural rights, the individual, the ego, had become the center and origin of the moral world, since man—as distinguished from man's end—had become that center of origin" (1953:248). For Strauss, the *Two Treatises* was a particularly modern political work and John Locke a particularly modern political writer. Indeed, he was the "most famous and the most influential of all modern natural right teachers" (1953:165). Many of the problems gripping contemporary thought could be directly attributed to the triumph of the natural-rights doctrines embodied in Locke's political thought.[4]

Along a considerably different line of thought, C. B. Macpherson (1962) provided a neo-Marxist reading of the *Two Treatises* that saw Locke's fundamental political ideas as the reflection of a new socioeconomic order. Like Strauss, Macpherson identified common themes that tied Locke's political thought to that of other liberals like Hobbes, the Levelers, and Harrington. His methodology for reading Locke, however, was strikingly different from Strauss's. By uncovering the "possessive individualistic" social assumptions that underlay Locke's arguments, Macpherson argued that the "contradictions and ambiguities" in Locke's thought were to be explained "by Locke having read back into the nature of men and society certain preconceptions which he generalized quite unhistorically, and compounded, rather unsystematically, with traditional conceptions such as those to which he assented in his frequent invocations of Hooker" (1962:197). The contemporary crisis in liberal democratic theory, in turn, was directly attributable to the triumph in modern thought of the possessive individualistic assumptions found in Locke's *Two Treatises*. As Macpherson explains, "the dilemma of modern liberal-democratic theory is now apparent; it must continue to use the assumptions of possessive individualism, at a time when the structure of market society no longer provides the necessary conditions for deducing a valid theory of political obligation from these assumptions" (1962:275).

In *Politics and Vision* (1960), Sheldon Wolin offered a third innovative reading of the *Two Treatises* that stood in sharp contrast to those of Strauss and Macpherson. For Wolin, the *Two Treatises* was best viewed as part of a larger movement in the history of Western political thought that saw the displacement of traditional political concepts by modern social and economic ones. The *Two Treatises* was a quintessential piece of liberal thought because of the social psychology and the constrained view of politics that was built into it. Like Strauss and Macpherson, Wolin attributed many of the problems facing contemporary political theory to the triumph of the liberal ideas found in the *Two Treatises*.

The bold interpretations offered by Strauss, Macpherson, and Wolin brought a new sensitivity to scholarly readings of the *Two Treatises*. Largely ignored passages were reread with different concerns in mind, and new appreciations emerged for the work's role in shaping modern political theory. Yet there were serious limitations to each, limitations that reflected in some ways the assumptions that had guided the earlier secondary literature. Neither Strauss, Macpherson, nor Wolin was particularly interested in pursuing historical questions such as who John Locke was as a real historical actor or why he wrote or published the *Two Treatises* at a particular time. Each wanted to fit excerpted passages from the text into a larger interpretive framework, one that accepted the existence and vitality of something resembling a liberal tradition. Their concerns were not so much to explain what the *Two Treatises* might have meant to Locke or his contemporaries on its own terms but to read the work as part of a larger story in the history of ideas that transcended the thought of any particular individual. Following the paths of earlier scholars, Strauss, Macpherson, and Wolin assumed that if the text were read carefully within the proper interpretive framework, its true meaning would emerge.

While the interpretations of Strauss, Macpherson, and Wolin were gaining popularity, three lines of inquiry began to raise questions about the proper way to read and interpret the *Two Treatises*. These, in turn, raised serious questions about the significance of the *Two Treatises* to Western thought in general and to the liberal tradition in particular.

Building upon and at times criticizing the pathbreaking work of Peter Laslett, scholars began a painstaking investigation to determine when the *Two Treatises* was written.[5] It was discovered that the manuscript originally had been written sometime between 1679 and 1682 and thus was a product of the pamphleteering debates during the engagement controversy. Far from being simply a philosophical defense of a revolution that had already occurred, the *Two Treatises* was shown to be a call to overthrow a regime whose legitimacy had come under question. This discovery sparked additional questions over the historical background to the document. Which treatise was written first? Did the arguments of one of the treatises presuppose the arguments found in the other? What was the political significance of Locke's publishing anonymously in 1689 a manuscript originally composed in the early 1680s?

In addition scholars began to investigate some of Locke's unpublished writings. In 1954 W. von Leyden edited Locke's *Essays on the Law of Nature*, a set of philosophic manuscripts written originally in Latin in his Journal in 1676. The *Essays* not only provided insight into the intellectual problems that Locke confronted as a young man but also shed light on the problems, contradictions, and tensions that commentators had found in the *Two Treatises* itself. It was discovered, for example, that many of the arguments and doctrines developed by Locke, particularly those associated with his doctrine of natural law, found their first articulation in the *Essays*. The *Essays* was followed in 1967 by the publication of *The Two Tracts of Government*, edited by Philip Abrams. *The Two Tracts*, probably written sometime between 1661 and 1664, was a polemical essay that presented strikingly authoritarian political conclusions along the lines of Hobbes. Along with other shorter pieces on justice, interest rates, the Glorious Revolution, and immigration, the *Essays* and *The Two Tracts* deepened the intellectual background that scholars could draw upon in their interpretations of the *Two Treatises*.[6]

A third line of inquiry that began to affect traditional readings of the *Two Treatises* lay outside formal Lockean scholarship. Beginning in the early 1960s, a debate broke out over the methodological foundations of political theory. Many leading political theorists began to question the legitimacy of reading any text in the history of political thought without a rich understanding of the historical and linguistic contexts within which the work's arguments operated.[7] The concerns of the audience and the intentions of the author were seen to be crucial elements of any interpretation of a text. Coupled to the other two lines of inquiry, this methodological debate laid the groundwork for a revisionist literature that challenged not only the traditional interpretations of the *Two Treatises* but also those of Strauss, Macpherson, and Wolin.

A major turning point in scholarship on the *Two Treatises* came in 1969 with the publication John Yolton's *John Locke: Problems and Perspectives* and John Dunn's *The Political Thought of John Locke*. Both books brought together many of the historical, textual, and methodological concerns that had begun to interest scholars in the 1960s. Yolton's book contained a number of insightful essays on aspects of Locke's political thought, including his theory of natural law and his notion of the state of nature, that would become classics for the next generation of scholarship. Dunn's book provided a comprehensive reinterpretation of the *Two Treatises* that directly challenged traditional scholarship on the *Two Treatises* and the interpretations of Strauss, Macpherson, and Wolin.

Dunn's goal was to free a reading of the *Two Treatises* from the assumptions that had dominated much of the earlier literature in order to provide "a more coherent and historically accurate account of what Locke was maintaining in the *Two Treatises* than has yet been given and a more coherent explanation of why he should have wished to maintain this" (1969:xi). Locke's religious preoccupations were, according to Dunn, the key to understanding the *Two Treatises*. Being neither a cunning defender of a modern notion of natural law, as Strauss had claimed, nor a bourgeois apologist for an emerging possessive individualist paradigm, as Macpherson had suggested, nor a champion of a depoliticized liberalism, as Wolin had argued, Dunn's Locke was instead a deeply committed

Christian whose political thought was part of a larger moral vision of the world grounded in the Puritan notion of the calling.

Dunn's book raised serious questions not only about the best interpretive framework from which to read the *Two Treatises* but also about its place in the liberal canon. If Locke was a committed Calvinist whose ideas on politics, epistemology, psychology, and rationality were premised upon a theological view of the world and the reality of the afterlife, how could he also be one of the founding fathers of a modern secular worldview such as liberalism? As Dunn notes, "the structure of Locke's thought may perhaps retain a certain potential embarrassment for the simpler devotee of liberalism" (1969:265). An article written by Dunn for the Yolton reader entitled "The Politics of Locke in England and America in the Eighteenth Century" (1969b) confirmed further this belief that Locke's relationship to later liberal thought was at best ambiguous. For Dunn, "the story of how *The Two Treatises of Government* was causally responsible (for what other sorts of responsibility could it bear?) for the direction of American political theory in the eighteenth century is, of course, largely false. Very similar judgements appear to be correct for the French, and to a lesser degree even for the English, experiences also" (1969a:7–8).

Dunn's conclusions about Locke's ambiguous legacy to eighteenth- and nineteenth-century Anglo-American thought received support from outside Lockean scholarship. In the late 1960s and early 1970s a series of books and articles appeared that reinterpreted seventeenth-, eighteenth-, and nineteenth-century thought in terms of a republican or civic-humanist tradition (see Bailyn 1967; Kramnick 1968; Pocock 1971a, 1971b, 1971c, 1975b; Robbins 1959; Wood 1969; Winch 1978). Stimulated by the work of J. G. A. Pocock, whose *Machiavellian Moment* supplied a breathtaking rethinking of Western political thought from sixteenth-century Florence to the American Founding, these republican interpretations effectively read liberalism, Locke, and the *Two Treatises* out of much of Anglo-American thought.

Throughout the 1970s and 1980s one new interpretation after another would uncover a previously misunderstood or not fully appreciated dimension to the *Two Treatises*. Geraint Parry (1978) and Eldon Eisenach (1981) offered scholars new insights into the religious dimensions of the work. James Tully (1980) and Richard Tuck (1979) respectively located Locke's theories of property and natural rights in the tradition of natural law and in the process provided readings of the *Two Treatises* that were both richer and more controversial than the traditional liberal reading of Locke had allowed. Tully in particular identified a communitarian dimension to Locke's arguments that effectively supplanted the notions that Locke was committed to the sanctity of property rights or to the separation of the political from the economic. Along another line of thought, Nathan Tarcov (1984) offered a different understanding of the moral concerns that lie embedded in Locke's political thought and in his theory of education. Julian Franklin (1978), meanwhile, discovered a radical Locke by reading his theory of sovereignty in light of the work of George Lawson, a political moderate of the later Interregnum who argued that one of the legal consequences of the conflict between king and Parliament in 1642 "was an entire dissolution of the government and reversion of power to the people, which was alone entitled to constitute a new authority" (Franklin:ix).

While this ongoing reassessment of the meaning and significance of the *Two Treatises* was taking place, scholars also began to draw upon and respond to a rapidly expanding literature on republicanism. Unwilling to blindly accept the pre-1969 characterizations of either Locke, the *Two Treatises*, or the liberal tradition, scholars nevertheless challenged the conclusion that neither Locke nor liberalism played an important role in defining political thought in the seventeenth and eighteenth centuries (see Appleby 1976a, 1978, 1986; Harpham 1984; Dworetz 1990; Wood 1991; Kramnick 1990). Perhaps the most intriguing outcome of this debate was the recognition that there were other viable traditions of discourse in the seventeenth and eighteenth centuries. Pocock himself came to accept the existence of a "civil jurisprudential" tradition whose "child" was liberalism, but curiously, he did not go into any detail explaining either the paternity or the legacy left to liberalism by civil jurisprudence (1983:249). Identifying Locke as part of a civil jurisprudential tradition enabled him to continue to reject conventional characterizations of a monolithic Lockean liberalism. Yet it also raised the sticky question of how Locke the civil jurisprudential thinker might have helped to articulate the problems and concerns of a later liberal tradition. The Locke that Pocock had thrown out the front door had effectively been allowed to return through the back.

The reassessment of Locke's *Two Treatises* culminated with the publication of two books by Richard Ashcraft in 1986 and 1987. The first, *Revolutionary Politics and Locke's Two Treatises of Government* (1986), was a masterful reconstruction of the intellectual and political environment within which Locke wrote the book. Moving beyond the work of Laslett and others who had located the initial writing of the *Two Treatises* during the engagement controversy, Ashcraft argued that Locke's ideas and conclusions were best understood as an expression of a radical political movement that posed a serious challenge to the existing social and economic order. Moreover, he suggested that the publication of the book in 1689 was not simply a defense of the Glorious Revolution but "one of the opening shots" fired in defense of a revived radicalism that was fearful of a growing conservatism among Court Whigs (1986:591). Working out of the background provided by his historical research, Ashcraft's second book, appropriately entitled *Locke's Two Treatises of Government* (1987), sought to provide an interpretation of the arguments and internal structure of the work. The book complemented his earlier work with an analysis of the religious and moral presuppositions that underlay the political language employed by Locke in the *Two Treatises*.

Ashcraft's works pulled together many of the historical and methodological concerns that had shaped revisionist scholarship on the *Two Treatises* for almost twenty years. They also helped to point out some of the questions about the *Two Treatises* that future scholars would have to confront in their own work. What did politics mean to John Locke in the *Two Treatises*, and how did his view of politics shape his view of political action? How far could a Calvinist reading of the *Two Treatises* be pushed? Had the picture of a radical communitarian Locke been pushed too far by revisionists like Tully and Ashcraft? How could the earlier radical Locke be reconciled with the conservative Locke of the later 1690s who sat on the Board of Trade and who called for recoinage along harshly deflationary lines? Was there any room left in our interpretations of Locke as a defender of modern rationalism or as one of the founders of a liberal political tradition? And finally, why have contemporary political philosophers come to read the *Two Treatises* in such a way that the historical Locke has all but disappeared?

The six essays in this volume were originally commissioned to address such questions for a conference sponsored by the Liberty Fund held in Dallas, Texas, on the *Two Treatises* in October 1988. The purpose of the conference was to assess the significance of the revisionist secondary literature on Locke's *Two Treatises* and to investigate the implications that this literature held for our understanding of various dimensions of the *Two Treatises*. The goal of the conference thus was not so much to seek closure on what might be considered the "right" interpretation or the proper methodological approach to reading the *Two Treatises* as it was to understand which doors had been opened by this scholarship, which had been closed, and which had been left ajar.

Four of the authors were asked to write on how the revisionist literature had transformed our appreciation of selected dimensions of the *Two Treatises*: its theory of politics, its religious underpinnings, its theory of rationality, and its understanding of the relationship between politics and economics in a commercial society. The remaining two authors were asked to inquire into how this literature had affected our understanding of the impact of Locke's *Two Treatises* on the development of Anglo-American thought in the eighteenth century and on contemporary political thought in the late twentieth century.

Richard Ashcraft's essay represents an extension of the arguments developed in his earlier work. His goals are twofold. First, he wants to show how the notion of politics found in the *Two Treatises* is premised upon certain ontological assumptions about the world and why Lockean politics can not be understood without reference to them. Second, he argues that there is a political realism to Locke's notion of politics, particularly in his theories of consent and elections, that is often missed or ignored by many commentators. Ashcraft's reading of the politics of the *Two Treatises* culminates in the defense of a Locke who is both theologically and philosophically more conservative as well as politically more radical than is generally granted in the literature. The recognition of this paradox, Ashcraft concludes, must be the starting point of any analysis of the politics of Locke's *Two Treatises*. Ashcraft also identifies a tension in Locke's thought between certain social practices and institutions that may be his true legacy to later liberal thought.

Eldon Eisenach investigates the religious dimensions to the *Two Treatises* by exploring three propositions that summarize the conclusions of recent scholarship on Locke's work: that Locke was a radical revolutionary whose *Two Treatises* was the basis of a left-wing critique of the regime established following the Glorious Revolution; that a deep skepticism regarding the reach of natural reason was built into Locke's thought, which was informed by a deep faith in the efficacy of biblical revelation as a source of moral and political duties; and that apocalyptic and millenarian notions of time are drawn from his theological speculations and built into his defense of reason and his theories of natural religion, natural law, and politics. In sharp contrast to earlier scholars who saw a cautious Locke revealed in his religious writings, Eisenach maintains that a "consistent and radical" anticlericalism ran throughout his religious writings and fed his radical politics. Viewing Locke's political thought from the perspective of his religious writings leads Eisenach to suggest that the trajectory of liberal ideas might not be linear but instead a complex series of spirals spinning from one topic to another.

Unlike Ashcraft's and Eisenach's essays, which expand upon recent revisionist interpretations of Locke, David Resnick's essay returns to a theme that had dominated much of the earlier literature: the idea that Locke was a rationalist who sought to create a theory of modern society. Although accepting the legitimacy of historicist approaches and the conclusions of recent scholarship, Resnick argues that we must nevertheless try to recover some of the insights of the older philosophical/analytical approach to reading Locke. From Resnick's perspective, Locke was committed to a critical rationalism that rejected traditional modes of political argument that appealed to custom and historical precedent and was grounded in a normative framework that was effectively free of modern criticisms of liberal social theory. By developing a Weberian interpretation of the *Two Treatises* Resnick explains how Locke articulated a liberal social theory that allowed him to criticize existing social and political institutions as irrational and to recommend rational means for their reformation.

In her essay "The Economic Background to Locke's *Two Treatises*" Karen Vaughn argues that Locke's understanding of the economic nature of human beings is the basis for his theory of civil government. Like Resnick, Vaughn is clearly dissatisfied with the tendency of recent scholarship to ignore or deemphasize certain dimensions of the *Two Treatises*. By viewing Locke's economic writings as important companion pieces to the *Two Treatises*, Vaughn shows how the political arguments developed by Locke in the *Two Treatises* were part of a larger view of a commercial society grounded in a sophisticated economic theory of value.

Ronald Hamowy's "*Cato's Letters,* John Locke, and the Republican Paradigm" is the first of two essays that attempts to assess the impact that the *Two Treatises* has had upon the Anglo-American tradition of political thought. A generation ago few would have questioned the importance of the *Two Treatises* to the development of Western political ideas in the eighteenth and nineteenth centuries. Indeed, much of modern political thought was identified with the rather nebulous term "Lockean liberalism." The emergence of a republican or civic-humanist interpretive paradigm over the past twenty years, however, has challenged this traditional view to the point that Locke has become for many a rather insignificant figure in the development of modern political thought. One of Hamowy's goals is to restore Locke to a central place in the history of eighteenth-century political thought. By examining the "Lockean" assumptions and arguments found in *Cato's Letters*, a work that for many is the paradigmatic example of civic-humanist thought in the early eighteenth century, Hamowy shows how Lockean ideas continued to shape political debate long after the events and context that had sparked the initial writing and publication of the *Two Treatises* had passed from the historical stage.

The final essay written by Stephen Newman uses the *Two Treatises* as a starting point for critically comparing two schools of contemporary political thought: libertarianism and communitarianism. The former school explicitly draws upon Locke's *Two Treatises* for inspiration in its militant defense of individualism and personal freedom in the modern world. The latter, on the contrary, views Locke as one of its archenemies and turns to supposedly anti-Lockean republican writers who championed the values of citizenship and public spiritedness over those of mean-spirited individualism. As Newman points out, however, the revisionist scholarship on Locke shows libertarians to be much less Lockean in their worldview and communitarians to be much more Lockean in their concerns than either ever imagined. Newman concludes that ironically both schools of contemporary thought might be well served by reexamining the theory of politics that lies embedded in the *Two Treatises*, a theory that is far richer than that offered by either side.

These essays are brought together in a single volume in the hope that readers will gain a deeper appreciation of how much our understanding of Locke's *Two Treatises* has changed over the last twenty years and of the importance that this has had for our understanding of the liberal tradition. The interpretive book on Locke and liberalism is by no means closed; indeed, it is probably more open today than it has ever been in the twentieth century. In coming to terms with Locke's *Two Treatises on Government* yet again, essays such as these should help us to understand more clearly the modes of discourse and forms of argument that have been and continue to be part of our liberal political culture. If it is even partly true that Americans are all Lockean, as Louis Hartz claimed, this is no small accomplishment. By understanding the *Two Treatises* and its legacy better, we may acquire a deeper appreciation of our collective past, our current dilemmas, and our future prospects.

NOTES

1. An excellent critical evaluation of the secondary literature on Locke can be found in Ashcraft's *Locke's Two Treatises of Government* (1987).

2. A notable exception to this dominant interpretive tradition is Willmoore Kendall's *John Locke and the Doctrine of Majority Rule* (1941). According to Kendall, Locke was a radical democrat who championed the cause of popular democracy rather than the interests of the propertied few. Significantly, he reached his conclusions through a creative, although rather tortuous, rereading of certain passages in the *Two Treatises*, adding nothing to our historical understanding of Locke's place in his own time.

3. A similar argument was developed by R. H. Cox in *Locke on War and Peace* (1960). See also Seliger (1968).

4. Strauss was explicitly ahistorical in his method, limiting himself to pointing out that the *Two Treatises* was the "civil presentation" of Locke's philosophy. "In the *Treatise*, it is less Locke the philosopher than Locke the Englishman who is addressing not philosophers, but Englishmen" (1953:220–21).

5. Among the most important contributions to this literature are Laslett (1956, 1960, 1988), Hinton (1974, 1977), Menake (1981, 1982), Goldie (1980a, 1980b, 1983, 1987), Tarlton, (1981), and Ashcraft (1980b, 1986, 1987).

6. See appendixes to Dunn (1968), Letwin (1965), Farr and Roberts (1987), and Resnick (1987).

7. Among the most important contributors to this debate are Quentin Skinner, J. G. A. Pocock, and John Dunn. Some of Skinner's most important essays have been collected along with essays by his critics in James Tully, ed., *Meaning and Context: Quentin Skinner and His Critics* (1988). See also Dunn (1962), Pocock (1971c, chap. 1), and Ashcraft (1986, "Introduction").

2 / The Politics of Locke's
Two Treatises of Government

RICHARD ASHCRAFT

In considering the politics of Locke's *Two Treatises of Government*, I propose to defend a broader definition of "politics" than the one generally found in the secondary literature on Locke. It is broader in two respects. First, Locke's conception of politics, as I will show, is premised upon certain ontological assumptions that supply the meaning and descriptive parameters for what counts as a "political" action. By this I mean not merely that a recognition of these—theological, philosophical, anthropological—presuppositions is useful as background information for an understanding of Locke's political thought; rather, I shall argue that Lockean political theory exhibits a structural dependence upon these assumptions such that its meaning cannot be understood without reference to them. Notwithstanding its contextual and contingent formulation in response to the political problems that emerged in Restoration England, therefore, there is a definite foundational framework upon which Lockean liberalism rests. Of course, this framework is itself rooted in certain cultural and intellectual developments that can be explained from a historical perspective, but the mere fact of historicity does not place all beliefs or social practices upon the same level of significance, nor do they display a univocal pattern of temporal change. The importance of this methodological pronouncement will become clearer as the argument of the essay proceeds, but it should be evident that I do not accept the view that Locke's *Two Treatises* must be read *either* as a compendium of philosophical statements about politics *or* as an occasional tract that polemically defends a partisan position with respect to the actions taken by a few politicians in late seventeenth-century England.

The second extension of the meaning of "politics," as I employ the term, addresses the latter interpretive standpoint, which is generally identified with a "historical" or "ideological" reading of the *Two*

Treatises. I shall argue that such interpretations, as presented in the secondary literature, are either too historically narrow in scope, focusing almost exclusively upon the particular sequence of events that constitutes the Glorious Revolution of 1689, or, paradoxically, that they are too abstract in their sociological formulation in characterizing the *Two Treatises* as an ideological defense of all the basic institutional features of capitalist society. Against the first view, I shall argue that Lockean liberalism provides a defense of specific social practices that both precede and transcend the particular events of 1689. Against the second view, I shall maintain that although it is true that some of these institutional features of Locke's society are also characteristic of capitalist societies, the latter are constituted, in part, by beliefs and practices that are quite alien to Locke's thought. Hence, Locke's *Two Treatises*, in its functional role as a work of politics, is a good deal more than a justificatory rationalization of a historical event and a good deal less than a conceptual expression of the complicated network of beliefs and social practices that, taken together, constitute a capitalist society.

In the first instance, I want to stress conceptual interdependence, a linking of ideas within a hierarchical theoretical structure—a worldview, if you like—as an essential feature of Lockean political theory. In the second instance, I shall emphasize the embeddedness of the meanings of those ideas in concrete social practices, institutions, and forms of collective action, where, from an explanatory viewpoint, beliefs are assumed not only to entail or to implicate other beliefs but also to function as reasons or causes with respect to social action. In short, the meaning of Locke's political theory, I shall argue, is rooted in a philosophical foundationalism and a sociological realism that, for the most part, Locke's interpreters have failed to grasp. Thus, against Strauss, I shall contend that Locke's belief in the Deity and in natural law commits him to a communitarian ethic and a politics of the common good rather than to a political order founded in subjective self-interest. Against Plamenatz (1963), Seliger (1968), and Dunn (1969a), I shall argue that Locke's discussion of "consent," for example, in the *Two Treatises* is not so philosophically abstract or confused as they assume but includes, as one of its meanings, the social practice of elections, reflecting a great deal more political realism on Locke's part than they are willing to concede in their interpretations of that work. Against Macpherson (1962), I shall insist that a society oriented toward amassing national wealth through trade—to which Locke was committed—cannot be simply equated with a society characterized by the social relations of capitalist production. Finally, against virtually all interpreters of Locke, I shall argue that their failure to give due emphasis to Locke's revolutionary objectives in writing the *Two Treatises of Government* effectively separates belief from action—political theory from practical action—in a manner that *necessarily* renders the meaning of "politics" abstract and vague, that is, divorced from those historical actors for whom Locke's political ideas were causally efficacious with respect to their efforts to achieve practical objectives.

Let me begin with an elaboration of the last point as a means of sketching the scope of the problem of reinterpreting Locke's political thought. Peter Laslett (1967) demonstrated in the introduction to his critical edition of the *Two Treatises* that that work was written as part of an endeavor to promote a revolution in the 1680s rather than to justify an already successful revolution in 1689.[1] Yet what exactly were the interpretive implications of this discovery with respect to Locke's political thought, viewed as a whole? Many scholars simply accepted Laslett's findings as constituting a minor adjustment as to the historical accuracy of the conditions surrounding the production of Locke's political theory, while the actual product, so to speak, remained substantially unaffected. Hence, no *theoretical* implications, it was assumed, were attached to the acceptance of Laslett's argument; and this was true, for the most part, even if one accepted that Filmer, not Hobbes, was Locke's chief opponent in the *Two Treatises of Government*. Lectures on Locke in university courses on the history of political thought could thus be preserved intact, and an uninterrupted flow of books and articles continued to present Locke as the defender of atomistic individualism, competitive self-interest, authoritarian liberalism, and capitalistic property owners.

For those interpreters who had constructed a mythical intellectual alliance between Hobbes and Locke, the latter's commitment to making a revolution ought to have served as a cautionary flag, signaling the need to rethink the presuppositions of their interpretive approach. Though Hobbes's ideas could be (and were) used to justify de facto a completed revolution, it certainly was not Hobbes's objective to urge his readers, as Locke does in the *Second Treatise* (no. 232), to resist the king, nor did anyone in seventeenth-century England understand Hobbes to be making such an argument. Moreover, this difference in intentional purpose and practical outcome between the political theories of Hobbes and Locke was not accidental or merely a contingent feature of the circumstances under which they formulated their respective political theories. Rather, it is a difference rooted in the very structure of the theories, such that absolute submission by the individual or collective resistance by the people *cannot* be a meaningful interpretation of the arguments advanced by Locke and Hobbes, respectively.

The question of how self-interested individuals could ever institute a sovereign through collective action has troubled readers of *Leviathan* from the outset, and, judging from the recent spate of books and articles in which interpreters have employed the precepts of game theory in their readings of Hobbes, the problem persists into the present. Yet even if the Hobbesian problem of collective action—viz., acting from a motive of fear to institute order in preference to chaos—were resolved, the answer would not satisfy Locke's requirements for collective action, which presuppose that the individual is obligated to the community to resist the rule of an absolute monarch to which the absence of any form of government at all (i.e., life in the state of nature) is to be preferred. It is, in short, an extremely difficult *philosophical* task—not to mention the issues relating to authorial intention, contextual evidence, or contemporaries' readings of the works by Hobbes and Locke—to formulate a theory of collective resistance beginning from the assumption of a Hobbesian war of all against all and the pursuit of individual self-interest. Not surprisingly, there is no discussion of Locke's commitment to revolutionary action in Macpherson's *Political Theory of Possessive Individualism* (1962) or in Leo Strauss's (1953) writings on Locke, where the interpretive objective is to make the reader believe that Hobbes and Locke share the same basic presuppositions about politics.

In addition to Laslett's research, a wealth of Locke manuscripts suddenly became available to scholars in the 1950s and 1960s. These unpublished materials provided a basis not only for a rethinking of the Hobbes/Locke relationship but also for a deeper understanding of the importance of Locke's religious beliefs to his political thought. The *Essays on the Law of Nature* (1954), in which Locke maintains a running argument against the Hobbesian perspective, is an especially significant work, one which Macpherson and the Straussians conveniently chose to ignore.[2] The otiose attempt to portray Locke as a secular thinker, either because he distanced his own beliefs from those of the masses (Macpherson) or because he concealed his true beliefs from public view for fear of persecution (Strauss), reflects a monumental obtuseness in the face of the massive evidence of Locke's religious convictions contained in these unpublished notebooks, journals, and private correspondence. True, these manuscripts include Locke's earliest writings in which he argues against religious toleration (1661–1662) in a most conservative, authoritarian, and Hobbesian manner, but Locke's reversal of his position on the question of toleration after 1667 (as well as natural rights, revolution, parliamentary sovereignty, and so on), should have been a sufficient reason for reinstating the intellectual distance between Hobbes and Locke for anyone familiar with the political debate over religious toleration in Restoration England.[3] Yet in fact a steady stream of interpreters of the politics of the *Two Treatises* persisted in ignoring the professions of Locke's religious beliefs and his conception of the Deity and the latter's relationship to natural law as well as to the political purposes to which Locke's writings were devoted; these elements were simply excluded from their interpretations of his political thought.

Supporters of the Hobbes/Locke paradigm, in other words, have been resistant, in the manner described by Thomas Kuhn in *The Structure of Scientific Revolutions*, to incorporating into their conception of political theory not only contextual evidence relating to Locke's intentions and political activity but also textual evidence that would extend the scope of Lockean political theory into the realms of theology and philosophy. Indeed this example provides only one illustration of the general tendency within the secondary literature on Locke to preserve a simplistic picture of his political thought—e.g., Locke the individualist, Locke the ideologue of capitalism, and so forth—when the evidence requires an interpretive approach that is both more comprehensive in scope and more complex in its structure. Such an extension of the meaning of politics, however, demands a defense of a paradoxical reading of Locke vis-à-vis the prevailing interpretive viewpoints. On the one hand, the philosophical/theological beliefs subscribed to by Locke are more conservative and traditional than the orthodox portrait of Locke as a modern secular thinker would suggest. On the other hand, the contextual evidence relating to Locke's political activity and his intentions in writing the *Two Treatises of Government* present Locke as a more radical and revolutionary thinker than the assumptions underlying the view of Locke as an exponent of orthodox Whiggism or as a cryptocapitalist allow (see Ashcraft 1986; 1987). Locke's thought is thus both philosophically more conservative and politically more radical than we have hitherto supposed. In short, Locke is at once closer to Aristotle and Hooker and to the Levelers and Sidney than the prevailing interpretations of his political thought maintain. It is with a recognition of this paradox and the complexity of the evidence that supports it—most of the evidence having been uncovered within the last three decades—that any analysis of the politics of Locke's *Two Treatises* must begin. Since I have dealt with these issues at considerable length elsewhere, my efforts in this essay to suggest the theoretical and the historical constraints operative with respect to the politics of the *Two Treatises of Government* must necessarily be rather schematic.

If one begins with the obvious, namely, Locke's definition of political power offered at the beginning of the *Second Treatise* (*ST*: no. 3), its notable features are its generic dependency upon conditions in which individuals are both free and equal with respect to each other and its employment on behalf of the public good. Neither of these aspects of political power can be understood, Locke insists, without reference to the Law of Nature, "which obliges every one," and which supplies the standard according to which specific determinations of the "public good" are made. This law is not only an objective rule of reason; it is also the intentional expression of a Deity's will (*ST*: nos. 4, 6, 8, 10). In the first few paragraphs of the *Second Treatise*, therefore, Locke makes it clear that political power operates only within the boundaries established by natural law and the "business" or purposes an "infinitely wise Maker" has set for his servants to accomplish (*ST*: no. 6).

This interconnection of politics, morality, religion—God-man-natural law—is neither incidental nor peculiar to the argument of the *Two Treatises*. "The belief of a Deity," Locke maintained, is "the foundation of all morality."[4] Without that belief the bonds of human society would dissolve, and, it follows, no political order could be established.[5] Since Locke viewed politics "as a part of moral philosophy," and the latter "comprehends religion too, or a man's whole duty," the conceptual linkage between religion, politics, and morality was a structural feature of Locke's thought (*Correspondence*, 6:215).[6] The key concept, common to all three provinces of life, was of course natural law. On the one hand, "the notion of a universal law of nature binding on all men necessarily" follows from a belief in God because, for Locke, existence always implies purpose (*ELN*: 133). That is, with an Aristotelian philosophical maneuver, Locke argues that God is that kind of being who not only must have given man a rule of reason to live by but who also intends that his subjects shall, as far as possible, be preserved (*ELN*:117, 199, 201). Philosophical knowledge of God's existence therefore presupposes, as a precept of Locke's theological conception of the Deity, the existence of a substantive law of reason directed toward the welfare of mankind.[7] Not surprisingly, Locke defines "the fundamental Law of Nature" as being "that all, as much as may be, should be preserved" (ST: no. 183; cf. nos. 7, 16, 135, 171). Hence, "the preservation of all mankind" constitutes "the true principle to regulate our religion, politics, and morality by" (STCE:116).

At the same time, the concept of natural law necessarily required, according to Locke, the presupposition of a lawmaker, for "without a notion of a law-maker, it is impossible to have a notion of a law" (ECHU, 1:4, 8; 1:3, 12; ELN:151, 173, 185). Thus, the Law of Nature is simply "the decree of the divine will," and as "the will of God," Locke insists, it is obligatory upon human beings "of itself and by its intrinsic force" (ELN:111, 113, 187; ST:135; ECHU, 1:3, 6). Whatever moral obligations human beings are presumed to have, therefore, can only be understood within a framework constructed from these basic presuppositions because "all obligation leads back to God, and we are bound to show ourselves obedient to the authority of His will because both our being and our work depend on His will, since we have received these from him, and so we are bound to observe the limits He prescribes" (ELN:183). Although it is true for Locke that "natural law stands or falls together with the nature of man as it is at present" (ELN:201), it is misleadingly narrow to suppose that Locke is simply offering another view of human nature to be contrasted with the one presented by Hobbes; rather, what is at issue is not merely a philosophical portrayal of mankind but also a different conception of natural law and a different understanding of the nature and role of the Deity vis-à-vis man from that contained in Hobbes's writings. Locke can therefore conclude that "since man has been made such as he is, equipped with reason and his other faculties . . . there necessarily result from his inborn constitution some definite duties for him, which cannot be other than they are" (ELN:199).

Moreover, for Locke, ought always implies can. That is, God would not have created individuals as they are and placed them under the "necessity" of performing certain "definite duties" if they were not in fact capable of fulfilling these obligations. To assume otherwise, Locke argues, would constitute an affront to "the wisdom of the Creator" (ELN:117). The ground of Locke's argument concerning natural law and the applicability of its precepts to the quasi-descriptive account of the actions of individuals in the state of nature in the Two Treatises therefore rests not upon the evidence relating to empirical human behavior but rather upon Locke's reading of the intentions of the Deity. "We cannot imagine," he asserts, that God "hath made anything with a design that it should be miserable" or that he would put human beings "in a worse state than destruction, misery being [a] much worse state than annihilation" (Locke, MS fol. 4, Journal, 1 August 1680; cf. *ECHU*, 2:27, 26).

If the Lockean state of nature is not a miserable Hobbesian condition of a war of all against all, it is not because Locke's reading of the record of human history is a peculiarly optimistic one but because, for Locke, man's ability to obey the Law of Nature follows from his presumption that "a manner of acting is prescribed to him that is suitable to his nature" by a God who cannot be assumed to have endowed man with reason and other capabilities that would remain unused by the vast majority of individuals (*ELN*:117). In short, "it is impossible," Locke declared, "that the primary law of nature is such that its violation is unavoidable." That statement occurs in an essay in which Locke argues that the Law of Nature is not premised upon the assumption that individuals pursue their self-interests.[8] If, therefore, natural law presupposes that individuals have obligations that extend beyond their subjectively defined self-interests, it must be possible, for the reasons I have suggested, for most people most of the time to fulfill those obligations in that natural condition in which God placed mankind.[9]

The specific "precepts of the law of nature," according to Locke, require us to demonstrate "sentiments of respect and love for the deity, obedience to superiors, fidelity in keeping promises and telling the truth, mildness and purity of character, a friendly disposition," and "love of one's neighbor" (*ELN*:129). Certain actions, such as theft, murder, and rape "are altogether forbidden" by natural law at all times and under all conditions. The Law of Nature, then, prescribes (or proscribes) specific sentiments, dispositions, and actions. In the seventh essay on natural law, Locke explains the several degrees of obligation attached to the various commands of that law. Not only is the prohibition on the actions mentioned above absolute, but also, Locke argues, individuals are required by the Law of Nature to entertain "certain sentiments" or "mental dispositions" at all times and under all conditions. Included in the latter category are a reverence for the Deity, affection for one's parents, and love and friendship for other human beings. Locke mentions a third area of obligation, viz., those actions that could be assumed to follow from the holding of such dispositions. These would include "the outward worship of the

Deity, the consoling of a distressed neighbor, the relief of one in trouble, and the feeding of the hungry," to cite only a few examples. With respect to these actions, however, Locke explains that "we are not under obligation continuously, but only at a particular time and in a particular manner." That is, "we are not obliged to provide with shelter and to refresh with food any and every man, at any time whatever, but only when a poor man's misfortune calls for alms and our property supplies means for charity" (ELN:193, 195; cf. ECHU, 1:3, 19). Some commands of natural law are therefore absolute; others are conditional as they pertain to human actions. Nevertheless, "the binding force of the law of nature is permanent, that is to say, there is no time when it would be lawful for a man to act against the precepts of this law" (ELN:193, 197).[10] In other words, there is no time in which an individual in the state of nature could entertain a hostile disposition toward others without violating the precepts of natural law.[11] Indeed, since Locke defines a state of war in dispositional terminology—a state of enmity and declared intention even in the absence of specific actions (FT:131; ST: nos. 16, 17)—he cannot help but characterize the state of nature, in part, by the holding of a different set of mental dispositions, i.e., those in accordance with the commands of natural law. Still, "this permanently binding force must not be supposed to be such that men would be bound at all times to perform everything that the law of nature commands." Taking into account the conditions that actually exist, both in the state of nature and in civil society, Locke believes that it will not always be possible for an individual to execute an action that follows from his maintaining certain sentiments. In the end, Locke concludes, "we can sometimes stop acting according to the law [of nature]," but we are never entitled to "act against the law" (ELN:193).[12] It is within this philosophical/theological framework—reaffirmed in Locke's writings on education and in his notebooks—that one ought to understand the meaning of politics as outlined in the Two Treatises.

Locke maintains that every individual has a "right" to enforce the Law of Nature and to assist others in enforcing it (ST: nos. 7–13). This right, like all Lockean natural rights, is premised upon a natural-law obligation, in this case, the individual's obligation to preserve mankind. That individuals in the state of nature are presumed capable of acting for the common good (the preservation of mankind) logically presupposes that they have "some sense of a common humanity, some concern for fellowship" (ELN:205; ST: no. 107). Thus, Locke argues, they are members of a "great and natural community" whose "common interests" and "fellowship" are established by the precepts of the Law of Nature (*ELN*:163; *ST*: nos. 128, 172). In other words, if political power as it emerges from the natural condition of mankind is inextricably bound to the realization of the common good, it is because Locke's conception of the state of nature allows for no other meaning. "So that the end and measure of this power, when in every man's hands in the state of nature, being the preservation of all of his society, that is, all mankind in general, it can have no other end or measure, when in the hands of the magistrate, but to preserve the members of that society in their lives, liberties, and possessions" (*ST*: no. 171).

If those who attribute to Locke a political perspective grounded in the pursuit of subjectively defined self-interest have failed to grasp the ontological foundations of Locke's cosmology or the ethical implications of his theologically centered worldview, it is no less true that Locke's theory of personal identity as an ontological/ethical characterization of the individual has rarely received the attention it deserves as a crucial ingredient of his political thought. Because Lockean political society is instituted by individuals who are endowed with specific powers and abilities, it is evident that the political argument of the *Two Treatises* is dependent upon certain philosophical assumptions concerning the internal constitution of man as a political actor. Any understanding of political power, according to Locke, depends upon the supposition that all individuals have "a perfect freedom to order their actions, and dispose of their possessions, and persons as they think fit, within the bounds of the Law of Nature, without asking leave, or depending upon the will of any other man" (*ST*: no. 4; cf. nos. 6, 22). What this means with respect to Locke's discussion of property and consent in the *Two Treatises* we shall see in a moment, but first it is necessary to consider the philosophical foundation for the concept of a "free man," which Locke employs in that work as his basic unit of politics.

Neither politics nor morality would be imaginable without the concept of a "person," which, Locke argues, "belongs only to intelligent agents capable of a law, and happiness and misery." The "self," that is, must be capable of consciously "appropriating actions" as its own and of experiencing "pleasure or pain; i.e., reward or punishment, on the account of any such action." For, Locke observes, "the personality extends itself beyond present existence to what is past, only by consciousness, whereby it becomes concerned and accountable, owns and imputes to itself past actions, just upon the same ground, and for the same reason, that it does the present" (ECHU, 2:27, 11, 17, 18). It is precisely this linkage between consciousness and action that allows us to treat the individual "as an intelligent being subject to government and laws, and accountable for his actions" according to some standard of morality (Works 1824, 2:320). Some understanding of Locke's concept of "personal identity" is therefore essential to any critical assessment of Lockean political theory, which explains the origins of political society in terms of the actions of "intelligent agents."

No one "can be capable of a law," Locke declares, "that is not a free agent" (ECHU, 1:3, 14). Since liberty consists "in a power to act, or not to act,". an individual must be in a position to exercise that power over his own actions through an act of will (ECHU, 2:21, 23, 47). "Every man is put under a necessity by his constitution, as an intelligent being, to be determined in willing by his own thought and judgment, what is best for him to do: else he would be under the determination of some other than himself, which is want of liberty" (ECHU, 2:21, 48). A free, intelligent agent, therefore, is an individual whose action is consciously guided by his own judgment, where the latter implies that "thought" determines the "will." Locke's argument in the Essay Concerning Human Understanding—here schematically stated—is that the individual has the power "to suspend the execution and satisfaction of any of [his] desires. . . . In this lies the liberty man has" (ECHU, 2:21, 47). "All the actions" of individuals, according to Locke, can be reduced "to these two, viz., thinking and motion." Thus, "so far as a man has a power to think, or not to think; to move, or not to move, according to the preference or direction of his own mind, so far is a man free" (ECHU, 2:21, 8). So that, "during this suspension of any desire, before the will be determined to action, and the action . . . done, we have opportunity to examine, view, and judge, of the good or evil of what we are going to do" (ECHU, 2:21, 47). Against Hobbes, Locke argues that "deliberation" cannot be equated with the pursuit of one's last appetite but must be seen as a conscious act of an intelligent agent who was free to act otherwise than he did. To put it simply, because Locke's discussion of action and the will "supposes knowledge to guide [the individual's] choice," Lockean man is by nature—that is, by "the necessity of his constitution"—a subject of reason rather than a slave to desire (ECHU, 2:21, 50, 52).[13]

Moreover, Locke believes that God "has put into [individuals] the uneasiness of hunger and thirst, and other natural desires" that "move and determine their wills, for the preservation of themselves, and the continuation of their species," all of which is "suitable to our constitution and frame" according to the wisdom of the Deity (*ECHU*, 2:21, 34; 2:31, 2; 2:32, 14). God has also "given a power to our minds . . . to choose amongst its ideas" and thereby a power to determine all our actions (*ECHU*, 2:7, 3). In other words, God "has furnished man with those faculties, which will serve for the sufficient discovery of all things requisite to the end of such a being" (*ECHU*, 1:4, 12; 2:23, 12). And since He "requires of us no more than we are able to do," (*ECHU*, 2:21, 53), it is evident to Locke that if we are "sent into the world by his order and about his business" (*ST*: no. 6), we must be capable of accomplishing that end. Human beings exist in a world structured by moral obligations, but they are endowed by their Creator with those natural powers that enable them to fulfill those obligations. To assume otherwise not only challenges Locke's philosophical explanation of the internal constitution of the individual as a rational free agent, but it also constitutes an affront to his theological conception of God.

It can hardly be surprising, therefore, that Locke's definition of a free man in the state of nature presupposes an individual capable of examining his various desires and of weighing them against each other in order to avoid acting upon "a too hasty compliance" with any desire rather than on the basis of a "mature examination" of the consequences of such an action (*ECHU*, 2:21, 52–53; cf. *ST*: no. 8). Such a "person," as a general characterization of mankind, simply cannot be supposed to exist naturally in a state of war where both the inclinations and the actions of individuals are contrary to the precepts of natural law. As Locke observes in the *Second Treatise*, "God having given man an understanding to direct his actions, has allowed him a freedom of will, and liberty of acting, as properly belonging thereunto, within the bounds of that law he is under" (*ST*: no. 58). And that law, according to Locke's definition, "prescribes no farther than is for the general good of those under that law," which he equates with "the direction of a free and intelligent agent to his proper interest" (*ST*: no. 57). "The freedom then of man and liberty of acting according to his own will," Locke argues, "is grounded on his having reason, which is able to instruct him in that law he is to govern himself by," so that, with reference to individuals in the state of nature, Locke insists that they must be "presumed to know how far that Law [of Nature] is to be [their] guide" (*ST*: no. 59). Thus, an individual can "be supposed capable of knowing the [natural] law, and so living within the rules of it" (*ST*: nos. 60, 170).

Locke's "philosophical" person, in short, is not only capable of making and obeying laws; he is also capable of suspending the gratification of a desire in his immediate self-interest in order to realize a greater good, such as the preservation of mankind. It would not be necessary to dwell on this point, which Locke emphasizes at length in the *Essay Concerning Human Understanding*, the *Essays on the Law of Nature*, and *Some Thoughts Concerning Education*, were it not for the fact that the politics of the *Two Treatises of Government* is so rarely discussed in terms of these writings or of the "internal constitution" of the political actors who inhabit Locke's state of nature.

Since a recognition of the structural importance of these philosophical/ theological presuppositions to Locke's political thought has been obscured in part by some interpreters' attribution to Locke of certain beliefs concerning the sociological constitution of political society, I want to shift the ground of discussion toward a consideration of those aspects of the argument in the *Two Treatises* that reveal what I earlier referred to as Locke's political realism. In *The Political Theory of Possessive Individualism*, C. B. Macpherson (1962:222, 226) argues that Locke excluded the laboring class from membership in political society on the grounds that they lacked sufficient rationality. This assertion was supported by Macpherson's contention that Locke subscribed to a view of "differential rationality"; that is, "when Locke looked at his own society he saw two classes with different rights and different rationality" (229). In Macpherson's reconstruction of Locke's thought, rationality is tied to property ownership and indeed to the unlimited accumulation of property (232–38). The latter endeavor is justified by Locke, according to Macpherson (218, 221, 231), as a natural right in the context of the discussion of property in chapter 5 of the *Second Treatise*. Only property owners give their express consent to the formation of political society; propertyless individuals, Macpherson writes (249–50), are obligated to obey the laws through the medium of tacit consent, notwithstanding the fact that they do not participate in the political process. Locke's political theory, Macpherson concludes (208, 221), supplies a justification for "the specifically capitalist appropriation" of property and for the institutions of capitalist society. In the discussion that follows, I shall argue that every one of Macpherson's propositions is mistaken. At the same time, however, I shall maintain that there is a clear and powerful argument in the *Two*

Treatises that draws its support from Locke's sociological realism, i.e., his recognition of certain social relationships and practices in seventeenth-century England.

As we have seen, Locke's political argument is grounded upon an assertion of moral egalitarianism with respect to the rationality of the individual, a normative proposition that, he believes, follows from his ontological description of the individual and ultimately from his theological conception of the Deity. At what point, therefore, does a standard of "differential rationality" set aside or displace this basic assumption? Macpherson (230, 232) concedes that there is no statement by Locke of such a position in the *Two Treatises*. Rather, he argues, the class-oriented definition of rationality is presented in *The Reasonableness of Christianity*, although he maintains that the distinction was implicitly relied upon by Locke in the *Second Treatise*. I have argued elsewhere (Ashcraft, 1987: 251–59) that Macpherson's misreading of *The Reasonableness of Christianity* cannot withstand a careful examination of the text or of Locke's purposes in writing that work. It follows that that misreading cannot be imported into an interpretation of the *Two Treatises*. With respect to the latter, let us take a closer look at the specific criteria upon which Locke relies for a determination as to when a person can be adjudged a rational agent for political purposes. Locke maintains that there are only two such criteria: age and the use of one's natural ability to reason. Is a person free according to the Law of Nature, Locke asks. "What gave him a free disposing of his property according to his own will, within the compass of that law? I answer; state of maturity wherein he might be supposed capable to know that law" and so "keep his actions within the bounds of it. When he has acquired that state, he is presumed to know how far that law is to be his guide, and how far he may make use of his freedom, and so comes to have it" (*ST*: no. 59). Twenty-one, Locke observes, is the age commonly accepted as evidence of one's maturity, so that upon reaching that age the individual must be accepted as a free man. Locke is even willing, contrary to the then existing laws of England, to extend his argument, insisting that an individual is technically "a subject of no country or government . . . till he comes to age of discretion; *and then he is a freeman*, at liberty what government he will put himself under; what body politic he will unite himself to" (*ST*: no. 118). Thus, "age and reason . . . leave a man at his own free disposal" (*ST*: nos. 55, 57–59, 61, 75, 170).

Locke cites an example to illustrate his argument for presumptive reason, which, like the statements above, has nothing whatever to do with property ownership. "Commonwealths themselves take notice of, and allow that there is a time when men are to begin to act like free men, and therefore till that time require not oaths of fealty, or allegiance, or other public owning of, or submission to the government of their countries" (*ST*: no. 62). In the seventeenth century, oaths were administered to civil servants, schoolteachers, members of the armed forces, the clergy, members of livery companies and corporations, and many other individuals. Oath taking is not a criterion that can be linked in any meaningful sense to property ownership of any type or amount, but it demonstrates, Locke believes, that governments act according to the customary belief that individuals at the age of discretion, whatever their social station in life, may be presumed to have sufficient reason to govern themselves in their political actions. Without such an assumption, it would be as foolish to ask them to swear their allegiance to the state as it would be to administer such oaths to children.

Locke's definition of a "freeman" is so clear and unequivocal and is not in any sense linked with property ownership that it is hard to know what to make of an interpretation that simply disregards the text so completely as Macpherson's reading of it does. When Locke writes that "*nothing but* the consent of any number of freemen capable of a majority to unite and incorporate into such a society . . . is that, and that *only*, which did, or could give beginning to any lawful government in the world" (*ST*: no. 99), there is not the slightest reason for believing that "freemen" in this passage is defined in any sense differently from Locke's explicit definition of a "freeman" offered forty paragraphs earlier.

Let us examine the relationship Locke establishes between political rationality, property, and consent more closely. Throughout the *Second Treatise*, and always at crucial points in the development of his argument, Locke repeatedly states his initial premise that every individual possesses the same freedom and natural rights as any other individual (*ST*: nos. 87, 95, 123). He is able to maintain this position because he makes it clear on three separate occasions that "by *property* I must be understood here, as in other places, to mean that property which men have in their persons as well as goods" (*ST*: no. 173; cf. nos. 87, 123). That is, the structure of Locke's political argument requires a broad definition of property in order to preserve the normative link between natural rights, political power, and the common good.

"Every man," Locke observes, "is born with a double right: first, a right of freedom to his person," which means "the free disposal of it lies in himself," and "secondly, a right, before any other man, to inherit, with his brethren, his father's goods" (*ST*: no. 190). "By the first of these, a man is naturally free from subjection to any government," and it is only through his consent as an intelligent agent that he places himself under a lawful government (*ST*: no. 191). However, if individuals wish to "retain a right to the possession of their ancestors," Locke argues, they may have to give their consent to the government on the conditions it offers them, and this consent they are free to withhold; they may withdraw themselves from that society and submit to a government more to their liking (*ST*: no. 192). Membership in political society, in other words, is in no way dependent upon ownership of property; on the contrary, the individual's ownership of property is conditional upon his having consented to be a member of political society, and the latter, in Locke's argument, follows directly from the presumption that *every* individual has a natural right to dispose of his "person" as he sees fit. Thus, referring to individuals as free men, Locke declares, "their persons are free by a native right, and their properties, *be they more or less*, are their own, and at their dispose" at the time they constitute political society (*ST*: no. 194). "By which means," Locke explains, "every single person became subject, equally with other the meanest man, to those laws, which he himself, as part of the Legislative had established" (*ST*: no. 94). As Laslett (1967:348n) remarks, the reference to "the meanest man,"—i.e., the individual's *lack* of property—as part of "the legislative power" of the community certainly suggests that he is a member of political society, exercising his political power through consent, notwithstanding the paucity of his possessions.

Moreover, when Locke amplifies the meaning of his pronouncement (on which Macpherson lays great interpretive weight) that "the supreme power cannot take from any man any part of his property without his own consent" (*ST*: no. 138), he does so with an illustration—not discussed by Macpherson—in which a common soldier is assumed by Locke to possess "an estate" that cannot be taken from him without his consent (*ST*: no. 139). This can hardly be surprising to any reader of the *Letter Concerning Toleration*, where the purpose of political society is defined in terms of preserving the "civil interests" of individuals, which consist of life, liberty, health, "and the possession of outward things, such as money, lands, houses, furniture, and the like," a list not notable for its exclusion of any particular group of individuals, except, possibly, the homeless (*Works 1824*, 5:10).[14] That "estates" or "property" necessarily carry a reference to aristocratic landowners is simply a fiction of Macpherson's making. It not only has no textual support, but Locke's persistent usage of an extended view of "property," his distinction between the natural rights of one's person versus the conditional or conventional rights or property in a narrow sense, and his application of consent, political rationality, and the exercise of political power to those with little or no property, narrowly defined, all point to a meaning of political rationality that is far more radical in its implications than Macpherson's perspective is capable of recognizing.

Macpherson's (1962:248ff.) confusion, which he ungenerously attributes to Locke, is manifest in his treatment of the distinction between tacit and express consent, into which he attempts to read a class differential, separating the propertyless subjects from the property-owning full members of Lockean political society. Locke, however, applies the concept of tacit consent to "*every man, that hath any possession or enjoyment, or any part of the dominions of any government,*" where possession is identified with land or "lodging only for a week" or use of the highway (*ST*: no. 119). In short, there is no class differential whatsoever contained in the concept of tacit consent; it applies to property owners and propertyless individuals alike. Locke wants to show that all property rights beyond subsistence are conventional, which is to say, conditional property rights; that there is a correlative relationship between benefits and obligation, mediated through the notion of tacit consent; and that only express consent by an individual—any individual—can make him a member of political society.

According to Locke, all individuals "have a right to their preservation, and consequently" to such things as maintain "their subsistence." This natural-rights claim is supported by both natural reason and revelation (*ST*: no. 25). "Man had a right to a use of the creatures, by the will and grant of God . . . and thus man's property in the creatures, was founded upon the right he had, to make use of those things, that were necessary or useful to his being" (*FT*: nos. 86–87). This natural "right everyone [has] to take care of, and provide for their subsistence," Locke argues, is justifiable, ultimately, because in acting "to preserve his being, [the individual] followed the will of his Maker" (*FT*: no. 86). A natural right to subsistence, in other words, is a necessary means of fulfilling the obligation of natural law to preserve mankind, which expresses the intentional design of the Creator in "willing" the Law of Nature in the first place. Thus, children have a natural right to subsistence, which is derivable in Locke's argument from the natural-law obligation parents have to nourish and preserve their children (*FT*: nos. 88–91, 93). More generally, Locke declares that "he that hath, and to spare, must remit something of his full satisfaction, and give way to the pressing and preferable title of those, who are in danger to perish without it." This declaration is defended by Locke through an appeal to "the Fundamental Law of Nature," which decrees "that all, as much as may be, should be preserved" (*ST*: no. 183; *FT*: no. 42). Elsewhere, Locke wrote that "everyone must have meat, drink, clothing, and firing. So much goes out of the stock of the kingdom, whether they work or no."[15] Although the natural right to subsistence follows from the natural-law obligation to preserve mankind and *not* from the activity of labor, a natural-rights claim does follow from that activity.

Labor is not only the reasonable means by which most people will, most of the time, provide for their subsistence, but Locke again offers a higher justificatory defense that labor is the individual's "title" to property. Thus, "God, when he gave the world in common to all mankind, commanded man also to labor." That is, he "commanded him to subdue the earth, i.e., improve it for the benefit of life" through cultivation. Therefore, "he that in obedience of this command of God, subdued, tilled and sowed any part of [the earth], thereby annexed to it something that was his property"—viz., his labor—"which another had no title to, nor could without injury take from him" (*ST*: no. 32). "So that God, by commanding to subdue, gave authority so far to appropriate" the materials He had provided to mankind, and the execution of this divine command in the state of nature "necessarily introduces private possession" (*ST*: no. 35). Now this is a very specifically structured argument that ties labor as an activity to the fulfillment of God's command (and intentional purposes), placing labor, as a necessary means to an end, in the category of the natural-rights claims already described.

Because Macpherson (1962:218, 231) pays no attention to the theological and hierarchical dimensions of Locke's thought, he simply interprets the meaning of natural right in the *Two Treatises* as anything that, in a quasi-descriptive sense, occurs in the Lockean state of nature. This will not do. Lockean natural rights always refer to natural-law obligations and, as we have seen, in a rather specific sense. Moreover, the individual's right to the products of his labor *may* have to give way to the superior-rights claim of another for subsistence, precisely because there is a higher obligation to preserve mankind, which must be fulfilled when the circumstances permit. And this obligation presupposes no special altruism on the part of individuals as an empirically descriptive account of human behavior; rather, it is referable to the will and intentional design of God.

Now it should be obvious that "the invention of money" through "the tacit agreement of men to put a value on it" introduces "by consent larger possessions, and a right to them," which is a conventional and not a natural right (ST: nos. 36–37, 45, 47, 50). Not only can no natural-law obligation—and therefore, no natural right—"be inferred from the general consent to be found among men," but in attacking this proposition in the *Essays on the Law of Nature*, Locke specifically cited the example of the acceptance of gold by individuals as an action that was not "decreed by natural law" (ELN:177). And in the *First Treatise* Locke wrote that "common tacit consent," such as that which accounts for the invention of money, creates "but a positive and not a natural right" (FT: no. 88). In short, consent in any form can neither create nor supersede a natural right. It follows that all property dependent upon the consent of men is a conventionally held right (see Ashcraft 1987:137–43; Tully 1980). Indeed, it is precisely this fact that in the state of nature necessitates some "umpire" to interpret and to adjudicate the conflicting claims arising from the agreements among individuals.

Moreover, when the individual incorporates himself into the community, he "submits to the community those possessions, which he has, or shall acquire" (ST: no. 120). Individuals now "have such a right to the goods, which by the law of the community are theirs" (ST: no. 138). The use or enjoyment of property by an individual is henceforth subject to the conditions imposed upon citizens by the commonwealth (ST: no. 120). Thus, Locke argues, "the laws regulate the right of property, and the possession of land is determined by positive constitutions" (ST: no. 50; cf. no. 45). This regulative function of government, according to Locke, is not merely negative or custodial but also extends to vaguely positive injunctions because "the increase of lands and the right employing of them" as well as the "encouragement [of] the honest industry of mankind . . . is the great art of government" (ST: no. 42). For reasons we will consider more fully in a moment, the rights of property ownership, excepting subsistence, are for Locke subject to *and not determinative of* the rights of political power.

Since the latter flows directly from "express consent," the problem for Locke is not, pace Macpherson, how propertyless individuals can be brought within the framework of political obligation through tacit consent but rather how the property owner—especially the landowner—who has *not* given his express consent can be said to be obligated to obey the government's laws. This issue arises, be it noted, because *ownership of property is, in itself, no evidence that the individual has expressly consented to anything.*[16] Not only does Locke not assume an identity between property ownership and membership in political society, but he presupposes a disjunction between express consent (membership) and property ownership for which the concept of tacit consent serves as the bridge. It can do so because Locke subscribes to the belief—held by many of his contemporaries—that there is a correlative relationship between benefits and obligations. Thus, referring to the landowner, Locke observes, "the obligation anyone is under, by virtue of such enjoyment, to submit to the government, begins and ends with the enjoyment; so that whenever the owner, who has given nothing but such tacit consent to the government, will, by donation, sale, or otherwise, quit the said possession, he is at liberty to go and incorporate himself into any other commonwealth" (*ST*: no. 121). In short, tacit consent and property ownership are conditional, but any person is at liberty to exercise his natural right to give his express consent to any government of his choosing because, Locke insists, the natural right of one person cannot be exercised or given away by another—e.g., one's father (*ST*: nos. 116–17)—nor can it be "bounded by the positive limits of kingdoms and commonwealths" (*ST*: no. 118).

We are therefore returned to the proposition that "submitting to the laws of any country, living quietly, and enjoying privileges and protection under them, makes not a man a member of that society. . . . Nothing can make any man so, but his actually entering into it by positive engagement, and express promise and compact" (*ST*: no. 122). Having dealt specifically with the landowner in relation to tacit consent, Locke reaffirms his association of express consent with the universalist language of "every man" (*ST*: no. 120) or "any man" (*ST*: no. 122). Locke's distinction between tacit and express consent does not provide evidence for differential class membership or rationality; it does provide, on the contrary, a defense of Locke's association of the "native right" an individual has over his person with an act of express consent as the exclusive condition for membership in political society where every person, without qualification, is assumed by Locke to possess such a natural-rights claim. Indeed, the structure of Locke's argument, as well as the specific criteria he incorporates into his definition of a free man, restates the position defended by the Levelers at the Putney Debates.

If one asks, what was it, really, that made the Levelers' argument appear so challenging to the conventional political wisdom, the answer, I think, has to be their notion that political power could be separated from property ownership. Harrington's neo-Aristotelian argument that changes in the form of property ought to be reflected in the redistribution of political power, as disturbing as that idea was to nonrepublican seventeenth-century Englishmen, seems positively conservative when set alongside the Levelers' insistence that "the poorest he" had a natural right to exercise political power. To put it simply, in their terms, owning property had a traditional but no reasonable relationship to the possession of political power. What Macpherson (and others) fail to grasp is that this is precisely the position adopted by Locke in the *Two Treatises*, and its appearance there carried no less a radical resonance with Locke's contemporaries than it had forty years earlier in the Levelers' tracts.

In the *First Treatise*, Locke launches a relentless attack upon Filmer's assumption that ownership of property supplies a "title" to political power. Even if "Adam was made sole proprietor of the whole earth," as Filmer claimed, Locke asks, "what will this be to his sovereignty?" That is, how could one suppose "that property in land gives a man power over the life of another" (*FT*: no. 41)? Not only does Filmer not provide any evidence to "prove that propriety in land . . . gave any authority over the persons of men," but, Locke maintains, this fact is hardly surprising because "it is clear that . . . private dominion *could* give [an individual] no sovereignty" (*FT*: no. 43; italics added). Filmer was not mistaken in his belief that Adam provided the best case for the notion that property ownership and political power were intrinsically conjoined, but Locke's rejection of that argument necessarily has the effect of calling into question the underlying general presumption that political authority is in some sense dependent upon and derivable from property ownership. "The power of making laws of life and death," Locke observes, "is indeed a mark of sovereignty" (*FT*: no. 129), but the question is what does this "political power of life and death" have to do with being a "proprietor of the goods and lands" (*FT*: no. 48) within a particular society? Locke's answer is that these are two quite different forms of power that have no necessary or essential relationship to each other.[17]

Moreover, even within the economic sphere, Locke argues that a property owner cannot force a propertyless individual into slavery through the use of the former's economic power (*FT*: no. 42). Thus, "the authority of the rich proprietor, and the subjection of the needy beggar began not from the possession of the Lord, but the consent of the poor man, who preferred being his subject to starving. And the man he thus submits to, can pretend to no more power over him, than he has consented to, upon compact" (*FT*: no. 43). Not "possession," but "consent" is the source of authority in Lockean society. Hence, political equality and natural rights manifest through express consent can coexist with various forms of social and economic inequality. Indeed, since this is *the* problematic issue built into the structure of liberalism as a political theory, not to recognize its appearance in Locke's political thought as *he* formulated it reflects a serious misunderstanding of his perspective and of the legacy he bequeathed to the tradition of liberalism.[18]

Finally, let us consider the charge that Locke's political theory is a justificatory defense of a capitalist society. The difficulty in formulating a response to this assertion arises from its unsuccessful attempts to connect two different levels of meaning and types of evidence. From a holistic or macro standpoint, capitalist society ought to display certain system-properties that distinguish it from other forms of society, and this definitional endeavor poses certain methodological problems with respect to the nature of the argument being advanced by Macpherson. From the micro standpoint, of course, the foundation of any interpretation of Locke's political theory rests upon what Locke wrote or did. The first level requires evidence in some objective (causal/structural) form, and the second relies upon an interpretation of phenomenological (intentional) activity. To state the point crudely, did capitalist society exist in seventeenth-century England? And did Locke mean to justify or defend its existence?

Marx describes the transition from "the feudal system of industry" to "industrial production" dominated by "the manufacturing system" as the outcome of "a long course of development, of a series of revolutions in the modes of production and of exchange" (Marx and Engels 1978:474–75). Historically, therefore, the transition from feudalism to capitalism occurs over several centuries. Yet, Marx (1906, 1:353) insists, "capitalist production only then really begins . . . when each individual capital employs simultaneously a comparatively large number of laborers" and production assumes "an extensive scale." These conditions "constitute, both historically and logically, the starting point of capitalist production." The problem is that these conditions are not historically specific to seventeenth-century England, a society dominated socially and politically by the owners of agricultural production, in which the largest proportion of workers were either resident servants performing services and producing few commodities or self-employed artisans without ties either to the process of manufacturing commodities or to industrial capitalists.[19] As Marx observes (Marx and Engels 1978:479), it is a historical step of several centuries from "the little workshop of the patriarchal master" to "the great factory of the industrial capitalist."[20]

It is Adam Smith, not Locke, who recognizes the importance of a large working class and the division of labor to the development of capitalism and who argues that that form of society must reproduce itself through the manufacture of goods rather than, as mercantilists such as Locke believed, through the expansion of foreign trade.[21] If, as Marx (n.d.:105) pithily put it, "the hand-mill gives you society with the feudal lord; the steam-mill, society, with the industrial capitalist," then the ideological role Macpherson attributes to Locke's political theory does not materialize in the stream of history until long after Locke's death.

As other scholars have noted, Macpherson unfortunately is not much interested in the historical specificity of either capitalism or the social relations characteristic of Restoration England. He employs an abstract heuristic model of society, simply assuming its correspondence to an existent "market society," which he frequently identifies with "capitalist production." Yet Macpherson never undertakes through historical investigation to demonstrate that such a society does exist or, even more implausibly, that a market society—which, as Marx observed, existed in the Roman Republic—is equatable with a capitalist system of production (see Ashcraft 1980b:32–33, 87; Ashcraft 1986: 150ff.; Wood 1984:7ff.). Of course there were wage laborers, a few manufacturing enterprises, and merchants' or bankers' capital in seventeenth-century England, but Marx argued that all of these things had previously existed in other societies (Marx and Engels 1978:243, 270ff). The crucial issue for him was the structural relationship between the owners of the means of production and the producers, between industrial capitalists and proletarian wage earners, and this system-defining relationship of capitalism simply did not exist in Restoration England (Marx 1906, 3:919).[22]

Macpherson's impatience with the complexities of history also manifests itself in the shortcuts he takes in his interpretation of Locke's writings. According to Macpherson (1962:221), once individuals have entered civil society, Locke removes the natural-law restrictions on property and hence any social constraints on the use of property, thus justifying the unlimited capitalist appropriation of commodities. Since Locke not only explicitly declares that "the obligations of the Law of Nature cease not in society" but also that "the municipal laws of countries . . . are only so far right, as they are founded on the Law of Nature, by which they are to be regulated and interpreted" (*ST*: nos. 135, 12), this is another instance in which Macpherson's interpretation of the text requires that Locke be confused or contradictory in the formulation of his argument. The problem is not that Locke is confused but that Macpherson never understood what the natural-law limitations imposed on the use of property were.

As I have suggested, Locke's conception of natural law (and of the Deity) provides a standard of use (viz., act to preserve mankind) and a dispositional framework supportive of such action (viz., maintain a friendly disposition toward others). In general, this means that no action of an individual should harm or injure another. Hence, no one is allowed "to hoard up more than he could make use of" (*ST*: nos. 46, 51) because in so acting he "offended against the common Law of Nature" by "invading his neighbor's share" (*ST*: no. 37) and by "robbing" others (*ST*: no. 46). No one "may engross as much as he will," Locke argues, because "the same Law of Nature, that does by this means give us property, does also bound that property too. . . . As much as any one can make use of to any advantage of his life before it spoils; so much he may by his labor fix a property in. Whatever is beyond this, is more than his share, and belongs to others. Nothing was made by God for man to spoil or destroy" (*ST*: no. 31). The key phrases in this argument are "make use of" and the reading of God's intentions in the last sentence. The former is tied, in the first instance, to Locke's defense of the natural right to subsistence as an integral part of his interpretation of natural law. The individual, therefore, "had no right, farther than his use called for any of [the goods]" he extracted from the state of nature (*ST*: no. 37). The important thing about the latter phrase is Locke's application of God's purposive designs to property rights in land. When "God gave the world to men in common . . . for their benefit," Locke argues, "it cannot be supposed he meant it should always remain common and uncultivated" (*ST*: no. 34), for then it would be a wasted resource (*ST*: nos. 36–38, 42–43, 45). Thus, referring to the precepts of the Law of Nature, Locke observes,

the same measures governed the possession of land too: Whatsoever he tilled and reaped, laid up and made use of, before it spoiled, that was his peculiar right; whatsoever he enclosed, and could feed, and make use of, the cattle and product was also his. But if either the grass of his enclosure rotted on the ground, or the fruit of his planting perished without gathering, and laying up, this part of the Earth, notwithstanding his enclosure, was still to be looked on as waste, and might be the possession of any other. (*ST*: no. 38)

The natural-law standard of productive use without injury to others, in other words, cannot be identified with unlimited appropriation because merely appropriating land through enclosure provides no guarantee that it will not be wasted; and if it is, the owner loses his right to the land, which can then be claimed by any individual who will make use of it, an argument reaffirmed by Locke later in the *Second Treatise* (no. 184). In other words, for Locke, ownership is not in itself a productive activity.

The question is, when Locke declares that "the same rule of propriety, (viz.), that every man should have as much as he could make use of, would still hold in the world . . . had not the invention of money, and the tacit agreement of men to put a value on it, introduced (by consent) larger possessions, and a right to them" (*ST*: no. 36), has he allowed this act of consent to suspend the natural-law standard of productive use and noninjurious behavior toward others? The answer to this question depends upon what "use" is assigned to money in the context of the social relations between individuals and specifically upon whether its use is consonant with the natural-law admonition to preserve mankind. Locke introduces money into his discussion of property in two contexts. The first is a sociological account of how people built cities, settled property boundaries, and engaged in trade with their neighbors. Hence, there is a type of society "where there is plenty of people under government, who have money and commerce," which has clearly advanced beyond the subsistence stage of existence (*ST*: nos. 35, 38, 45). The second context presents an ethical dilemma facing the "industrious and rational" producer whose overproduction of goods would, if allowed to rot, brand him a violator of the Law of Nature. If he gives these goods to someone who needs them or barters with someone where mutual needs can be met, the problem is resolved since everyone has benefited and these actions are consonant with the preservation of mankind. "And thus came in the use of money, some lasting thing. . . that by mutual consent men would take in exchange for the truly useful, but perishable supports of life" (*ST*: nos. 46–47).

Money, that is, is useful in the context of trade, and trade, Locke believes—not "unlimited appropriation"—is beneficial to everyone. "What reason could anyone have," Locke asks, "to enlarge his posses- sions beyond the use of his family" if "he had no hopes of commerce with other parts of the world, to draw money to him by the sale of the product?" Land "would not be worth the enclosing" if one were cut off from "all possible commerce with the rest of the world" (*ST*: no. 48). Money is as "necessary to trade as food is to life." Its function is to serve as a medium of exchange, i.e., as "a universal commodity" and a "standing measure" of all other commodities (*Works 1824*, 4:7, 14, 44). "Considered in its proper use as a commodity passing in exchange," Locke argues, money performs a useful service by extending the meaning of productive labor beyond the limits of subsistence (*Works 1824*, 4:42). Moreover, commerce not only does no injury to anyone but is positively beneficial to mankind, making everyone, even day laborers, better off than they were in more primitive forms of society (*ST*: no. 41). It is an extension of the very reason that individuals join civil society, namely, that they expect to benefit from "the labor, assistance, and society of others in the same community" (*ST*: no. 130). It is precisely in terms of Locke's consistent belief in the precepts of natural law and not their suspension, in other words, that his argument concerning property must be understood. Social benefits and the public good, in short, *always* take precedence over individual self-interest in the structuring of Locke's political theory.

What Locke advocates, then, is productive labor, not unlimited appro- priation, and national wealth gained through foreign trade, not capitalist appropriation for individual profit.[23] It is England as a commercial, trad- ing nation—as, indeed, seventeenth-century England was—that supplies Locke with a socioeconomic model of his political society and not the Britain of Birmingham, Manchester, and the industrial revolution. It is Locke, not Macpherson, who displays a realistic grasp of the sociological dimensions of Restoration England. This is hardly surprising, given their importance to the political argument that he and other Whigs were ad- vancing in the 1680s (see Ashcraft 1986:214–24, 251–85). To pretend that the differences between a mercantilist and a capitalist perspective or between the social conditions of Restoration England and those obtaining more than a century later do not matter with respect to the meaning of capitalism merely so' that Locke's ideas can be viewed as endorsing capitalist appropriation reflects a poor understanding of history, a sloppy interpretive approach to Locke's authorial intentions and the text of the *Two Treatises*, and a seriously defective methodological endeavor to ascertain the relationship between ideology and social action. Of course commerce *leads* to a capitalist society through a series of historical changes, as Marx recognized, just as Locke's ideas are revised and reshaped by Adam Smith or Bentham. But who ever doubted this? Telescoping the course of history for the sake of producing simplistic heuristic models is no intellectual gain from the standpoint of understanding political theory.

As a further illustration of Locke's political realism, I shall focus very briefly upon the concept of consent. To paraphrase Humpty-Dumpty in *Alice through the Looking Glass*, "consent" is one of the hardest-working concepts in the *Two Treatises of Government*. Earlier I argued for the importance of (express) consent as a political concept in the context of Locke's ontological definition of a person, his commitment to the moral framework of natural law and natural rights, and his theological belief in man's free will. Now I wish to suggest that one of the several meanings of "consent" in the *Two Treatises* has a concrete referent in the social practice of elections and that Locke's reliance upon this meaning of consent gives his political theory a much more historically specific and ideologically structured meaning than most interpreters of that work have recognized.

In paragraph ninety-four of the *Second Treatise*, Locke declares that individuals "could never . . . think themselves in civil society, till the legislature was placed in collective bodies of men, call them Senate, Parliament, or what you please." In the remainder of that paragraph, Locke contrasts "civil society" so defined with the state of nature. A few paragraphs earlier, Locke had rejected absolute monarchy as being "inconsistent with civil society" and as "no form of civil government at all," equating it with a state of nature (*ST*: nos. 90–91). The question is, does Locke mean to argue, as this juxtaposition of passages suggests, that only a civil society with some sort of legislature chosen by the people meets his standard of legitimate government? To this question two types of answers are possible. The first maintains that Locke sets out formal criteria of legitimacy, broadly defined, according to which a number of different forms of government, past and present, qualify as legitimate. The second answer directs attention to the fact that the *Two Treatises* is a defense of a particular form of government with a specific set of political institutions whose legitimacy is the focus of the political debate in the 1680s.

If one reads the *Two Treatises* as a work of abstract philosophy, there are passages, certainly, which present formal criteria of legitimacy, such as consent and government's acting for the public good. Yet since Locke believes that *all* governments are founded in consent and instituted for the public good (*ST*: nos. 102, 104, 106, 112, 175), this formal latitude places tremendous interpretive weight upon consent in those instances where, for example, all power is in the hands of a single individual, precisely the *political* situation Locke is arguing against. Moreover, Locke places great importance upon "settled, standing laws" and "indifferent judges" to interpret them as essential (formal) ingredients of his definition of political society (*ST*: nos. 124–25, 131, 136–37, 142). He insists that political society *only* exists where individuals have resigned their power to "the community," which then gives to particular individuals the authority to execute and to interpret the rules made by the community (*ST*: no. 87).[24] These decisions allocating authority to particular individuals, Locke explains, are made by majority consent, and even his remarks describing this formal decisionary principle seem to presuppose some kind of "public assembly" (*ST*: nos. 96, 98). Yet in the primitive societies of the Indians in America or the paternal monarchies of "the first ages," *these* formal conditions of legitimacy were not met. Power is generally resigned into the hands of father or chieftain, not to the community (*ST*: nos. 74–76, 105, 107–9).[25] Government is, in essence, the prerogative of the ruler and not subject to the will or consent of the majority (*ST*: nos. 111, 162). There are no "settled, standing laws" made by the community nor even "express conditions limiting or regulating his power" (*ST*: no. 112). Members of the society have no indifferent judge to whom to appeal against the decisions of the ruler, who embodies both executive and legislative power in his actions, which is after all the *formal* definition of absolute monarchy (*ST*: no. 91).

At the very least, I would maintain that Locke offers a developmental framework for legitimacy. Monarchy is a "simple and most obvious" form of government to meet the conditions of primitive existence. That is, in a subsistence society where individuals have few possessions, there are "few controversies and so no need of many laws to decide them," (*ST*: no. 107; cf. nos. 31, 39, 162) and "no contest betwixt rulers and people about governors or government" (*ST*: no. 111). The latter's function was essentially to provide individuals with a "defense against foreign invasions"; hence, the ruler was generally a person who could best "conduct them in their wars" (*ST*: no. 107). Yet Locke reminds us that the power of making war or peace "will not prove that every one that does so is a politick ruler." Not only is it "no proof of any other power" but also "this power in many cases any one may have without any politick supremacy" (*FT*: nos. 131–32; cf. *ST*: nos. 108–9), which, as I read Locke, means that the holding of this power—the chief mark of ancient monarchies—is not sufficient to qualify them as political societies (Ashcraft 1987:153ff.).

In any event, what Locke clearly does want to show is that "express limitations and restraints" must be put upon the ruler's power and that there is a need "of balancing the power of government, by placing several parts of it in different hands" (*ST*: nos. 107, 110–23). The complexity of government, Locke believes, expands proportionately to the increased complexity of society, and the major factor in this process is of course the development of various forms of property. The latter gives rise to more controversies and more laws and hence to the need for judges to interpret them. The riches and power of society increase and, Locke argues, it is dangerous to place this power in the hands of one man, or even a few men, because they "will think themselves to have a distinct interest, from the rest of the community" (*ST*: no. 138; cf. no. 111). As Locke explains,

> because it may be too great a temptation to human frailty apt to grasp at power, for the same persons who have the power of making laws, to have also in their hands the power to execute them, whereby they may exempt themselves from obedience to the laws they make . . . to their own private advantage, and thereby come to have a distinct interest from the rest of the community, contrary to the end of society and government: Therefore in well ordered commonwealths, where the good of the whole is considered, as it ought, the legislative power is put into the hands of divers persons who duly assembled, have by themselves, or jointly with others, a power to make laws. (*ST*: no. 143; cf. no. 153)

If we recall that Locke argues that the use of money and the development of a commercial economy occurred in the state of nature "out of the bounds" of political society (*ST*: no. 50), it would appear that Locke's "civil society," or a "well ordered commonwealth" is not only the legitimate response to this situation, but it must also follow, temporally, those conditions of nomadic subsistence that characterize life under "simple" monarchies. For it is certainly the case that Locke, like other exclusion Whigs, mounted a political argument against one-man rule as an appropriate or legitimate form of government for a commercial society such as seventeenth-century England.[26] Hence, even if monarchy had at one time represented a legitimate political response to a simple social existence, it could no longer retain its political legitimacy in the face of much more complex socioeconomic conditions.

I have developed this argument more fully and presented my reasons for rejecting the view that Locke's argument for political legitimacy remains on the formal/theoretical level elsewhere. What I wish to stress in this essay is the strong case for representative government that Locke makes in the *Two Treatises* once we understand—as his readers surely did— "consent" to refer to the institutional practice of holding elections. Locke assumes as an integral aspect of his assertion that "the supreme power cannot take from any man any part of his property without his own consent" and that this consent is represented by and mediated through some sort of assembly that meets for short periods of time to pass laws (*ST*: no. 138). Thus, in explaining the dependency of taxation upon consent, Locke defines the latter concept in terms of "his own consent, i.e., the consent of the majority, giving it either by themselves, or their representatives chosen by them" (*ST*: no. 140). Indeed, two paragraphs later this point is repeated as part of the boundaries that "the Law of God and Nature have set to the legislative power of every commonwealth, in all forms of government," that is, that "the consent of the people [be] given by themselves, or their deputies . . . to be from time to time chosen by themselves" (*ST*: no. 142). An election may not be the only procedural means of satisfying this restrictive condition—now incorporated into the Law of Nature as a standard of legitimacy for every commonwealth and all forms of government—but it is certainly the procedure that Locke and his contemporary readers had in mind. If the legislature "be made up of representatives chosen . . . by the people," Locke writes, "this power of choosing must also be exercised by the people, either at certain appointed seasons, or else when they are summoned to [hold] new elections" (*ST*: no. 154). From this point on, Locke's argument in the *Second Treatise* grows imperceptibly more specific. He remarks upon the need to reform the system of representation so that more numerous towns and "new corporations" can be more equitably represented in "the grand assembly of law-makers" (*ST*: nos. 157–58). The latter becomes "Parliament" (*ST*: no. 167), made up of "an assembly of hereditary nobility" and "an assembly of representatives chosen, *pro tempore*, by the people" (*ST*: no. 213).

Yet this descriptive familiarity should not be allowed to obscure the fact that the people having the opportunity of "choosing their deputies from time to time" has, through its association with natural law, become a "native right" to be exercised by or on behalf of the people. Thus, those "forced to submit to the yoke of a government by constraint, have always a right to shake it off" and to replace it with a government of their own choosing (ST: no. 176). "For no government can have a right to obedience from a people who have not freely consented to it: which they can never be supposed to do, till either they are put in a full state of liberty to choose their government and governors, or at least till they have such standing laws, to which they have by themselves or their representatives, given their free consent" (ST: no. 192; cf. no. 196). When Locke associates "the consent of the people" with the recovery by the people of "their just and natural rights" as the outcome of the Glorious Revolution in the preface to the *Two Treatises*, it is clear—if only from William III's publicly stated intention for his coming to England—that it is the reinstatement of a freely elected Parliament that satisfies both these conditions.[27]

Having assisted the Whigs, led by Shaftesbury, in their successful efforts in winning three parliamentary elections between 1679 and 1681, Locke may be presumed to have had a realistic understanding of the conceptual linkage between elections and consent of the people. In the *First Treatise*, written in support of that electoral campaign, he juxtaposed "tyranny and usurpation" to "election and consent" (FT: no. 148). However, Charles II not only refused to accede to the will of the majority, i.e., their representatives in the Commons, repeatedly dissolving Parliament, but after 1681 he also refused to call for new elections. With these actions, Locke argues, the king put himself in a state of war with the people, subverted the meaning of consent, and dissolved the form of government heretofore dependent upon the existence of an elected assembly (ST: nos. 155, 168, 212, 215).

Not surprisingly, Locke is primarily preoccupied throughout his discussion of resistance in the *Second Treatise* with the executive's interference with the elections of the people's deputies. Apart from the refusal to call for elections, Locke lists a number of specific indictable offenses— changing the rules of the election, bribing the electors or representatives, prescribing what laws they must enact, and so on—all of which have the effect, Locke argues, of dissolving a form of government where the people have "reserved to themselves the choice of their representatives" (ST: nos. 216, 222). Such interference with the ways in which the people "choose and authorize a legislative" is "as perfect a declaration of a design to subvert the government, as is possible to be met with" (ST: no. 222), and the people have every right to resist these actions and "to reinstate their legislative" assembly (*ST*: nos. 155, 212). Since the argument of the *Second Treatise* has now come full circle, interference with representative government having dissolved the form of government, returning power into the hands of the community in a state of nature, it seems clear that Locke does believe that he can employ his concept of the Law of Nature and his criteria for political legitimacy in defense of the specific political institutions and social practices characteristic of Restoration England.

What I have tried to suggest in this essay is that many of the problems alluded to in the secondary literature on Locke arise from the adoption by contemporary scholars of a much narrower conception of politics than the one subscribed to by Locke or his contemporaries. It is true that, in general, we do not believe or act upon those religious and philosophical presuppositions that were important to Locke, nor can we accept as our socioeconomic framework for political action the conditions that existed in Restoration England. In both respects, we are in some sense cut off from Locke's political thought and the meaning it had for the initial readers of the *Two Treatises*. It seems pointless to deny this reality or to pretend that Locke's (or anyone else's) political theory can be reduced to a few timeless truths vaguely stated, as if in so doing one has in actuality managed to escape the vicissitudes of change in meanings and social conditions in which political theories are deeply embedded.

Of course, as I indicated at the outset, some problems, institutions, social practices, and beliefs do persist over a relatively long time, and it is important to try to discover why this is so. But I insist that the answer to this question will always be an empirically specific answer, showing, as I have tried to show, why certain beliefs are assumed to be true and causally efficacious with respect to action, why certain institutions are preferable to others, given the contextual circumstances that exist, and so forth. It may be difficult to understand how a Lockean concept of property can be meaningfully applied to Exxon or IBM, but that is a problem the solution to which does not include reading back into our interpretation of chapter 5 of the *Second Treatise* a defense by Locke of the capitalist system of appropriation. At the same time, it seems apparent that many social practices in twentieth-century capitalist society are dependent upon the belief that political power is separate and distinct from social or economic power, and it can be argued that some of Locke's arguments supportive of this viewpoint retain much of their relevance to our current understanding of politics. My point is that any determination of the place of Locke's ideas or the politics of the *Two Treatises* in the context of twentieth-century liberalism therefore requires, in the first instance, a careful assessment of the gains and losses with respect to the beliefs and social practices that gave meaning to those ideas for Locke. Indeed, I am arguing that such an assessment *is* a constitutive feature of any comprehensive understanding of *our* context.

NOTES

1. A number of Laslett's particular assumptions regarding the writing and specific dating of the *Two Treatises* are erroneous (see appendix to "The Composition and Structure of the *Two Treatises of Government*," Ashcraft 1987:286–97), but I am concerned here only with the general point to which he drew attention.

2. C. B. Macpherson makes no reference to Locke's text in *The Political Theory of Possessive Individualism* (1962), though he does cite W. von Leyden's introduction to that work once (258) in order to make a point against it. Leo Strauss's *Natural Right and History* (1953) appeared before the publication of the *Essays on the Law of Nature*. Neither Strauss nor Macpherson, however, ever reconsidered or reexamined their positions in light of the evidence contained in the Locke manuscripts or in the scholarly work based upon them.

3. For Macpherson (1962:258–61), there is an "essential identity" between Locke's earliest writings and the *Two Treatises*, as if the difference between unqualified support for the Stuart monarchy (1660) and active resistance to it in the 1680s represented no "fundamental change" in Locke's political perspective. See also Kraynak (1980).

4. *Essay Concerning Toleration* (1667). This passage is printed in the appendix to Gough (1956:197), which is a collation of two drafts of this essay. "The idea of a supreme Being, infinite in power, goodness, and wisdom, whose workmanship we are, and on whom we depend; and the idea of ourselves, as . . . rational beings . . . [supplies] the foundations of our duty and rules of action" (John Locke, *ECHU*, 4:3, 18).

5. It is on this ground that Locke excludes atheists from toleration or membership in civil society (*Works 1824*, 5:47).

6. Locke MS fol. 2, Journal, 6–10 April 1677. Hence, the "matters of the highest concernment" are "religion, law and morality" (*ECHU*, 3:9, 22).

7. "That God has given a rule whereby men should govern themselves, I think there is nobody so brutish as to deny" (*ECHU*, 2:28, 8; cf. *ELN*:109).

8. That is, such a violation of natural law would be "unavoidable," Locke argues, if one accepted the Hobbesian assumption that "men are . . . by the law of nature in a state of war." Such a view renders impossible "all justice, friendship, and generosity" among human beings in their natural, God-created condition (*ELN*:211, 213; cf. 201).

9. In the *Essay Concerning Human Understanding* (2:28, 11) Locke observes that human behavior corresponds "in great measure" to the dictates of the Law of Nature. In the *Second Treatise* (123), Locke remarks that "the greater part" of mankind are "no strict observers of equity and justice." Much depends upon

whether one places the interpretive weight upon "the greater part" or upon "strict" in this sentence. The former can be used to support a Hobbesian reading of Locke; the latter simply represents a comment on the fallibility of man. The fact that individuals are "biassed by their interest" or "ignorant" of their duty (*ST*: no. 124) or subject to "negligence" (*ST*: no. 125) seems to me to apply to most individuals, while Locke's reference to "the corruption and viciousness of degenerate men" (*ST*: no. 128) is applicable to those few criminals in the state of nature who have "renounced" the law of reason as their guide (cf. *ST*: no. 10; see Ashcraft 1968:898–915).

10. "The duties of [natural] law, arising from the constitution of his [man's] very nature are of eternal obligation; nor can it be taken away or dispensed with, without changing the nature of things, overturning the measures of right and wrong, and thereby introducing and authorizing irregularity, confusion, and disorder in the world" (*Works 1824*, 6:112). Nevertheless, "some" of God's commands are "suited to particular circumstances of times, places, and persons" and therefore carry with them "a limited and only temporary obligation" (*Works 1824*, 6:13).

11. "The law of nature neither supposes nor allows men to be inflamed with hatred for one another" (*ELN*: 163; cf. *STCE*: 143–45). Hence, "we are bound to maintain and promote" sentiments of "universal charity, goodwill and love" toward others under all conditions whatsoever, according to natural law (*Correspondence*, 4:758; Locke MS fol. 3, Journal, 20 March 1678). It is in the context of the fact that we may "stop acting according to the law" without acting against it or abandoning the dispositions it prescribes that one should interpret Locke's statement that the individual, "when his own preservation comes not in competition, ought he, as much as he can, to preserve the rest of mankind" (*ST*: no. 6). Self-preservation, that is, is an obvious and necessary means to the end of preserving mankind, but it is neither an end in itself nor a warrant for engaging in an aggressive Hobbesian war of all against all, as Strauss (1953:224, 234), for example, maintains.

12. "All negative precepts" or prohibitions of the Law of Nature "are always to be obeyed," but "positive commands only sometimes upon occasions" when this is possible, although "we ought to be always furnished with the habits and dispositions to [execute] those positive duties" when the occasion permits (Locke MS fol. 3, Journal, 20 March 1678).

13. Following the publication of the *Essay Concerning Human Understanding*, Locke rewrote chapter 21 of that work, inserting his revisions into the second edition of the *Essay*, published in 1692. Although a few of the statements cited in the text are from this edition, I am not making a post hoc propter hoc argument; rather, my aim is simply to demonstrate the congruity and similarity of Locke's definition of person in the *Essay Concerning Human Understanding* and his definition of free man in *The Two Treatises of Government*. The statements and presuppositions concerning the latter concept were already established in Locke's thought before the *Essay* appeared in print. Hence, one might even argue that Locke's philosophical position in the *Essay Concerning Human Understanding* was revised in such a way as to bring it into greater conformity with the assumptions underlying the political perspective in the *Two Treatises*. In any event, much of the basic argument to which I have referred was already present in the first edition of the *Essay Concerning Human Understanding*.

Indeed, the fundamental points were recorded in Locke's journals and notebooks prior to the publication of either work. Thus, as Hans Aarsleff has observed, one must not exaggerate the significance of Locke's revisions or the extent to which they constitute a restructuring of the fundamental precepts of his thought (Aarsleff 1969:110–26).

14. In the *Letter Concerning Toleration*, Locke defines the meaning of his reference to "the estates of the people" as the securing "of every particular man's goods and person." This objective is reaffirmed a few pages later in language that recalls Locke's definition of "civil interests," where the purpose of political society is identified with the protection of "every man's possession of the things of this life" (*Works 1824*, 5:40, 43).

15. Locke's memorandum to the Board of Trade on the employment of the poor, printed in H. R. Fox-Bourne (1876, 2:382).

16. Contrary to what Geraint Parry (1978:106), for example, asserts.

17. Locke argues that while a son has "a right to succeed to his father's property . . . this can give him no right to succeed also to the rule, which his father had over other men" (*FT*: no. 93). I emphasize the point that Locke is arguing against a necessary and/or symmetrical relationship between property ownership and political power, and not that, as a matter of empirical observation, there is no relationship between forms of property and forms of government.

18. Of course, Macpherson recognizes this problematic in liberalism, but since he does not take seriously the democratic or egalitarian impulses in Locke's thought, he reads into Locke's universalist language a rhetorical camouflage for his conscious intention to justify socioeconomic inequality. This interpretive approach, I am suggesting, not only misstates Locke's authorial intentions and commitment, but it also misses something important with respect to the structural dilemma internal to liberalism as a set of social practices and institutions, namely, to put it crudely, that the conflict between democracy and capitalism is not simply a function of the false or unenlightened consciousness of the historical actors within a democratic capitalist society.

19. A point, of course, recognized by Marx (1906:788n) as he notes in his comment on his citation from Macaulay's *History of England*.

20. See also his association of commerce, money, merchants' capital, and "an *urban artisanate* resting *not* on capital, but on the organization of labor in guilds" as descriptive characteristics of this historical period (seventeenth-century England) (Marx and Engels 1978:272).

21. For Marx's discussion of Smith on these points, see Marx (1906:502ff.).

22. On the importance of this structural analysis to Marx's thought, see Ashcraft (1984:637–71).

23. Macpherson (1962:205–8) recognizes these points (e.g., Locke's mercantilism, money as a medium of exchange, national wealth rather than individual profit as the goal of Locke's economic perspective, and so on), but he simply identifies them with unlimited capitalist appropriation of land, capital accumulation (money), and Hobbesian individualism (Ashcraft 1986:278; Vaughn 1982:53–4, 102).

24. "When the people have said, we will submit to rules, and be governed by laws made by such men, and in such forms" through what Locke calls "a positive voluntary grant for [the] institution" of the legislative power, thus ensuring that the subsequent exercise of that legislative power must operate within the

limits of "what that positive grant conveyed" (*ST*: no. 141; cf. nos. 134, 212), then *and only then* has a legitimate form of government been established. Without this positive and specific action, the people would exist in a community where no one was authorized to act for the community, which one could interpret, ipso facto, as either a democracy (where majority consent is naturally taken for the whole) or the state of nature (where equal authority leaves collective association a contingent matter). For a discussion of this issue, see Ashcraft (1987:113–19, 183ff.).

25. In his *Second* and *Third Letters Concerning Toleration*, Locke discusses the Indians who have "no private possessions of land" nor any "enlarged desires after riches or power." Hence, they are content with "the spontaneous provisions of life" provided by "the rivers and woods." They live "without any municipal laws, judges, or any person with superiority established amongst them." This statement, Locke believes, is reconcilable with his recognition that the Indians do have a chieftain, whose duties are limited to the defense of "the commonwealth." That is, "their captain, or prince, is sovereign commander in time of war; but in time of peace, neither he nor anybody else has any authority over any of the society" (*Works 1824*, 5:225; cf. 121).

26. For a further discussion of this point, see Ashcraft (1986:202–6, 213–24).

27. On the importance of a freely elected Parliament to Locke, the Rye House Plotters, participants in Monmouth's Rebellion, and the radical exiles in Holland, see Ashcraft (1986:538ff.). On William III's commitment to this objective, see Ashcraft (1986:549).

3 / *Religion and Locke's* Two Treatises of Government

ELDON EISENACH

One of the early reviews of John Dunn's 1969 *The Political Thought of John Locke* compared it to Martin Seliger's *The Liberal Politics of John Locke* published the previous year. The *Times Literary Supplement* headline to this review said it all: "John Locke: Liberal, Yes; Calvinist, No." Judging from the patterns of Lockean scholarship over the next two decades the reviewer got it almost exactly wrong. A headline for a review of this literature might now read, "John Locke: Moderate-Anglican-Calvinist, Yes; Liberal-Bourgeois, Not Yet; Radical-Revolutionary, A Qualified Yes; Enlightenment-Rationalist, A Qualified No."

To address the question of religion and the *Two Treatises of Government* in light of recent Lockean scholarship is necessarily to plunge deeply into the same historical framework that has been the locus and the engine of this new scholarship. This historical context makes the task of relating religion to the *Two Treatises* much simpler than before—and for a very simple reason: the *Second Treatise* is no longer assumed to be disembodied text (or one twinned with *Human Understanding*), whose meaning can be uncovered by performing analytical operations on it. Indeed, historicizing Locke changes the kinds of meaning we look for. No longer are we engaged in the philosophical task of either helping Locke along in perfecting his reductionist project (i.e., a self-enclosed and logically coercive civil philosophy) or of exposing his failure to do so. The game now afoot is to treat the various propositions of the *Treatise* as so many intimations, the meanings of which will become clear only when tied both to the whole range of his other writings and to the languages and audiences clustered about the religious and political conflicts in Britain from the early Restoration period through the turn of the century. Suddenly, the *Second Treatise* is a room with many doors—and some of those doors open into Locke's writings on theology, biblical interpretation, church polity, and sacred history. Indeed, even that previously cluttered passageway from the *Second Treatise* to the *Essay Concerning Human Understanding* has been, if not cleared, at least by-passed by a rerouting through Locke's writings on religion.

Some preliminary discussion of the new views will help clarify the ways in which historical location itself has paved the way for relating the meanings of the *Second Treatise* to Locke's writings on religion. The most obvious preliminary was the 1960 publication of Peter Laslett's research dating the initial writing of the *Two Treatises* in the period of the exclusion controversy. This dating should have had the immediate effect of forcing our attention to the republication of Filmer's treatises in 1679 and *Patriarchia* in 1680 and therefore to that group of High Churchmen and courtiers who were seeking to reinstitute royal absolutism. Thus, the first door opening out from the *Second Treatise* is the notoriously unread and misread *First Treatise*, i.e., a work centered not in the freedom of unaided reason, tabula rasa, and the state of nature but in the duties commanded by an authoritative biblical text and a God who created and intervenes in human history. Despite the invitation from Laslett, this door has not been opened until quite recently (Thompson 1976; Tarlton 1978; Goldie 1980a, 1980b; Tully 1980:53–61).

A second opening was suggested even earlier, namely, W. von Leyden's 1954 translation and publication of Locke's *Essays on the Law of Nature*. But, like the Laslett invitation, the religious and more specifically Christian elements in these essays were slighted, until recently, in favor of melding these natural-law writings into the more philosophical "Locke as rationalist—Locke as hedonist" debate that had structured scholarship on the *Second Treatise* and *Human Understanding* ever since Lamprecht's *Moral and Political Philosophy of John Locke* (1962: chapters 3 and 4), first published in 1918 (see also Ashcraft 1987:298–305; Rapaczynski 1987:150–70).

A third door opened was the translation and publication in 1967 of Locke's *Two Tracts on Government*. These tracts, one in English and one in Latin, were written in the early Restoration period (1660–1661) and urge what in effect was the moderate Anglican solution at that time to church-state issues. Philip Abrams's extensive introduction (1967) and notes were another invitation (and challenge) to see both the *Two Treatises* and *Letters on Toleration (Works 1823*: vol. 6) as arising out of these decidedly conventional and moderate origins. Thus, prior to Dunn's book, textual availability and historical scholarship had already suggested that the *Second Treatise* needed to be reread in light of the *First Treatise*, the *Essays on the Law of Nature*, and the *Two Tracts*—that is, in light of biblical hermeneutics, Christian and Stoic natural law, and Anglican church doctrine and theology.

John Dunn's (1969a) book was the first and remains the most complete attempt to relate the text of the *Second Treatise* both to Locke's earlier writings and to his later ones, especially the *Letters on Toleration* and the *Reasonableness of Christianity*. That same year, Richard Ashcraft's "Faith and Knowledge in Locke's Philosophy" (1969) sought to rescue Locke's epistemology from analytic philosophers by placing Locke's *Essay Concerning Human Understanding* within the theological context of the seventeenth century.[1] By so doing, he underlined the importance of Locke's theology as found in the *Reasonableness* and its *Vindications* for his philosophy and deprived *Human Understanding* of its status as a nonproblematic wall around the endless debates about the meaning and philosophic integrity of the *Second Treatise*. Again, the importance of Locke's biblical hermeneutics was raised, and some students of Locke's political theory began to examine the primary and secondary sources of British theological writings from the Elizabethan Reformation through the first decades of the eighteenth century. These studies have had the direct effect of ridding Locke's early and late religious writings of interpretive anachronism and the indirect effect of depriving prevailing understandings of the *Second Treatise* of buttress from those previously misread sources. Thus, for example, Marxist understandings of the *Second Treatise* can no longer dismiss *Reasonableness* as proletarian opiate and *Toleration* as a strategic ploy of the rising bourgeoisie (Macpherson 1962:224–26; Wolin 1960:335–38). For those understandings of the *Second Treatise* grounded in epistemology and the analytic tradition of philosophy, this scholarship has induced some healthy skepticism and (dare we hope) an element of humility in assumptions about the meaning of key concepts in this work.

In addition to these new elements in Lockean scholarship, a series of books and articles have recently appeared that make systematic attempts to relate both the *First* and *Second Treatises* to cognate pamphlet literature at the time of their primary composition during the exclusion crisis, 1679–1681, and at the time of their publication during what is now called the allegiance crisis, 1689–1694. And because the largest part of this literature on both sides in these controversies was written by churchmen and includes issues of church polity, biblical exegesis, and sacred history, this cognate literature casts new light on the religious import and religious assumptions of Locke's larger political theory (Goldie 1980a, 1980b, 1983; Kenyon 1972, 1977; Miller 1973; Straka 1962a, 1962b; Tarlton 1981, 1985).

Finally—and this is more a hope than a fruit of recent scholarship—there is an emerging sense that Locke's place in the history of philosophy must be reconsidered now that both the *Second Treatise* and *Human Understanding* are being reexamined in historical and religious contexts. Indeed, one might put this in a more radical way: Because Locke as previously understood played such a central part in defining the boundaries and developments in the history of early modern philosophy, a reconsideration of what he means and says might force a reconsideration of how that history of philosophy is written. If Locke's political theory and epistemology cannot be understood apart from his writings on religion, can we understand Locke's predecessors and successors—Hobbes and Hume, for example—without a reexamination of *their* religious thought? And if Locke's writings are located in sixteenth- and seventeenth-century hermeneutical discourse and had a profound influence on that discourse in the eighteenth century, can we even speak of a self-contained history of philosophy or a history of "liberal political theory" absent its theological elements? Fortunately for students of early modern British political theory, Henning Graf Reventlow's *The Authority of the Bible and the Rise of the Modern World* has been translated and published (1984). This study of English philosophy and theology from the Reformation through the Enlightenment now makes clear the political and ecclesiastical stakes involved in disputes over biblical authority, natural law, natural religion, and the meaning of sacred history.

Given all this recent scholarship, students of Locke's political theory can no longer plead ignorance or specialization; the doors from and to the *Second Treatise* are now clearly labeled and relatively easy to open. In this essay, I want to suggest where those doors labeled religion in its many forms and guises might lead us.

At the start of Richard Ashcraft's (1987:2) recent study of the *Two Treatises* he states, "The *Two Treatises of Government* has become a work which is at once philosophically more conservative"—that is, less trusting of the sufficiency of reason and scientific method—and "politically more radical"—that is, less tied to the moderate settlement and modes of legitimating the Revolution of 1688. At the end of this same study, he suggests an explanation for this conclusion: "The radical dimensions of Locke's thought are rooted in the areas of religion and morality" (1987:260). If we then add a corollary to these propositions that Locke's economic and social theory is now seen as much more traditional and complex and much less bourgeois, reductionist, and market dominated than previously viewed (Pocock 1985: chaps. 3 and 6; Tully 1980; Wood 1984), we confront the first set of tasks of this essay, namely, to clarify the import of these separate propositions and to show their interrelationships. Since nothing clarifies more quickly than bare dogmatic assertion, I shall begin by overstating the conclusions of recent scholarship in the form of three propositions:

> *Proposition 1*: Locke's politics are radically revolutionary and the *Two Treatises* is the basis for a left-wing critique of the institutional settlements, dominant modes of legitimation, and major public policies of the regime established following the Glorious Revolution of 1688.

> *Proposition 2*: Locke's metaphysics, epistemology, and philosophy are bounded by a deep skepticism regarding the reach of natural reason and informed by deep faith in the efficacy of biblical revelation as the source of our moral and political duties.

> *Proposition 3*: Locke's theology and biblical interpretation are grounded in the spiritualist tradition of the radical reformation and incorporate apocalyptic and millennial ideas of time into his defense of reason and in his theories of natural religion, natural law, and politics.

PROPOSITION I: LOCKE AS REVOLUTIONARY

The changing view of Locke from post hoc defender of the settlement of 1688 through cautious spokesman of resistance to attain the exclusion of James II and finally to revolutionary activist insisting on a radical understanding of the events of 1688 has necessarily changed our understanding of the *Two Treatises*. Enough has now been written to suggest the scope of those changes regarding the *Second Treatise*, especially in underlining its politically egalitarian elements and its provisions for popular resistance and the use of force. So also has this view focused attention on the *First Treatise* as a pamphlet of "exposure"—a conspiracy, largely clerical, to institute divine-right monarchy and Catholicism—and a pamphlet of warning and menace, advising Charles that power erected on those twin pillars might quickly fall victim to rebellion and regicide (Ashcraft 1987: chaps. 2, 5, and 8; Ashcraft 1986: chaps. 7 and 8; Goldie 1980a, 1983; Tarlton 1978, 1981; Thompson 1976).

Somewhat slighted in this more revolutionary reading of Locke, however, is the import of equating tyranny with (variously) Catholicism and High Church Anglicanism. Whether or not Locke helped write Shaftesbury's virulently anti-Catholic pamphlet of 1676, *A Letter from a Person of Quality to His Friend in the Country*, it is certainly true that "antipopery feeling was the glue that held together the various constituencies comprising the political movement that emerged during the exclusion crisis" (Ashcraft 1986:140–41). The popish plot not only was part of parliamentary mobilization for exclusion, but it also revived and ratified the millennialist and antinomian impulses of reformed Protestantism (Kenyon 1972; Miller 1973; see also Hill 1971)—not, surely, on the scale of the Puritan Revolution (Hill 1975; Reventlow 1984:91–146) but sufficient to arouse almost all Dissenters and a good portion of moderate Anglicans. The attempt to sever biblical authority from mandating particular forms of church polity and church office *jure divino* was an integral part of this reinvigoration of reformed Protestantism. While the hermeneutical forms of this severance were clearly established in the Elizabethan Reformation[2] and clearly accepted by Locke even at his most authoritarian (*TT*:239), the institutional forms through which this biblical doctrine could be expressed are many and various. The actual and theoretical possibilities regarding church-state relationships are necessary to note here, not only because they provided the staple of much political argument but also because they intruded into fundamental assumptions of sixteenth- and seventeenth-century political theory, especially Locke's political theory.

Primitive Free Church. This most radical form of severance posits a return to the earliest voluntarist church form as expectation and sign of the Second Coming. All intervening church polity and liturgy and supporting doctrines are human invention, unbiblical, and part of the antimillennial "kingdom of darkness." Hobbes raises this free-church possibility in chapter 47 of *Leviathan* (Eisenach 1982); Locke's *Two Tracts* and *1667 Essay* oppose it but his *Letters* celebrate it.

Godly Prince (Protestant Royal Erastianism). This Elizabethan doctrine sees the king as political head of a national church whose reforming bishops are to be the shock troops to purge the lower clergy and laymen of their idolatry and priestcraft and to prepare his subjects for the coming kingdom. A variant would be "prerogative toleration," with the king imposing toleration or comprehension of Dissenters and mandating latitudinarian doctrine within the church against a recalcitrant Parliament and/or clergy. Locke held this position in the period 1669–1672 (Goldie 1983).

Godly Parliament (Protestant Parliamentary Erastianism). To prevent the always-tempting alliance of king and sacerdotal church (see *FT*), Parliament has the constitutional right and duty to subordinate ecclesiastical governance to the ends of civil government. The possible forms of this subordination are:

Variant no. 1: a latitudinarian and *comprehensive state church*, making legal provision for a mixed authority of bishops, presbyters, and laymen. No toleration is needed because all sensible Protestants would subscribe. If one adds "King in Parliament," Locke's *Two Tracts* expresses this conventional position of moderate Anglicanism in the early Restoration period. After 1688, the old or "true" Whigs were particularly in favor of comprehension.

Variant no. 2: a latitudinarian and *voluntary state church*, with toleration of all dissenting Protestant sects. Locke's *Letters* express this position, which is usually combined with a hope that toleration will lead to comprehension of all Protestants *within* the state church. Harrington's *Oceana* takes this position (Goldie 1987).

Variant no. 3: *a latitudinarian state*, requiring that all churches be voluntary organizations and proscribing churches that implicitly or explicitly teach doctrines subversive of civil society and/or disobey laws established to maintain the ends of civil society. Locke's *Letters* approach this position.

Note that this last and most "liberal" variant of parliamentary Erastianism is also the "radical" demand of left-wing Puritanism in the English Revolution, but even the "commonwealthmen" immediately following the Glorious Revolution refrained from so extreme a position (Goldie 1980b). The early Puritan demand was biblical and eschatological; the latter calls seem constructed additionally on a position of an extreme latitudinarianism cum Deism and could even be viewed as a subtle way to construct a secularized "civil religion" with a Christian content (Zuckert 1986; Goldie 1987; Kraynak 1980). Rather than force a choice on Locke at this point we should remember that Hobbes's *Leviathan* suggested all of these possibilities, from free churches through royal Erastianism. The only independent variable for Hobbes was the prevailing requirements of civil order and the prevailing ideological/theological beliefs of the various forces in organized religion such as bishops, lower clergy, laymen, and universities (Eisenach 1982). Note also that "Puritans" within and without the state church took a variety of positions between Elizabeth and the Glorious Revolution (George and George 1961; Goldie 1980b; Hughes 1965) and that High Church Tories shifted position as well (Goldie 1980b). The point to remember, then, is that the determining factor for serious reformed Protestants was to protect the integrity of their religious teachings by preventing the ordained clergy from making *jure divino* or biblical claims for their own authority and for the internal constitution and liturgy of the church. Institutional methods for achieving that end varied with circumstance, but once a connection was seen between *jure divino* clerical claims tied to royal prerogative and doctrines of passive obedience, the potential for resistance and revolution immediately arose. It is this factor that helps explain not only why Locke's politics were so politically revolutionary but also why Locke could appear so moderate, so pragmatic, so lacking in consistent principle regarding issues of church and state.

The axis of Locke's writings on church-state issues is primarily political and moral: What duties do reason and revelation teach that create and sustain political and religious order on earth and warrant hope for salvation after death? Despite this central axis, a survey of Locke's writings on church polity and church-state relationships from 1660 to 1692 demonstrate two quite separate movements of thought. One shows a principled and progressive movement toward free churches and toleration; the other shows a remarkable continuity of ends sustained by a series of changing recommendations to achieve those ends (see Kraynak 1980). The case for the first logic appears almost prima facie. What Philip Abrams has termed "the authoritarian and rationalistic" *Two Tracts* (107) becomes the more liberal plea for "prerogative toleration" in the *1667 Essay*, finally to evolve as the demand for broad toleration resting in the power of the elected legislature. This movement is accompanied by a corresponding and progressive shift in Locke's theory of the nature and reach of political obligation. The *Two Tracts* gives the magistrate power to impose uniform rules governing "indifferentia" in the realm of religion, extending even to all forms of external worship and dress, because the peace of the realm depends upon preventing disputes over religion, disputes that necessarily undermine political authority. The grounds of political obligation, however, are not resolved, even as the issue of the extent of the magistrate's power is:

> Not that I intend to meddle with that question whether the magistrate's crown drops down on his head immediately from heaven or be placed there by the hands of his subjects, it being sufficient to my purpose that the supreme magistrate of every nation what way soever created, must necessarily have an absolute and arbitrary power over all the indifferent actions of his people. (122–23, cf. 230–31)

Locke does not deny that the Scripture is "a perfect rule [providing] general standards of conduct from which all other particular rules derive and can be deduced" or that "Scripture is a perfect rule of the inward and necessary worship" (*TT*:234). Nor does he deny that each Christian is an equal judge of the meaning of Scripture and that, as a Christian, the magistrate is only an equal "brother to his fellow Christians" (140). But the passage from inward or "speculative" belief, on the one hand, to particular rules of external conduct, on the other, must pass through the treacherous and uncertain territory of practical moral opinions. These opinions are so distorted by personal interest, popular prejudice, and prevailing beliefs and circumstances that the real choice is between lodging the power over rulemaking in sovereign authority or plunging society into anarchy (234–41). This stark choice leaves little room for conscience:

> The law of conscience we call that fundamental judgment of the *practical intellect* concerning any possible truth of a moral proposition about *things to be done in life*. For it is not enough that a thing may be indifferent in its own nature unless we are convinced that it is so. God implanted the light of nature in our hearts and willed that there should be an inner legislator (in effect) constantly present in us whose edicts it should not be lawful for us to transgress even a nail's breadth. Thus our liberty in indifferent things is so insecure and so bound up with the opinion of everyone else that it may be taken as certain that we do indeed lack that liberty which we *think we lack*. (225, some italics added; cf. 63–66 and 161–62)

Thus, "a law for toleration" imposed by the magistrate "would offend [some] consciences as of limitation [some] others" (*TT*:140; see also *1667 Essay*, 2:176–79). Reason is powerless among a people that are ready to conclude God dishonored upon every small deviation from that way of his worship which either education or interest hath made sacred to them; . . . who are apt to judge every other exercise of religion as an affront to theirs, and branding all others with the odious name of idolatry, superstition or will-worship, and so looking on both the persons and practices of others as condemned by God already, are forward to take commission from their own zeal to be their executioners, and so in the actions of the greatest cruelty applaud themselves as good Christians. (*TT*:161 –62)

But if the determining factor is civil peace, which is the clear responsibility of the magistrate, Locke's logic does not necessarily dictate that the magistrate's plenary power is the only solution. In the *Two Tracts*, this logic did lead to a state church and the imposition of external uniformity; in the *Essay on Toleration* of 1667, his same logic led to urging prerogative toleration, i.e., urging the king with supporting bishops, against the law of Parliament and the lower clergy, to impose toleration in order to fulfill his duty as *conservator pacis*. In the *Two Tracts*, passive obedience is urged as a necessity; in the *1667 Essay*, passive resistance is urged as an inducement to the king to impose a toleration on acts of worship (178, 180–81, 183). Following the accession of King James, Locke still based toleration on the expediential grounds of civil peace in the face of religious disagreement. To this point then, the continuities appear to outweigh the "progress" in Locke's writings on church and state. But what of Locke's final words on this subject?

The *Epistola de Tolerantia*, first printed anonymously in Holland in 1689 and then translated and published in England later that year, appears to support an unambiguous "progressive" reading of Locke's thought. One can point to a resting of government solely on popular consent, which confines the ends of government to secular/civil interests and those "practical moral opinions" that sustain such a government. Royal prerogative does not extend to church polity, liturgy, or doctrine, and any group has a right peaceably to assemble and worship as they choose. Despite the familiarity of these principles to contemporary ears, Locke continues to base toleration on the same pragmatic grounds on which he had earlier based both imposition and prerogative toleration, i.e., on grounds of political convenience and not on conscience (George and George 1961:181–210, 331–41; Hughes 1965:161–88, 225–62).

Other continuities among the three sets of writings can also be found: In all three he absolutely denies toleration to Catholics; in all three he denies the right to teach practical moral doctrines thought by believers to be part of their speculative religious beliefs but judged by authority to be dangerous to the ends of civil society. And in all three sets of writings he clings to the Elizabethan ideal of an embracive national religion. In his plea for toleration in 1667, for example, Locke concludes "that toleration conduces no otherwise to the settlement of government than as it makes the majority of one mind, and encourages virtue in all, which is done by making the terms of church communion as large as may be; i.e., that your articles in speculative opinions be few and large, and ceremonies in worship few and easy, which is latitudinism" (*1667 Essay*:194). Though the means differ, the *Two Tracts* and the *Letters* share these same ends (see Reventlow 1984:243–85).

The final caveat against reading Locke's views as a progression toward increased secular enlightenment is found in the relationship between his epistemology and his position on toleration. Running through all three sets of writings on toleration as well as in *Human Understanding* and the *Reasonableness* is an insistence on the incapacity of most men rationally to derive stable and just sets of practical moral norms from general truths. Minimally this leads to a systematic denial of the recognition of conscience-claims against the political needs for order, but more importantly it pushes Locke in the direction of a "voluntarist" or "will-centered" source of duty, a stress more on knowledge of the lawgiver and his punishments than on knowledge of the specific and applicable content of those duties. The translation of general obligations into specific rules is always contingent, always dependent upon time, place, and circumstance. Responsibility for maintaining civil order in the face of this contingency must rest ultimately with a publicly recognized translator. For the subject-citizen, this voluntarism can be expressed as consent to government (whether primarily rational or in response to a felt obligation to God). For the ruler, responsibility consists in a clear identification of his duties to God and a clear knowledge of the secular and divine punishments for violating those duties.

Once this same practical and moral impulse is recognized in Locke's writings on church polity and toleration, a number of their more political elements fall into place. First, Locke's stress on the requirements of civil order and expedience is always and directly connected to isolating and protecting the purely religious sanctions of practical moral opinion—the God behind the earthly sovereign. It is this protection of source, this concern to keep interest and party and prejudice from clouding apprehension of moral rules and their divine sanctions that impels Locke's writing on both ecclesiology and on church-state relations. The twin political dangers are always the same: on the one hand, giddy multitudes who unleash irrational desires under the justification of conscience; on the other, "priestcraft"—"popish priests," seducers of magistrate and people, sowers of superstition to achieve earthly power and advantage. The vehicles on which these machinations ride can vary considerably over time: Sometimes scheming bishops ally with kings; often the lower clergy allies with the upper to exploit the gullible populace; always a corrupt clergy at all levels seeks to dominate the universities; always human addition is annexed to the Bible; and clerical complexity threatens to cloud the clear light of the gospel. Whether Locke looked nostalgically to the godly bishops under Elizabeth, or to a godly king against the corrupt Parliament and upper clergy, or to a godly Parliament against a corrupt court, or to a saving remnant of lay and clerical dissenters, the primacy of political obedience and moral goodness remains fixed.

A clear knowledge of moral and legal duties that are seen to flow from a just God, enforced by a disinterested magistrate, and taught by an upright and modest clergy are the prerequisites to achieve both political obedience and moral righteousness. Combined with a saving faith in Christ, man's highest ends on earth and highest hopes after death are vouchsafed. In politics this led Locke increasingly in the direction of popular consent and the right of revolution and in religion in the direction of anticlericalism and toleration. But the causes of both movements are not necessarily to be found in a putative progressive enlightenment nor in Locke's discovery of the state of nature. If the fixed axis of Locke's concern is practical moral beliefs and actions—how we get them, why we follow them—then one must explore Locke's writings on knowledge, on the relationship of philosophy and religion, reason and revelation, natural religion and Christianity, works and faith.

PROPOSITION 2: LOCKE AS SKEPTIC

Locke's metaphysics, epistemology, and philosophy are bounded by a deep skepticism regarding the reach of natural reason and informed by a deep faith in the efficacy of biblical revelation as a source of moral and political duties.

Given the recent writings on Locke's epistemology, which stress his skepticism and his limitations on the reach of reason, it may seem somewhat superfluous to begin with Locke's use of this skepticism in his last published defense of toleration in 1692. In the *Third Letter (Works 1823*: vol. 6) he defended freedom for "speculative religious truth" because that truth is

> faith . . . and not knowledge, persuasion, and not certainty. This is the highest the nature of the thing will permit us to go in matters of revealed religion, which are therefore called matters of faith; a persuasion of our own minds, short of knowledge, is the last result that determine us in such truths. . . . Knowledge, then, properly so called [is] not . . . to be had of the truths necessary to salvation. (*Third Letter*:144)

This same set of distinctions forms the core of analysis in Book 4 of *Human Understanding* and lies at the foundation of his argument defending revelation in the *Reasonableness of Christianity*. The most important feature of these inward or speculative beliefs is that they lie outside of the motivational structures by which we acquire knowledge of practical truths. Because speculative opinions "are required only to be believed . . . and to believe this or that to be true does not depend upon our will," these beliefs *"are not in men's power to perform"* (*Works 1823*, 6: 39–40). Thus, although speculative religious beliefs are absolutely necessary for salvation, they exist on a plane quite removed from those beliefs and opinions that *do* depend upon the will, *are* within men's power to perform, and *can* be known. Practical opinions are beliefs about "those moral rules which are necessary to the preservation of civil society" (*Works 1823*, 6:45). Whether rationally grounded or the product of revelation, these opinions and rules are what Locke means by natural law (Tully 1980:8–22).

The location and status of these practical moral rules and opinions, however, are somewhat ambiguous. Each person knows that both inward religious belief (faith) *and* the performance of moral duties (works) are necessary for salvation. As divinely commanded natural laws, they are part of our "religious interests" and therefore are of "the highest obligation that lies upon mankind . . . because there is nothing in this world that is any consideration in comparison with eternity" (*Works 1823*, 6:41). At the same time, these same moral obligations are closely tied to the necessities of our bodies, to the protection of our worldly or "civil interests"

(Works 1823, 6:10). Thus, knowledge of these rules and motivations to obey them seem to emanate from two different sources: On the one hand, these rules are commanded by a supernatural god through direct or written revelation communicated subjectively to each sincere Christian. Punishment for their breach is hell. On the other hand, knowledge of these rules can be attained rationally by reflection on our physiology, our own sensations, and our ideas. By listening to the insistent voices of our natural bodies as they speak the language of self-preservation and by reflecting on those voices we are led to a knowledge of our moral and political duties. Obedience to their dictates is pleasure; disobedience is pain. Assuming that natural law is written and enforced as civil law by political sovereigns, motivation to follow these dictates of reason is augmented by fear of physical punishment—i.e., by the desire (necessity) for self-preservation. As Locke so clearly puts it in his *Letter on Toleration* *(Works 1823,* 6:42):

> The necessity of preserving men in the possession of what honest industry has already acquired, and also of preserving their liberty and strength, whereby they may acquire what they farther want, obliges men to enter into society with one another; that by mutual assistance and joint force, they may secure unto each other their properties, in the things that contribute to the comforts and happiness of this life.

At the extremes then, natural law or practical moral rules and opinions lie suspended between the utter subjectivity and inwardness of speculative religious belief and the utter subjectivity and inwardness of bodily sensations. It would seem that only a wholly unreconstructed Calvinist would suspend our active duties on such distant hooks as an utterly remote god and an utterly depraved body. Or to put the image in another way: The Bible is written revelation, but each man is absolutely the only human judge of his understanding of this revelation. No social or political institutions have any titles to command rules whose authority is based on *their* understanding of biblical revelation. The only publicly commanded belief derived from biblical revelation is "Jesus is the Messiah." Obedience to any rules commanded by political authority that are believed to threaten the hope for eternal life is not obligatory. Thus, it is a matter for each individual to see (or not to see) the connection between his particular set of speculative beliefs and the moral rules or natural laws that are obligatory. But what of the naturalistic and reasonable side? Here, too, no social or political institution has any title to command rules the obedience to which are seen (or felt) to threaten the rights to preservation of the individual. The "right of nature" usually trumps the law of nature and the civil laws that declare and enforce the natural law (cf. Tully 1980:60–64, 115–30, 151–54, 166–70).

Locke's epistemological location of practical moral and legal rules has an institutional parallel: The state is the putative protector of our bodies, our "civil interests," and its authority is bounded by the logic of those interests. Churches, meanwhile, express our "religious interests." They are organizations whose members share speculative beliefs and who collectively engage in external acts of worship believed to be appropriate to those beliefs. The distance between these two institutions appears as great as that between spiritual perfection and bodily corruption: "The church itself is a thing absolutely separate and distinct from the commonwealth. . . . He jumbles heaven and earth together, and things most remote and opposite, who mixes these societies, which are in their original, end, business, and in every thing, perfectly distinct, and infinitely different from each other" (*Works 1823*, 6:21).

In graphic terms, here is what Locke seems to have done:

Soul	Body
Religious Interests	Civil Interests
Heaven/Hell	Pleasure/Pain
Church	State
Belief	Sensation
Supernatural God	God of Nature
Sacred History and Prophecy	Natural History/State of Nature

Put in this bald way and with no recourse to innate ideas to mediate and lend coherence, how can the realm of natural law, practical moral opinions, and moral actions be constructed to preserve the integrity of these distinctions and to integrate them into collective life? Indeed, the problem is still more difficult. The very studies that have stressed historical and ideological context and have called our attention to the limits of reason and the importance of religion have also stressed Locke's insistence on the utter contingency of almost every mediating institution, method, or value that might fill the space between the voids (Ashcraft 1987; Dunn 1969a; Rapaczynski 1987; Tully 1980; Wood 1983). Between body and soul are moral practices and opinions of almost infinite variety among different cultures and times; between the eternal interests of heaven and the temporal interests on earth are found greed, corruption, and exploitation; between church and state lie scheming priests, tyrannical kings, and giddy multitudes; between pure religious faith and the testimony of our own senses lie frenzied enthusiasm, false philosophy, and corrupt morals; between the promise of a heavenly kingdom and the purpose, beauty, and harmony of the natural order lies secular history as the story of bloodshed and depravity. From Locke's earliest Latin *Tract* of 1660 to his posthumously published *Reasonableness of Christianity* and its *Vindications* this contingency becomes almost a litany: "The perverting influence of customs, the frivolity of opinions, the allurements of pleasures, the violence of passions and the enthusiasm of parties confuse and mislead our feeble minds in such diverse ways" (*TT*:237); "these thousand years and upwards; schisms, separations, contentions, animosities, quarrels, blood and butchery have harassed and defamed" Christian Europe (*Second Vindication, Works 1823,* 7:358). Given this contingency, civil and religious peace is a miracle (*TT*:119, 211).

Against these odds and this history, what chance has reason; indeed, what chance have the simple truths of the gospel? And against such odds what chance does Locke have in extricating us both epistemologically and historically from the many binds he has placed us in? Is it mere whistling in the dark that both Dunn (1969a) and Ashcraft (1987), respectively, title chapters near the end of their studies of the *Two Treatises* "The Coherence of a Mind" and "The Coherence of Locke's Thought"?

Attempts at resolution between Locke's epistemology and politics in this new, historically located Lockean scholarship are quite different from earlier attempts at resolution. Earlier argument took place almost wholly within the confines of Locke's formal epistemology bounded by the reach of sensation (and hedonism) on the one hand and the role of reflection (and rationalism) on the other. The former position was sustained by reference to Locke's discussion of "Power" and "Will" in Book 2 of *Human Understanding,* and the appropriate Hobbesian and possessive individualistic conclusions are drawn from the *Second Treatise,* starting with appropriation of property and ending with the invention of money. Arrayed on the other side were those who began with Locke's discussion of morality as a "mixed mode," considered variously in Books 2, 3, and 4 of *Human Understanding.* This discussion centered on complex ideas, reflection, and choice and suggests a deistic and natural-law reading of the

Second Treatise. Coherence is achieved by the resolute pursuit of one or the other logic. Third parties and textbook writers were left to conclude only that Locke muddled his way through.

Without resolving this earlier debate, Lockean scholarship, reflected most recently in Tully's (1980) and Rapaczynski's (1987) studies, asserts that in Locke man's natural desires are always assumed to be historically mediated through religious beliefs, custom, habit, and the whole complex of social and economic institutions established in any given society. Thus, a simple hedonistic reading of Locke is rejected: Locke assumes that men are motivated primarily by ideas of happiness and not by feelings of pleasure, by complex and socially constructed ideas of good and evil and not by simple and natural desires (Rapaczynski, 1987:154–68; Tully 1980: part one). Locke assumes that every man has what he considers a "life plan," whether handed him by custom or produced by morally serious reflection, whether composed of bits and pieces of rationally indefensible superstition or of logically coherent and morally praiseworthy norms.

This same perspective, then, locates Locke's realm of practical moral opinions and norms *in history*—that is, time, place, and circumstance shape and help to determine the institutions and rules that make up this realm. This historical contingency ascribed to Locke holds true for him whether or not these same norms can be justified at the bars of reason and revelation. Some norms and opinions are truly good, and some are not; some practices and institutions are in accord with Scripture and reason, and some are not.

Locke's writings on education and on epistemology can both be seen as addressing the very practical problems of how to instill the proper values in children and how to be assured as adults that the values we hold can be justified. At the level of the individual, then, Locke outlines an *ontogenetic* model of development—a "natural history" or cause-and-effect movement from a childhood of unreflective desires and sensations to an adulthood of self-conscious and reflective conduct. Indeed, the "natural history" of ideas from simple sensations to complex moral judgments is a microcosmic parallel to this learning theory. Neal Wood's recent study of *Human Understanding* is an excellent summary of this kind of analysis (1983), especially because it points to the need for purgation and self-reform in societies where moral norms and moral education are historically corrupt.

Yet if *Human Understanding* from this individual perspective can be seen as having a "politics"—that is, political life sustains the environment in which men are well or ill taught—so, too, does this side of Locke's analysis have a religious dimension. At the simplest, churches are major sources of moral and legal education, and Locke's writings on church-state relations attest to their importance. Yet this side of religion as institution can be and was subsumed by Locke under politics and the various configurations of institutional arrangements touched on in Proposition 1. At a deeper level, however, an individual's moral development has a religious dimension because his salvation is largely dependent upon fulfilling the obligations of natural law as commanded by God and ratified by reason. But if each person exists in history, subject to prevailing "laws of opinion," how can he be expected to conduct himself according to eternal and timeless standards of conduct? How can one expect him to stand outside of time, place, and circumstance, at least to the extent of attaining reflective self-consciousness regarding moral choice and moral responsibility? One answer is found in the power of reason; whether we look to Locke's early *Essays on the Law of Nature* (1954: Questions 1, 2, 4, 6, 7) or to his last writings in the *Reasonableness (Works 1823*: vol. 7), the message is the same: "The duties of [natural] law, arising from the constitution of his very nature, are of eternal obligation; nor can it be taken away or dispensed without changing the nature of things, overturning the measures of right and wrong, and thereby introducing and authorizing irregularity, confusion, and disorder in the world" (*RC*: no. 180). From first to last, then, reason is seen by Locke as the "spark of divine nature" (*RC*: no. 231), "the light of nature revealed to them" (*RC*: no. 232).

Still, to any reader of the *Reasonableness,* from the point where Locke asks "What need is there of a Savior?" (*RC*: no. 234) to the end of the essay, it becomes clear that the resources any individual has through his own reason both to discover the rules of right conduct and to act on them are slim indeed. And when one adds Book 4 of *Human Understanding* (chaps. 2, 3, 11, and 15–18), on the gap between what we *must* know to achieve righteousness and what we *can* know with certainty through unaided reason, each individual's *natural* history would necessarily lead straight to a natural hell—i.e., to eternal death. The requirements of both knowledge and motivation mandate the intervention of sacred history, moments Locke calls "the fullness of time" (*RC*: no. 228) or revelation, which transform both the understandings and the actions of men. In short, religious faith or revelation is a transforming moment *in each man's natural history* and is necessary for both worldly happiness and redemption and eternal life. Understood in this perspective, *Human Understanding* outlines both a natural history of knowledge and a path to salvation.

At the ontogenetic level, sacred history appears in the form of an individual act of faith or conversion and the beginning of a new life. Hypocrisy, corruption, and greed are cut away, and the clear duties taught by reason shine through in the clearing. This penetration of sacred history into natural man and natural reason is possible only because God supernaturally intervenes in history, first at various moments in the Old Testament, then by sending Christ, and finally by promising a final and collective "fullness of time" at the Second Coming and final judgment.

Although all of this parallel or typology between biblical sacred history (God entering history) and personal experience (Christ entering a natural man) is fairly standard Protestant hermeneutics, one can easily miss its importance in Locke's epistemology by dismissing its relevance. This dismissal is understandable because acts of faith, personal transformation, and renewal of purposes are discussed in such abstract, individual, and subjective ways in *Human Understanding*. At most, this dismissive reading could say that Locke's politics might require sturdy Calvinist saints with their self-discipline and sense of calling to usher in and sustain his politics—and this conclusion has been used either to praise Locke or to bury him. Yet what is ontogenetic in *Human Understanding* and in his educational writings is phylogenetic or social in both *Reasonableness* and the *Second Treatise*. Mankind also has a "natural history" from simple subsistence and simple sensations, desires, and actions to a complex society of specialized institutions, social roles, and moral and civil laws. The process of ontogenetic moral development can become corrupt and distorted by succumbing to base desires and from the pressure of social institutions and popular opinion (see Wood 1983:109–12, 129–35, 153–67). Individuals require faith and grace to renew lives of righteousness. Mankind, too, can become corrupt (fathers become despots); "mankind . . . under a corruption of manners and principles, which ages after ages had prevailed, and must be confessed, was not in a way or tendency to be mended" (*RC*: no. 243), so Christ was sent to renew the collective life of man. From a phylogenetic standpoint the natural limits of reason and the natural barriers to moral development in individuals can now be restated as a *historical* limitation in the collective moral development of mankind:

Though the works of nature, in every part of them, sufficiently evidence a Deity, yet the world made so little use of their reason that they saw him not where, even by the impression of himself, he was easy to be found. Sense and lust blinded their minds in some, and a careless inadvertency in others, and fearful apprehensions in most . . . gave them up into the hands of their priests, to fill their heads with false notions of the Deity, and their worship with foolish rites, as they pleased; and what dread or craft once began, devotion soon made sacred, and religion immutable. In this state of darkness and ignorance of the true God, vice and superstition held the world. Nor could any help be had or hoped for from reason, which could not be heard, and was judged to have nothing to do with the case, the priests everywhere, to secure their empire, having excluded reason from having anything to do in religion. (*RC*: no. 238, and see *RC*: nos. 241 –43; compare *ELN*, 1954:133 –35)

To which period in history is Locke here referring? On the most obvious reading, he is referring to the Jews and the Gentiles in the time of the Old Testament. The Gentiles are gripped in polytheistic paganism, the Jews in idolatry, and both in priestcraft. Into this "darkness" Christ was sent as a supernatural intervention to redeem nature and natural reason and natural law. But there is also a second dark period in history, a Christian "kingdom of darkness," that "thousand years and upwards [of] quarrels, blood and butchery." Ontorevelation and phylorevelation meet in the Reformation and in those crucial moments in history in which its teachings are instituted and defended. Christ metaphorically reappears in history in these critical moments of collective renewal; priestcraft is challenged, corruption is battled, and the light of nature—that *natural* revelation—again penetrates the darkness, but this time, a darkness of the collective soul.

This reading is also a standard Protestant understanding of itself and the Bible. Whether it takes a radically apocalyptic and millennial turn as it did among the Diggers, Fifth Monarchists, and Muggletonians in the English Revolution (Hill 1975) or suddenly explodes in the form of "popish plots" and anti-Christs before the Glorious Revolution (Hill 1971; Kenyon 1972), or whether it makes a more philosophically mediated appearance as political opposition to the cultural and institutional barriers to the appearance of reason, the logic and periodization of Locke's sacred history and prophecy is much the same.

In Locke's writings, both radically Puritan and moderate Anglican formulations of this sacred history can be found, often in rough parallel to his changing positions on church-state issues. There is more reliance on reason to be found in the *Essays on the Law of Nature* than in *Human Understanding* and more in *Human Understanding* than in *Reasonableness*. Institutionally there is more faith in moderate Anglican and enlightened churchmen (largely bishops) in the *Tracts* and the *1667 Essay* than there is in the *Letter on Toleration*, with its defense of sects and saints. Yet to see this is not necessarily to conclude, as some have strongly suggested (Ashcraft, Dunn, Philip Abrams), that Locke moved on a line from youthful rationalist and middle-aged enlightened philosopher to older and wiser believer. I want to suggest that Locke's developing position argues in favor of an increasingly confident assertion of an *interpenetration* of reason and revelation, of natural history and sacred history, of what the title of the classic study of nineteenth-century English romanticism called "Natural-Supernaturalism" (M. H. Abrams 1971) and Reventlow's study of British hermeneutics called "rational supernaturalism." An examination of the dimensions and import of this interpenetration is the subject of the third and last proposition.

PROPOSITION 3: LOCKE AS CHRISTIAN

Locke's theology and biblical interpretation are grounded in the spiritualist tradition of the radical reformation and incorporate apocalyptic and millennial ideas of time into his defense of reason and his theories of natural religion, natural law, and politics.

Just as our understanding of Locke's *Second Treatise* has been altered by seeing it in light of political writings contemporary with the exclusion crisis and the allegiance controversy, so, too, has our understanding of Locke's religious writings undergone great change by seeing them in light of contemporary writings on religion. Although specialization has tended to keep these two bodies of scholarship somewhat isolated, I want to suggest ways in which the findings of this latter body of scholarship might further alter our understanding of the *Second Treatise*.

Accept the fact that Locke was a devout member of the Anglican confession and one sees immediately that his epistemology and theology reflected and influenced the latitudinarian and Low Church party of Anglicanism (Reventlow 1984:223–34; James 1949:63–114; Hunt 1871, 2: chaps. 8–10). The stress on a few simple articles of faith, on the accessibility of all to the simple truths of the gospel, and on the use of plain reason to understand the Scripture are all leading tenets of this group and for very sound reasons. One reason is that it expressed the theological values of the radical reformation, which were powerful in English church life from the Elizabethan period onward. Also, these tenets were important adjuncts to a Restoration policy of "comprehension" and intrachurch tolerance in opposition to High Church ideals of uniformity and imposition. Finally, these religious perspectives were anti–High Church, anti-Catholic, and anticlerical, valuing the pastoral over the official roles of the clergy and encouraging the role of laymen in the life of the churches. Rather than opiate, then, Locke's defense of these themes in the *Reasonableness* and its *Vindications* is traditional doctrine, albeit supported by a complex and new "way of ideas." As such, they were an integral part of exclusion ideology and, later, true or old Whig party values from 1688 through the first three decades of the eighteenth century (see Goldie 1980b; Straka 1962b; Kenyon 1977; Reventlow 1984:327–34).

In addition to locating Locke's theological writings in latitudinarian Christian apologetic, a second feature of those writings reflects another persistent strain in Reformation hermeneutics, namely, the idea of a progressive revelation. To be sure, Christian doctrine assumes that, to some degree, the law of the New Testament supplants the law of the Old. In the view of the radical side of the Reformation, however, this supplanting becomes a transcending and supplies the core of its millennial antinomianism: To be transcended are not only laws but priests and kings; not only complex liturgy but all official ceremony; not only idolatry but all physical and institutional barriers between God's spirit and the true believer.

One can take the logic of progressive revelation even farther—much farther as it turns out. Biblical history repeats itself as allegory and typology, and each cycle of repetition, each higher "age," brings the pure spirit of God closer to man. The passage from Old to New Testament is a sign that men are "now" prepared to receive a higher law than that given the Jews; Christ is not only a New Adam, but represents the promise of a new and higher mankind. And, given the fall back into the "kingdom of darkness" after Christ's first appearance—that millennium of idolatry, priestcraft, and corruption—the Christ as liberator from the Jewish law becomes Christ as liberator from the historic church and even the historic Bible. Direct revelation, the direct infusion of spirit into matter, transcends the historic and literal New Testament, symbolized by the church's teachings of the Epistles, to become pure gospel, pure expectation, pure eschatology. Whether expressed as Quaker, Ranter, or Fifth

Monarchist movements on the one hand or in the language of humanism, the new science, natural law, and Deism on the other, the hermeneutical framework is the same.

Within the framework of progressive revelation an individual can hold two sets of beliefs simultaneously: If matter and spirit become one, a Baconian scientist can also be a Christian mystic (Newton), a materialist can also be a spiritualist (Hobbes), a believer in natural law can also see that law as part of Christian revelation (Locke). What Pocock has called the hylozoistic features of this side of Reformation theology—the conflation of matter and spirit in history—is a common theme in studies of early and mid-seventeenth-century Puritanism. These features are readily recognized in, for example, Part 3 of *Leviathan* or in Winstanley's *The Law of Freedom* (Hill 1975:387–94). What has not been so readily seen, however, is the more philosophical and methodological expression of this same idea of conflation in late seventeenth-century writings.

Another way of seeing this ideal of conflation is through the use of the radical reformation's understanding of the millennium. One form of this understanding is apocalyptic, with the radical twist that the Second Coming is just around the corner and that the saving remnant of saints know this and are preparing for it by climbing the nearest hill or by organizing a revolutionary army or by occupying common lands. Again, this is now commonplace in studies of the English Revolution. A more communal and individualistic expression of this way of understanding the millennium is through perfectionism—the millennium has already arrived in the souls of the faithful; they need no laws, no Bibles, no churches, no marriage vows, for they are no longer part of the ordinary world. A third form of understanding and one that had the most profound effect on British philosophy and literature in the late seventeenth and early eighteenth centuries is to see the millennium as a historical process, a gradual unfolding of time, the revelatory marks of which can be seen through the "evidences" of antitypes and the reasonable signs through moral, social, and intellectual progress. What Sacvan Bercovitch (1975) calls "the myth of America" is precisely this reading of millennialism.

In the case of Locke and his latitudinarian and Deist contemporaries, this latter reading of progressive revelation was the dominant hermeneutical assumption. Latitudinarian apologetic tended to stress the themes already noted: the simplicity, accessibility, and morality of the Gospels are the absolute center of the Bible and the Bible the core of Christianity. All else in the Bible and in historical church doctrine and practice should be treated publicly as "indifferent" to the issue of redemption or simply rejected as not relevant for Christians any longer. This spiritualist view of the Bible is accompanied by a strong streak of moralistic rationalism. Except for faith in Christ and belief in the Resurrection the Bible must be read through the lens of reason and not through the institutional mediation of church tradition or corporate clergy. The remainder of essential Christianity is morality. While moral action flows from the act of conversion, the moral norms must be justified at the bar of nature and reason. Unlike Deists, Locke and other latitudinarians did not deny miracles or denigrate belief in them; but they insisted that each individual was responsible for believing biblical revelation and the recounting of miracles only so far as he could, and they proceeded to provide guidelines to aid in this process. Indeed, Locke's *Human Understanding* can be read as a handbook for Protestant salvation, such was its twin insistence on the standards of reason and morality and on the necessity of faith.

Periodization and the stress on the future transformed biblical history more and more into an allegory of a reason-based universal or natural history. Clerical writings that express this movement began within the latitudinarian framework. William Chillingworth's highly influential *The Religion of Protestants a Safe Way to Salvation* (1638) is an early seventeenth-century example (cf. Reventlow 1984:147–52) of the stress on reason and morality as progressive revelation. During the Restoration period, John Tillotson and Edward Stillingfleet are the best-known exponents of this same position. Tillotson, who later became Archbishop of Canterbury, stressed the centrality of the Gospels and the "obedience to the moral and eternal law of God" as the "sum and essence of all religion." The Old Testament law is consigned to the dustbin of history by the theory of condescension: "The Jewish law was an institution of religion adapted by God in great condescension to the weak apprehension of that people" and was designed to prepare them for a higher moral and ethical law. Christianity incorporates this higher law directly (Reventlow 1984:240).

Stillingfleet, who became Bishop of Worcester, was even more direct in equating biblical revelation with natural law. By distinguishing between the historical and contingent "positive commands of God" and the eternal "Law of Nature," biblical periodization becomes a progressive revelation of nature and a progressive diminution of miracle. "The Law of Nature binds indispensably, as it depends not upon any arbitrary constitution, but is founded upon the intrinsical nature of good and evil in the things themselves, antecedently to any positive declaration of God's Will" (Reventlow 1984:230). In both writings, spiritualism and rationalism converge. Reventlow's conclusion is most apt: "Once the inner light as a charismatic force has been made into a sure possession, it has only to be turned into the light of reason which all human beings have at their disposal as creatures and later as autonomous subjects" (129).

John Toland's *Christianity Not Mysterious* (1696) and Matthew Tindal's *Rights of the Christian Church Asserted* (1706) and *Christianity as Old as the Creation* (1730) carry this process to its rationalist conclusion. These moderately Deistic writings are, like the latitudinarian ones, Whig political documents addressed against High Church, Non-Juror, and Tory claims that forms of church government, religious ceremony, and doctrines of faith are divinely commanded and that the church as an institution is of divine right. In asserting the claims of reason and morality against the Old Testament specifically and biblical legalism generally, Christianity for Toland and Tindal becomes the teaching of the gospel as a reasonable morality. Christianity is as old as creation, on this reading, because Christ was sent by God to reform morality by reinstating natural law and natural reason.

Locke's *Reasonableness of Christianity* exactly centers on this reading of the New Testament, although, unlike the Deist writings, it does not dispense with the need for faith to open one up to reason, to teach its main conclusions, and to stimulate dedication to a new life. But this "newness" is really an instauration, a renewal of the original and eternal values of natural law. Behind the Jehovah of history is the original God of Nature; behind ceremonial law, church polity, and historic dogma is pure religion as pure morality.

There are two interesting variants on these notions of progressive revelation. The first is biblical and states that the Gospels are not contrary to reason; indeed, properly understood, they are a historical "republication" of the eternal Law of Nature. Tindal, the Lockean apologist for the true Whigs at the turn of the century, subtitled his last work, *Christianity as Old as the Creation*, "the Gospel, A Republication of the Religion of Nature." Later Christian apologetics, especially Joseph Butler's highly influential *The Analogy of Religion, Natural and Revealed, to the Constitution and Course of Nature* (1736), made almost exactly the same point: The Bible is "a republication, and external institution of natural or essential religion, adapted to the present [i.e., prevailing] circumstances of mankind" (Reventlow 1984:347). This same "rational supernaturalism" is also found in Anthony Collins's defense of natural religion, where he says that Christian teaching contains a predetermined moral standard and that the Bible "does but republish the law of nature" (Reventlow 1984:369). Pure Christianity as morality and pure revelation as reason are, then, another expression of the interdependence of spiritualism and rationalism in sixteenth- and seventeenth-century Reformation theology in Britain. Beginning with Lord Herbert of Cherbury at the time of Hobbes, this same equation was made in assertions that a pure reason lies behind and infuses all historical revelation. Daniel Whitby, one of the great theologians in the Church of England, not only states Locke's argument that early Christianity made its way in the world because of its reasonableness but concludes that the doctrines of the Apostles "were conformable to the principles of natural religion which were known *from the beginning*" (Hunt 1871, 2:459, italics added).

In addition to the republication theory, a second variant of sacred history as progressive revelation is that *all* religions in the beginning, not just Judaism and Christianity, were pure morality, pure natural religions, and that all religions became corrupt. Lord Herbert of Cherbury's five *notitiae communes circa Religionem* in his *De Veritate* (1633) is the first statement of this depravation thesis by an Englishman, but the notion of the original purity of all religions and the assumption that this original purity is now reclaimed through the gospel (latitudinarianism) or through pure reason (Deism) has a long history, running from Martin Bucher in the early sixteenth century through the Enlightenment and the later era of romanticism. Within this early literature, one finds the beginnings of a "natural history of religion," i.e., a rational explanation for the rise of patterns of religious belief and practices within a larger theory of human progress or the process of civilization. Locke's contemporaries, Toland and Thomas Morgan, for example, suggest this idea (Reventlow 1984:303−8, 396−404).[3]

Locke himself broaches these theories both directly and indirectly. His use of condescension theory to explain (and dismiss) the Old Testament incorporates ideas of progressive revelation having implications outside of literal biblical history and prophecy. Next, his explanation for religious superstition and the rise of priestcraft often suggests that this took place because men had not yet developed their rational faculties because they were not yet ready to receive the gospel. If reason is an evangelical imperative, then its appearance (or reappearance) in history is contingent on the workings of faith. As so much of this apologetic literature does, Locke mixes the images of the Reformation as a *recovery* of the pure gospel and the Reformation as a critical moment in the progressive *discovery* of higher truth—a notion of time spiraling upward but also cycling through fixed typological axes.[4]

A third and more direct Lockean instance of this mode of natural history is in his ethnographic and economic arguments in the *Second Treatise*. The two successive states of nature are also a "natural" succession and explain not only the historic rise of paternal/hereditary kingship but also why that rule could become hedged with divine right and cultivated by priestcraft and superstition (see Schochet 1975). Here, the natural history of human invention complements his phylogenetic theory of ideas.

Putting all of these paths of time together, then, suggests a revelatory convergence when pure faith and pure reason meet, when quantitative social and economic developments stimulate a sudden rediscovery of natural rights and popular consent, when political and religious despotism are finally confronted and destroyed. These intimations in Locke and in the cognate literature of Puritanism, Low Church Anglicanism, Dissent, and later Deism make perfectly understandable the tendency to locate the state of nature in this history as both recovery and discovery. Only when the Gospels have purged men of priestcraft and superstition and only when economic development has made possible leisure and learning does the light of Nature shine through clearly and natural law become obligatory.

> Our Savior found mankind under a corruption of manners and principles, which ages after ages had prevailed, and . . . was not in a way or tendency to be mended. . . . Natural reason nowhere had cured, nor was likely to cure, the defects and errors in them. Those just measures of right and wrong . . . were looked on as bonds of society and conveniences of common life . . . but where was it that their obligation was thoroughly known and allowed, and they received as precepts of law—of the highest law, the law of nature. (*RC*: no. 243)

But of course Christ's first coming did *not* suddenly cause philosophers to prevail over priests. Only now, when true biblical revelation has been recovered, has reason a chance to prevail. Contracts and markets and property rights and interest rates and balance of trade were hardly of central concern to Christ's disciples or to the moral teachings of the early church. The causal mechanisms of natural history are the causal mechanism of the God of Nature, and together they become evangels of this reappearance of Christ and the appearance of reason as a power in history. It becomes but a short step to the Scottish Enlightenment's answer to the question of where the state of nature is to be found. Adam Ferguson replied, "We may answer, It is here" (1980:8).

The new historical scholarship has led to some paradoxical results, some of which are suggested in the arguments of this essay. The most obvious is an almost complete reversal in judgment about what is radical and what is moderate in Locke's writings. The clearest expression of this reversal concerns Locke's politics versus Locke's philosophy. The old reading tended to be that Locke's politics were moderate, commonsensical, and temporizing; his philosophy radical and reductionist. Now the judgment is almost reversed: Locke's politics are revolutionary; his epistemology and moral theory temporizing, contingent, and grounded in convention.

But what about Locke's religion? Earlier scholarship tended to see Locke's religious writings either as part of his legendary caution (perhaps to cover his "real" philosophical radicalism) or at one with his political moderation. The dissonance is critical only when Locke wrote on church-state relations: Then his radical philosophy urging unconditional religious freedom clashes with his prudent politics that urges proscription of Catholics and atheists, and prudence wins. The newer historical scholarship also makes the distinction between principle and prudence but draws the lines of separation at very different places in his work. Whether urging latitudinarian imposition in the early 1660s or qualified toleration in the 1690s, Locke's position consistently sought to purge political and cultural life of priestcraft. Anticlericalism was a consistent and radical strain in Locke's writings. When it became obvious to Locke that proponents of clericalism were attempting to further their designs through the king and court, this same radicalism fed into Locke's politics. Earlier, Locke's anticlericalism was usually viewed as a secular and antireligious stance; in the eyes of more recent scholarship, this secularism is seen as a religious imperative, a protection of biblical Christianity from priestcraft, whether Catholic or High Church. That Locke changed his views on the appropriate institutional weapons in this battle does not derogate from the consistency of his ends. And when one compares Locke's institutional shifts to those of other writers—indeed, writers much less obviously pious Christians—the older view attains even less force. Rein-terpretations of Hobbes (Eisenach 1982), or of Harrington (Goldie 1987), or of Anglican latitudinarianism generally (Reventlow 1984) have stressed the interdependence of the logic of the secular state and the theology of the English Reformation. Indeed, the shifts back and forth between Protestant Erastianism and toleration are so pervasive historically that it makes very little sense to posit a major philosophical difference, not to speak of difference in political ideology, between them.[5]

A parallel reversal, I think, is taking place regarding judgments of the relationship between Locke's epistemology and his politics. With some notable exceptions (James 1949; Aaron 1971), the older scholarship never took Locke's humble protestations in *Human Understanding* very seri-ously because they saw Locke's epistemology as the powerful engine of the triumphal train of secularization. Correspondingly, they discounted his confident confessions of biblical faith. Recent scholarship has taken Locke's protestations both of humility and of faith more at face value by seeking to reconstruct the connections Locke sought to make between reason and faith and between outward behavior and inward belief. The conclusions have not been an exact reversal because the older scholarship was always divided over the hedonist/economic and rationalist/natural-law components of Locke's epistemology and moral theory. Recent scholarship has come down squarely on the side of the rationalist in-terpretation, but not on the same terms. To be sure, what Locke isolates as the realm of practical moral opinion, "mixed modes," relations, and moral sanctions in *Human Understanding* is now linked more to his writings on natural law and less to the bodily nexus of desire, will, and action. To this linkage of Locke's theories of moral knowledge and moral action to natural law, however, is now added the linkage of natural law to the law of the gospel. This linkage immediately established, as I have suggested earlier, a *historical* connection to what might soon become a litany of names in the new scholarship, some of whom I have invoked, e.g., Cumberland, Collins, Chillingworth, Toland, Tindal, and Morgan. And once this historical connection is made, Locke's epistemology as tabula rasa and politics as state of nature become located in biblical time and sacred history. This, indeed, is the conclusion of any study that as-serts the interdependence of spiritualism and rationalism or the close relationship of Reformation hermeneutics and the emergence of Protes-tant Christianity as morality. The reassertion of the rationalist Locke over the hedonist one in his epistemology is in the new scholarship also the recognition of a spiritualist and assertively evangelical Locke as well. This side of Locke is simply not evident in the older defense of his rationalism. The older understanding had the effect of making the *Second Treatise* very Kantian (e.g., Pitkin 1965 and Riley 1974) even if it did rescue Locke and the history of liberalism from the hedonistic grasp of Hobbes.[6] The newer historical scholarship does no such thing. By seeing the institution of the Law of Nature as in part a religious imperative of reborn Christians, the *Second Treatise* becomes more obviously revolutionary because its rationalism and moralism are so closely tied to revolutionary transformation and biblical apocalypse.

All of these suggested reversals are having and will continue to have a major impact on the place of Locke in the history of philosophy and in the history of liberalism. The latter history has been so radically rewritten in the recent past as to be almost unrecognizable. Both politics and time have been rigorously reinserted into the political thought of early modern England by insistence on the two paradigms of civic humanism and Protestant millennialism. While these two paradigms have not always proved easy to integrate with each other—Christopher Hill's use of millennialism is often quite removed from John Pocock's or Quentin Skinner's—both paradigms have challenged the liberal enlightenment view. This challenge, moreover, is not simply over textual interpretation but over the more fundamental issues of the role of economic interests, classes and institutions, the place of religious and theological conflict, and the importance of constitutional and legal traditions in the major upheavals of seventeenth-century England. And this broader challenge over the issue of the relationship between historical change and change in ideas has had effects not only on how we write the history of "liberalism" (which now must appear in quotes) but on the history of philosophy in this period as well.

The older history of liberalism was essentially an intellectual product of Victorian reform liberalism and continued to be written in that spirit by Marxists, who, after all, remain quite Victorian in their views of history, science, and progress. This history of liberalism was a linear history resembling nothing so much as a train on one track with many coaches labeled, variously, secularization, rationality, positivism, empiricism, or utility and passing through such quaint villages as custom, religion, superstition, magic, and Natural Law. The newer history of liberalism denies that there is such an unambiguous animal and writes history not in the mode of a train but on the model of a series of complex spirals.

Movements along these spirals cause periodic encounters with the same vertical axes, though now seen in a slightly different light. Older ideas or symbols do not simply die, as if passed by, but are only submerged and usually reappear in a slightly new guise. Much like d'Entreves's (1951) discussion of Natural Law, in which he says that every time it is kicked out the front door it reappears in the back, so, too, do biblical notions of time, Stoic notions of virtue, and classical ideals of the polis continually reappear. Both civic-humanist and radical-reformation political ideas have carried with them nonlinear or "cyclical-progressive" notions of time, and this has affected not only how we write the history of liberalism and the history of political thought but the history of philosophy generally.

Midway through Reventlow's *Authority of the Bible and the Rise of the Modern World*, he puts the issue quite simply: "The history of philosophy needs the history of biblical exegesis as a presupposition for understanding" (283). Locke occupies a central place, not only in Reventlow's study of English hermeneutics but in every history of ideas in early modern England. Thus, reinterpretations of Locke's *Second Treatise* in light of Locke's writings on religion will, if persuasive, almost automatically occasion a reconsideration of the history of early modern philosophy. Indeed, this process has already begun.[7] I say "almost automatically" because the ways in which we interpret texts often provide the guidelines for how we read and understand history and the place of that text in history. To reintroduce Locke's religious writings into his understanding of politics is also, then, to reintroduce forms of biblical time as understood by Locke and his contemporaries into our own understanding of history. I suppose that one can then conclude—and perhaps with Locke's consent—that we who study Locke are not born free after all but inquire within a preexisting history of inquiry. Like Locke, we are born within a framework of authoritative understandings, which no amount of unaided reason can dispel. And, like Locke, we discover that our interpretive truth is a small clearing in a rather tangled hermeneutical circle.

NOTES

1. Though others had written on this feature of *Human Understanding* (James 1949:63–114; Aaron 1971:296–301, 335–51; Hunt 1871, 2:183–90), this earlier work was largely ignored by students of Locke's politics and philosophy.

2. See George (1961:181–210 and 331–41), Hughes (1965:161–88 and 225–62).

3. This argument gets carried even further in Shaftesbury: Only *after* one has found the God of Nature is one prepared to receive historical or biblical revelation (Reventlow 1984:312).

4. See M. H. Abrams (1971:17–70), Frye (1983), and Reventlow (1984:369–83) on the relationship of allegorical and typological exegesis and later Deistic thought.

5. This same recognition is evident in studies of American Protestantism and of the development of American civil religion as an embracive national Protestantism in the nineteenth century.

6. This rescue has proved rather late in view of the fact that Hobbes is also being reinterpreted in this direction (Eisenach 1981:55–71; Pocock 1971c:148–201).

7. The most obvious example is the publication of the "Ideas in Context" series by Cambridge University Press. Examples of this series are Pocock (1985); Rorty, Schneewind, and Skinner (1984); and Pagden (1987).

4 / *Rationality and the* Two Treatises

DAVID RESNICK

In my view, Locke's great contribution to modern liberal thought arose from his commitment to a critical rationalism that undermined the foundations of traditional society and thoroughly rejected traditional modes of thought grounded in irrational appeals to custom and historical precedent. Locke was aware of social change and the need to defend new and more rational approaches to solving the problems of social order created by a society in transition. Though he wished to rationalize social and political practices, he did not yield to the temptation to substitute a ruthless commitment to absolute power for traditional sources of authority. He believed that human reason could delineate the rational purposes of human institutions and could discover appropriate rational methods for achieving them.

Despite all the obstacles to progress that he identified—ignorance, superstition, intellectual lethargy, the rage of party and religious dogmatism as well as simple greed and selfishness—Locke still held that humanity was able to create a more moral and just society because it was capable of learning from experience. He demonstrated that the structure of a modern society could be grounded in human reason. Locke participated in and helped to conceptualize two fundamental processes in the transformation of a traditional society into a liberal society: the articulation, clarification, and rational defense of the structure and function of distinct spheres of social activity and the rationalization of norms and practices appropriate to the efficient operation of these social activities.

In this essay I shall provide a reading of Locke's *Two Treatises* (1963) based upon his commitment to rationality. This commitment helped him to construct a liberal theory of society and politics invulnerable to the now fashionable criticism of liberalism as a theory that destroys community, relies on atomistic self-seeking individuals, celebrates private interest above the public good, and so on. Locke's worldview is grounded in a belief in God's providence and in natural law, which provides a moral framework for analyzing the various social activities of human beings. Rather than yielding an endless and meaningless pursuit of self-interest that reduces all morality to subjective assessments of instrumental value, his rationalism provides a normative social theory in which human action is structured to achieve morally justifiable ends.

For Locke, human social institutions and practices have moral purposes that are objectively knowable, but there is also a distinct and significant instrumental dimension to Locke's social theory. Locke's natural-law rationalism is wedded to another type of rationalism, a utilitarian strain that seeks to discover practical and efficient means for achieving rationally defensible ends. The moral grounding of his social theory in natural law gave Locke a secure place from which to criticize social and political institutions as irrational and to investigate and recommend rational means for their reformation.

My assertion that Locke's great contribution to modern liberalism flows from his critical rationalism builds upon recent scholarship emphasizing the religious dimension of his thought. Rationalism, as I understand it, is a process that occurs in both the sacred and the secular spheres and affects both the church and the state. To hold that Locke demonstrated that the structure of modern society could be grounded in human reason is, among other things, a statement about Locke's intent. If Locke was skeptical about the reach and power of human reason, he was just as skeptical if not more so about the claim of faith to be a sure and certain guide for delineating the structures characteristic of modern society. Assuredly faith itself is no simple substitute for human rationality.

It might seem that my emphasis upon rationality in Locke means that I am claiming Locke for the side of reason in some historic struggle between reason and faith or that I hold that Locke should be understood as a secular thinker trying to replace religion by reason. This is certainly not my intent. Locke's rationalism does not entail any conflict between reason and revelation; he believed that revelation and true religion could aid reason in the historical task of rationalizing the world.[1] My reading of Locke as a rationalist does not imply any doubts about the depth and sincerity of Locke's own religious convictions. He did not see true faith and religion in a cynical way as merely a useful means to establish a modern rational society, but he believed in the power of human reason to judge matters of faith. In the chapter on faith and reason in the *Essay*

Concerning Human Understanding he writes, "Whatever God hath revealed is certainly true: no doubt can be made of it. This is the proper object of faith: but whether it is a *divine* revelation or no, reason must judge" (*ECHU*, 4:18).

The relationship between reason and faith in Locke's writings is very complicated. He defended himself vigorously against those who claimed that his philosophical and religious writings undermined Christianity. Those polemics often involved controversies about the relationship between reason and faith, but such controversies in the seventeenth century are not the same as nineteenth-century debates over science and religion or science and superstition. He argues for keeping distinct boundaries between faith and reason, but he also concludes that "to this crying up of faith in *opposition* to reason, we may, I think in good measure ascribe those absurdities that fill almost all religion which possess and divide mankind" (*ECHU*, 4:18).

Any reading of Locke such as mine, which relies on Max Weber for inspiration, must be sensitive to the religious dimension of Locke's thought. Yet an attempt to take Weber seriously must go beyond a traditional narrow Weberian reading of Locke that relies on the Protestant ethic and that sees Locke's "Calvinism" reflected in the *Second Treatises* in passages about God's giving property to "the use of the Industrious and Rational" (*ST*: no. 34). To me, Weber's great theoretical contribution lies in his account of the process of rationalization, which is unique to the West. This process encompasses new ways of thinking about religion as well as politics, economics, and culture.

LOCKE AND RATIONALITY

To read Locke as a rationalist social thinker was once a commonplace of Lockean scholarship. Unfortunately, this led to the belief that his rationalism made him an almost hopelessly abstract thinker. It fostered the belief that he had an unrealistic view of human motivation that prevented him from appreciating the hard and messy facts of human experience. Sterling Lamprecht (1962:132), one of the first and most influential modern scholars who emphasized Locke's rationalism, asserted that

> he viewed political organization as due to one momentous change, engineered by men who, before as after this change, exhibited the

same nature and qualities. He had no conception of a gradual growth from relatively simple to relatively complex forms of social organization, each stage of which prepared the way for the next by altering men's desires, motives, ideals and moral sentiments.

This assertion is totally mistaken. Indeed as I shall argue, one of the great strengths of Locke's liberalism was his appreciation of the growth of society from a simple to a relatively complex form of social organization.

Locke's rationalism in no way entailed the naive view that human beings were perfectly rational, nor did his commitment to natural law and reason prevent him from understanding social change. Early scholarly discussion of Locke's rationalism ignored so much of the actual text because of a tendency to see him as a philosopher whose real concern was to solve abstract philosophical problems. The only practical interest that was attributed to Locke in the writing of the *Two Treatises* was the defense of the Revolution of 1688, but this did not affect in any meaningful way the interpretation of Locke as an abstract thinker.

Recent significant scholarly contributions to the study of Locke's political writings have fundamentally transformed our understanding of Locke's purposes and enabled us to read the *Two Treatises* in a new way. They have exhibited a much greater sensitivity to the need to recover the intentional meaning of the text. This attempt at recovering the intentions of the author entailed a more thorough examination and appreciation of the historical context of Locke's writings—both intellectual and political—than that shown in previous Lockean scholarship. At the same time, as Ashcraft (1987:298) notes, this more historicist reading of Locke has meant a shift away from what he calls the "philosophical/analytical" approach.

These new readings have deepened our understanding of Locke by identifying him as a much more politically radical thinker and activist than the familiar characterization of him as a reluctant revolutionary and conventional defender of Whig orthodoxy (Franklin 1978; Ashcraft 1986). James Tully's (1980) detailed study of Locke's theory of property situated Locke's account within the context of seventeenth-century natural-law theory and emphasized the theological and epistemological premises embodied in his understanding of the relationship between God and man. These foundations of religious and natural law bring out the communal and moral dimension of Locke's thought. Because these aspects of his thought are more traditional, they save him from the accusation that he was at heart a defender of radical individualism and selfish self-interest. The more recent scholarship portrays Locke as a political radical and in no sense as an apologist for liberal capitalism. If anything, Locke seems now more like a precursor of democratic socialism.

The beginning of the contemporary historicist turn was marked in 1969 by the publication of John Dunn's pathbreaking study, *The Political Thought of John Locke*. Dunn's emphasis on the centrality of Locke's religious thought in his politics broke new ground. It directly challenged an emerging scholarly consensus that viewed Locke primarily as a secular thinker who embodied the principles of "possessive individualism" (Macpherson 1962) or whose natural-right theory justified the "emancipation of acquisitiveness" and the "spirit of capitalism" (Strauss 1953). The radical, one-dimensional readings of both Strauss and Macpherson rescued Locke from textbook interpretations such as Sabine's, which viewed him as a confused and inconsistent thinker whose influence could be explained because his work was commonsensical, containing a simple surface that covered over irreconcilable complexities and contradictions (Sabine 1961). Yet the rescue operation failed since the Locke who emerged from the operation bore scarce resemblance to the real Locke.

The contemporary emphasis on the historical context of Locke's political thought exposed the historical and textual inadequacies of Strauss and Macpherson and avoided barren exposés of the supposed philosophical confusions of Locke. However, one focus of earlier Lockean scholarship has been more or less shunted aside: the belief that Locke is a rationalist, and rationalism is the key to understanding his philosophy. Though earlier accounts of Locke as a rationalist suffered because they portrayed his rationalism as entailing an abstract, unhistorical, individualistic worldview that necessarily ignored empirical reality, they did contain a core of truth worth recovering.

One significant early controversy that took Locke's rationalism as a serious interpretive problem involved the philosophical grounding of Locke's moral and political theory. The question was whether it was based on a rationalist-metaphysical ethical theory on the one hand or on a utilitarian or hedonistic one on the other. In 1918 Sterling Lamprecht analyzed what he perceived to be these two different ethical theories in Locke. Though arguing that Locke was not totally successful in his attempt to deduce a purely rationalist ethics, he concluded that the *Second Treatise* basically reflected Locke's reliance on metaphysical rationalism and natural law rather than the hedonism that he saw in Locke's other writings (Lamprecht 1962).

Writing in 1920, about the same time as Lamprecht, Harold Laski also saw Locke as a rationalist and argued that the *Second Treatise* suffered because of this rationalism. Though his views were superficially similar to Lamprecht's, Laski actually meant something entirely different by rationalism. Laski, following in the footsteps of Leslie Stephen, who saw Locke as one of the founders of British utilitarianism (Stephen 1962), insisted that Locke's rationalism was a defect in his political theory that arose because of his commitment to a utilitarian ethical theory. "And with Locke, as with the Benthamites, his clear sense of what utilitarianism demanded led to an over-emphasis of human rationalism" (Laski 1920:66). This rationalism, according to Laski, led to a simplistic, mechanical view of the state and a shallow view of human psychology.

Another scholar of the 1920s, C. H. Driver, recognized the presence of both metaphysical rationalism and utilitarianism in Locke's politics and argued that there was a dualism throughout Locke's thought. One side was experimentalist and utilitarian and the other relied on deductive mathematics, logic, and a Cartesian universe. He asserted that "in politics it gives us the great compromise between (a) empirical organization based on the sole criterion of utility, and (b) the idea of a determinable and delimiting system of rights" (Driver 1967:86–87). Although I would not agree with his precise formulation of the dualism nor with his assertion that it entails "a great compromise," Locke's politics certainly contain both of these elements. Both also deserve to be called rationalistic: One is the rationalistic metaphysical natural-law aspect of Locke emphasized by Lamprecht, and the other is the rationalistic utilitarian strain discussed by Stephen and Laski.

The older philosophical/analytical approach focuses on the contradictions between two philosophical doctrines: rationalistic metaphysical natural law and utilitarianism. It leads us to try to place Locke in one camp or the other or to figure out which strain is more fundamental to his political thought. From the perspective of intellectual history, it asks us to see him either as one of the first of the utilitarians struggling to free himself from an outmoded metaphysical theory or as a muddleheaded theorist whose work, however confused, still helped clear the ground for later, more competent thinkers.

We need to recover some of the insights of the older philosophical/ analytical approach to Locke's political and social thought, which struggled to understand his rationalism, without giving up the new sensitivity to the historical context and practical intentions of the author. We also need a deeper understanding of rationality that is more appropriate to analyzing Locke as an engaged social theorist whose intellectual activity was directed to the creation of a theory of modern society.

I suggest that Max Weber's sociological approach to the interaction of ideas and social structure provides a way to understand Locke's rationalism that avoids the barren controversies plaguing the philosophical/ analytical approach. It also allows us to build on the great advances of the newer historicist approach to Locke, with its concentration on authorial intentions and historical context. At the same time, Weber helps us appreciate Locke's role in the creation of modern liberalism. Furthermore, by introducing a more complicated and sociologically sophisticated understanding of rationalism and rationalization as a social process, Weber sensitizes us to aspects of Locke's thought that were almost totally ignored in earlier studies of his rationalism.

LOCKE AS SOCIAL THEORIST

One way of understanding the significance of Locke's rationalism is to approach him as a social theorist and to see the two sides of Locke—the natural-law rationalist and the utilitarian rationalist—not as competing philosophical theories but as complementary aspects of a coherent social theory. Weber reminds us in many passages that rationalism can mean several different things. It means one thing if we think of the kind

> of rationalization the systematic thinker performs on the image of the world: an increasing theoretical mastery of reality by means of increasingly precise and abstract concepts. Rationalism means another thing if we think of the methodical attainment of a definitely given and practical end by means of an increasingly precise calculation of adequate means. These types of rationalism are very different, in spite of the fact that ultimately they belong inseparably together. (Weber 1946:293; see also Habermas 1984; Kalberg 1980)

Like Weber, John Locke uses the notion of reason in a number of different ways, but the two types of rationalism that Weber points to are crucial to understanding Locke's intentions and mode of argumentation in the *Two Treatises*. Locke develops systematic concepts to comprehend social reality in order to establish a rational social theory, and he evaluates various social practices in terms of their purposive rationality—their adequacy as technical means to achieving well-defined rational ends.

Locke attempts to master reality, in this case social reality, by using "precise and abstract concepts," which he holds conform to reason in contrast to the use of imprecise and confused concepts employed by his opponents. Locke's deeply held theological convictions about the existence, benevolence, and rationality of God ground his reasoning in a metaphysically stable framework. In the first essay in *The Law of Nature* Locke asserts that "there will be no one to deny the existence of God, provided he recognizes either the necessity for some rational account of our life, or that there is a thing that deserves to be called virtue or vice" (*ELN*:109; Ashcraft 1987:36). He goes on to assert that "there is nothing so unstable, so uncertain in this whole constitution of things as not to admit of valid and fixed laws of operation appropriate to its nature" (*ELN*:109). This old assumption of natural-law thinking—everything has its own fixed principles that can be known and used to orient inquiry—provides the basis for arguments about society that give Locke's thought its rationality.[2]

In broad outline, the rationality of human social practices can be discovered and defended by uncovering their nature or function—the human, and by extension the divine, purposes, ends, or goals that they are to achieve. This rationalistic natural-law perspective is used to criticize opponents who pervert the nature of social institutions by twisting them to their own purposes. These polemicists do this by implicitly or explicitly attributing values to these institutions that are incompatible with the true nature of the institutions or by defending their actions or theories with arguments that are irrational—arguments that are incompatible with human nature and reason. Either the values themselves, such as the notion of arbitrary power, are irrational, or arguments such as appeals to divine authority or tradition and custom are defective. In practice these two distinct errors are intertwined. An adequate defense of the rationality of an institution or social practice must encompass both aspects; that is, it must demonstrate that the values to be achieved are rational and can be defended in a rational manner.

The rationality of social institutions entails rational technique, the use of means that are consciously chosen to achieve ends. Means can be more or less efficacious in achieving ends. In the case of social practices, the means employed can be evaluated in terms of their success; there can be technical improvements and advances that signal a gain in purposive rationality. Instrumental rationality depends upon the accumulation of experience and knowledge; it requires a flexible approach to received practices and a willingness to depart from traditional ways of doing things in order to achieve ends. Custom and tradition are often sources of irrationality in this sense because they prevent innovation—they are barriers to change.

In his analysis of human history, Locke also sees an increasing rationalization. While the most important human social practices that Locke discusses, such as procreation and childbearing, religion, productive labor, and politics, have relatively fixed purposes from the point of view of his value theory, they are embodied in changing social institutions. Society becomes more complex, and its complexity is reflected in a movement from the primitive unity of the family to a structurally and functionally differentiated modern society. At the beginning of social development, the family performed political, religious, and economic—as well as childbearing and educational—functions. The head of the family, the father, was political ruler, priest, property owner, and ultimate authority in educating and disciplining his children.[3]

At the dawn of history these distinct functions were all exercised by the same man, legitimately. Locke quotes Filmer's assertion that "*Adam was the Father, King, and Lord over his Family; a Son, a Subject, and a Servant or Slave, were one and the same thing at first*" (FT: no. 8). Locke insists that although the same person exercised different powers, the powers themselves were not the same nor were the power relationships identical. While rejecting Filmer's analysis of the nature of political power, he still finds it plausible to believe that political power evolved from domestic rule (ST: no. 74).

The primitive family unit underwent a process of differentiation; religion, politics, and the economy spun off as relatively independent spheres of social activity, operating according to their own principles. Each of these spheres can be analyzed in terms of its own purposive rationality. Since the *Two Treatises* focuses on politics, it does not contain much detail regarding the rationalization of social practices such as religion, economics, childbearing, and education; but it is important to remember that Locke was deeply concerned with problems in these areas. The works he wrote about them also show his concern with values and purposive rationality. His major works on education and religion define and elaborate rational principles that ought to govern these spheres of social activity (STCE; Works 1823: vols. 6, 7). Even his relatively minor work on specific economic problems betrays a similar commitment to rationality—to clear arguments and the appropriate relation of means to ends (SC).

For Locke, maintaining the boundaries of each sphere is crucial since fundamental social problems stem from applying principles and practices that are appropriate in one sphere to another. Although the various spheres of social life in modern society are not and cannot be totally autonomous, they still must be allowed to develop according to their own principles and purposes. Any attempt to collapse distinctions radically— to return to a more primitive social order before these spheres had differentiated themselves from the primitive patriarchal family—leads to oppression and irrationality. Modern society requires more complex social institutions than those appropriate to simpler times.

In the very first chapter of the *Second Treatise* Locke insists that it is absolutely necessary to define political power correctly so that "the Power of a *Magistrate* over a Subject, may be distinguished from that of a *Father* over his Children, a *Master* over his Servant, a *Husband* over his Wife, and a *Lord* over his Slave." It is necessary to make these distinctions among the types of power that are exercised in society because they can be held by the same person: "All which distinct Powers happening sometimes together in the same Man, if he be considered under these different Relations, it may help us to distinguish these Powers one from another, and shew the difference betwixt a Ruler of a Common-wealth, a Father of a Family, and a Captain of a Galley" (*ST*: no. 2). More is at stake in setting forth these distinctions than the need for intellectual clarity and conceptual neatness. In the chapter of the *Second Treatise* in which he considers paternal, political, and despotic power together, he observes that "the great mistakes of late about Government having, as I suppose, arisen from confounding these distinct Powers one with another" (*ST*: no. 169).

The most basic threat to a rational account of social relations is the collapsing of distinct spheres of social power into one and confusing this power with despotism. Despotism, for Locke, stands as the direct antithesis to all relations based upon rationality: "*Despotical Power* is an Absolute, Arbitrary Power one Man has over another, to take away his Life, whenever he pleases. This is a Power, which neither Nature gives, for it has made no such distinction between one Man and another; nor Compact can convey, for Man not having such an Arbitrary Power over his own Life, cannot give another Man such a Power over it" (*ST*: no. 172). Such an arbitrary absolute power cannot arise through consent or compact because all men are God's creatures: "They are his Property, whose Workmanship they are, made to last during his, not one anothers Pleasure," and each "is *bound to preserve himself*, and not to quit his Station wilfully" (*ST*: no. 6). No one can alienate a power that he does not have, for no one has an absolute arbitrary power over his own life.

The only way such a power can come into existence legitimately is through the willful conscious renunciation of reason itself:

> *It is the effect only of Forfeiture*, which the Aggressor makes of his own Life, when he puts himself into the state of War with another. For having quitted Reason, which God hath given to be the Rule betwixt Man and Man . . . and so revolting from his own kind to that of Beasts by making Force which is theirs, to be his rule of right, he renders himself liable to be destroyed by the injur'd person and the rest of mankind . . . And thus *Captives*, taken in a just and lawful War, and such only, are *subject to a Despotical Power*. (*ST*: no. 172)

Despotic power, except in this very narrow and circumscribed case, is always illegitimate. It cannot be equated with political power or paternal power. For Locke, a rational account of all other fundamental social relationships must always exclude any element of despotism.

Any accounts of the origins of political or paternal or economic power (with the exception of slavery) that justify despotism must be flawed because they conflict with Locke's fundamental rational-value premises. A basic axiom of Locke's thought is that by nature human beings are free and equal. By equality he means a condition where "all the Power and Jurisdiction is reciprocal, no one having more than another" (*ST*: no. 4). Thus all unequal power relationships stand in need of some rational justification.

PATERNAL POWER

Locke demonstrates the rationality of paternal authority in terms of his own basic-value commitments to natural freedom and equality. The authority of parents over children would seem to be an obvious counterexample of such natural freedom and equality. Indeed, the attraction of paternal authority and the family as a model of political power for Filmer and others is that it substitutes subjection for freedom and hierarchy for equality (Schochet 1975). Locke admits that the statement that all men are equal by nature does not mean all sorts of equality (*ST*: no. 54). Children are an exception but one that can be justified in terms of a deeper understanding of Locke's basic values:

Children, I confess are not born in this full state of Equality, though they are born to it. Their Parents have a sort of Rule and Jurisdiction over them when they come into the World, and for some time after, but 'tis but a temporary one . . . we are born Free, as we are born Rational; not that we have actually the Exercise of either: Age that brings one, brings with it the other too. (*ST*: nos. 55, 61)

There are other exceptions to the claim to natural freedom and equality, such as "Ideots, Lunaticks and Madmen" (*ST*: no. 80), but all these deviations from the general rule can be explained in terms of a defect in rationality.

Freedom and equality become rationally defensible values only when the subject can exercise his will in a reasonable manner. "The Freedom then of Man and Liberty of acting according to his own Will, is grounded on his having Reason, which is able to instruct him in that Law he is to govern himself by, and make him know how far he is left to the freedom of his own will" (*ST*: no. 63). It would be irrational to accord men freedom if they are deficient in reason. "To turn him loose to an unrestrain'd Liberty, before he has Reason to guide him, is not allowing him the privilege of his Nature, to be free; but to thrust him out amongst Brutes, and abandon him to a state as wretched, and as much beneath that of a Man, as theirs" (*ST*: no. 63).

God has given man understanding to direct his will within the bounds of law, but when he does not have sufficient understanding to direct his will he "is not to have any Will of his own to follow: He that understand for him, must will for him too: he must prescribe to his Will, and regulate his Actions" (*ST*: no. 58). A child's defect in understanding justifies paternal power, the substituting of the rational will of a parent for the irrational will of the child. It would seem that this would entail a form of absolute government. Locke himself notes in *Some Thoughts Concerning Education* that "I imagine every one will judge it reasonable, that their Children, *when little*, should look upon their Parents as their Lords, their Absolute Governors" (*STCE*:41). But the great art of successful parenting is to reduce absolute governing gradually and replace it by love and affection, to encourage the germs of rationality in children and enable them to grow into adults who are capable of using their own reason to guide their actions (Leites 1979).

Paternal power by contrast is a fundamental category in Filmer's political theory. Used to support an authoritarian account of political power, Filmer's theory is based on absolute natural right, which is possessed by fathers. Locke is willing to grant that there is a natural right arising through procreation and supported by both reason and revelation, but it is a very different natural right from the one that appears in Royalist thought and has nothing whatsoever to do with politics. One of the props of Filmer's argument for Adam's sovereignty is "a Supposition of a natural Right of Dominion over his Children, by being their Father" (FT: no. 50), and he cites Grotius to the effect that the act of begetting children creates this right. This natural right, according to Filmer, entails the denial of natural freedom and is one of the bases of royal authority.

Filmer's argument appeals to natural law, and Locke generates a natural-law argument to refute it. Filmer assumes that this natural right entails an absolute supreme power of fathers over the lives of their children. Locke observes that others argue that "Fathers have a Power over the Lives of their Children, because they give them Life and Being" (FT: no. 52).[4] Locke points out that it is really God who gives them life and who forms and shapes them. Yet even if it were true that fathers give children their life and being (and Locke is always insistent that the same argument applies to mothers), the natural right that flows from this act of creation is not the right of dominion or power but the right to honor. This natural right is absolute and cannot be limited by positive law or prescription (FT: no. 63); it has nothing to do with power and cannot be used as a justification for political or even domestic authority. The natural right to honor gives "no Authority, no right to any one of making Laws over him from whom they are owing" (ST: nos. 69–70). The bare, natural act of begetting creates a natural right to honor, but this is not the source of parental authority.

Locke argues that the right to paternal power is not a result of the natural act of begetting; rather, it follows from the natural duty of parents to take care of their children (ST: no. 58). The right to exercise power follows from a duty imposed by natural law and is limited in scope and extent. This duty is a fiduciary one. Locke explains that all parents "were by the Law of Nature, under an obligation to preserve, nourish, and educate the Children, they had begotten, not as their own Workmanship, but the Workmanship of their own Maker, the Almighty, to whom they are accountable for them" (ST: no. 56). Paternal power is thus analogous to legitimate political power in that it is a trust, though in this case it is God, rather than the people, who is to judge how well the trust is performed.[5]

Locke emphasizes the difference between this power and a natural right by noting that it ceases if the duty is not fulfilled: "Nay, this power so little belongs to the Father by any peculiar right of Nature, but only as he is Guardian of his Children, that when he quits his Care of them, he loses his power over them, which goes along with their Nourishment and Education, to which it is inseparably annexed, and it belongs as much to the Foster-Father of an exposed Child, as to the Natural Father of another" (*ST*: no. 65). Locke is careful to note that, according to natural law, paternal power is authorized for a purpose, and if that purpose is not fulfilled it will cease.

As is generally the case with Locke, natural-law duties are supported by natural dispositions. It is not simply that *ought* implies *can*—that men are formed so that they are able to perform their obligations; God has implanted in them appropriate feelings and sentiments to support their duties, to make it more likely that the duties will be performed and performed in the right way (Ashcraft 1987:42). Locke argues that the child's lack of understanding authorizes parental power; but God has not simply placed the duty of care and nurturing on parents, he "hath placed in them suitable Inclinations of Tenderness and Concern to temper this power, to apply it as his Wisdom designed it, to the Childrens good" (*ST*: no. 63). Though parental power entails two functions that are analogous to political power, the power to command and the power to punish, we need not worry about the abuse of this power since "God hath woven into the Principles of Humane Nature such a tenderness for their Off-spring that there is little fear that Parents should use their power with too much rigour" (*ST*: no. 67).

Even though a family partakes of some attributes of absolute government, in no sense does it or can it become a model for political rule. Parental power, which is directed to nurturing children, lacks fundamental attributes of political sovereignty. Once the purposes of paternal or parental power are clear, it is evident that not all the attributes of political power appropriate to government are appropriate to domestic rule. The sphere of family life cannot support rights and powers that are legitimate only when exercised over consenting rational adults.

Locke further undermines paternal power as a model for political power by rhetorically asking us to consider the absurdity of attributing such powers to the head of a family, who could be the mother just as well as the father in some cases. He asks whether "she can make standing Rules, which shall be of perpetual Obligation, by which they ought to regulate all the Concerns of their Property, and bound their Liberty all the course of their Lives? Or can she inforce the observation of them with Capital

Punishments? For this is the proper *power of the Magistrate*, of which the Father hath not so much as the shadow" (*ST*: no. 65). He points out again that the power he exercises is but temporary and then argues that "though a *Father* may dispose of his own Possessions as he pleases, when his Children are out of danger of perishing for want, yet *his power* extends not to the Lives or Goods, which either their own industry or anothers bounty has made theirs; nor to their Liberty neither, when they are once arrived to the infranchisement of the years of discretion" (*ST*: no. 65).

Locke refutes Filmer by arguing that the natural right created by bringing children into the world is a right to honor and has nothing to do with paternal power or with command and coercion. Paternal power properly understood flows from a paternal duty to nurture and to educate children and is limited in a number of ways: It is temporary and alienable and is a fiduciary trust; it does not extend to life and death or to property. Neither political nor paternal power can be exercised legitimately in an arbitrary way. Both are limited, but while paternal power is more absolute than political power in the sense that it cannot be challenged by those under it, it is also much more restricted in scope.

Filmer's argument from revelation and natural right is fundamentally different from another type of argument that threatens a rational account of paternal authority. This is the argument from history and precedent, which is also employed to support an absolute and despotic account of paternal power. Locke, however, dismisses historical and anthropological examples when they contradict a natural-law account of authority. He has nothing but scorn for those who attempt to defend a despotic theory of authority on the basis of past practices: "They who alledge the Practice of Mankind, for *exposing or selling* their Children, as a Proof of their Power over them, are with Sir *Rob*. happy Arguers, and cannot but recommend their Opinion by founding it on the most shameful Action, and most unnatural Murder, humane Nature is capable of" (*FT*: no. 56). With some relish, he quotes from a history of Peru that purports to give a Swiftian account of parents begetting and raising children to eat them (*FT*: no. 57): "Thus far can the busie mind of Man carry him to a Brutality below the level of Beasts, when he quits his reason" (*FT*: no. 58).[6]

Locke asserts that history can be the source of the greatest irrationality because it contains examples of the most perverse and immoral human behavior. When men quit their reason their "fancy and imagination" is almost unbounded and "the will, reason being laid aside, is ready for every extravagant project" (*FT*: no. 58). The great danger to rationality is that some "extravagant project" will become the basis for a tradition that will prove most resistant to rational argumentation. He observes that "when Fashion hath once Established, what Folly or craft began, Custom makes it Sacred, and 'twill be thought impudence or madness, to contradict or question it" (*FT*: no. 58). A rational account of social practices cannot be grounded on historical examples without holding them up to the bar of human reason. From his very earliest work on natural law Locke is insistent that we cannot infer moral values from the general consent of mankind, or from custom, tradition, or precedent.

Locke provides a rational account of the value of paternal authority but is willing to accept natural sentiments as a sufficient restraint upon the abuse of parental power. There is no need, as he sees it, for a further rationalization of the relationship between parents and children by the introduction of legal restraints on the behavior of parents in the way he advocates restraints on political power. The formal institutional limitation on political power arises when rulers come to believe that they have a distinct interest separate from that of the people, and the people decide that it is too dangerous to rely simply upon unbounded trust. Locke further assumes that his contemporaries are not suffering from perverse and immoral customs that are recorded in the historical record. If either of these two assumptions does not hold, that is, if it is found that parents abuse their children or adopt truly perverse and irrational practices, then there is room for legal restraints on parental authority. The autonomy of the family sphere is only a relative autonomy, and Locke's natural-law account of the family permits limitations on paternal authority.

ECONOMIC RELATIONSHIPS

Just as Filmer's account of paternal power occasioned Locke's alternative explanation, so Filmer's theory of property prompted Locke to provide a rational alternative account. In both cases Locke's polemical point is to undercut the ground of a theory of absolute arbitrary political power. Just as Locke grants that there is a natural right associated with paternity, he acknowledges a natural right connected to private property. But, once again, this natural right cannot in any sense support a theory of absolute government.

According to Locke, Filmer offers two distinct foundations for absolute monarchical power, fatherhood and property (*FT*: no. 73). By adding property to fatherhood as another distinct foundation for political power, Filmer confuses two different spheres of power, natural dominion (or paternal power) and private dominion (or ownership of land and goods). Not only does he confuse each sphere with the other, he also confuses both of them with political power. It is necessary for Locke to sort out this confusion and untangle the three distinctly different arenas of social action: the family, the economy, and the state.

As I have shown, Locke distinguishes political power from paternal power. Each has its own distinctly different purpose, and neither accords with Filmer's absolutist account of political power as paternal power. This would suffice to refute Filmer's mistaken account of the origin and extent of political power were it not for Filmer's claim that the "*Grounds and Principles of Government necessarily depend upon the Original of Property*" (*FT*: no. 73). This claim impels Locke to investigate the nature of private property itself and the relationship it has with political power. Filmer justifies Adam's private dominion or ownership of the whole earth by biblical interpretation, claiming that it is the result of a direct grant or donation by God. Locke notes that once again Filmer confuses two distinct arguments in that he "begins here with *Adam's* propriety, or *Private Dominion, by Donation*: and his conclusion is, *which shews the Title comes from Fatherhood*" (*FT*: no. 22).

Locke refutes Filmer's interpretation of the origin of private property by his own biblical exegesis. This leaves him with the task of providing an account of private property that is in accord with both reason and revelation. Momentarily leaving aside his own alternative account of the origin of private property, Locke assumes for the sake of argument that God did give Adam private dominion over the earth. Locke then asks the crucial political question, "How will it appear, that *Property* in Land gives a Man Power over the Life of another? Or how will the Possession even of the whole Earth, given any one a Soveraign Arbitrary Authority over the Persons of Men?" (*FT*: no. 41) The most direct and according to Locke the most specious argument is that the owner of the whole earth could starve them into submission, forcing them to "acknowledge his Sovereignty and Obey his Will" (*FT*: no. 41). He concludes that if this were true it would be a good argument *against* any such private dominion because it is more reasonable to think that a God who bid mankind to increase and multiply would give each person a right to subsistence.

Any such argument would be inconsistent with justice: "We know God hath not left one Man so to the Mercy of another, that he may starve him if he please" (*FT*: no. 42). God has given the needy a right to the surplus of goods, and it would always be a sin for one man to let another perish. Justice gives a man a title to the products of his own labor and what he inherits from his ancestors, but charity also gives a right to subsistence from any individual surplus.

Thus, Locke argues that "a Man can no more justly make use of another's necessity, to force him to become his Vassal, by withholding that Relief, God requires him to afford to the wants of his Brother, than he that has more strength can seize upon a weaker, master him to his Obedience, and with a Dagger at his Throat offer him Death or Slaver" (*FT*: no. 42). Because of the natural-law limitation on the use of property, it is impossible for property to be the foundation of a just-sovereign authority. This argument shows that private property cannot be a source of legitimate political power if it entails unjust coercion. We might note that for Locke this argument goes both ways: Just as property cannot be used to gain political power over others, those who wield political power cannot use it to acquire private property. Force cannot be used to bridge the gap between two distinct spheres of life. Like private property, political power has its own origin and purpose.

An even more pernicious confusion between the spheres of private property and political power arises when they are simply conflated. Rather than being considered as the unjust origin of political power, the subjects of political power, human individuals, are treated as if they were objects—as if they were the private property of their rulers. This entails the grossest form of categorical mistake. Locke cites Filmer's assertion that "*a Son, a Subject, and a Servant or Slave, were one and the same thing at first. The Father had Power to dispose or sell his Children or Servants . . . we find the Sale and Gift of Children to have been much in use in the Beginning of the World, when Men had their Servants for a Possession and an Inheritance*" (*FT*: no. 8). He accuses Filmer of believing that "the Societies of Men, were made as so many Herds of Cattle, only for the Service, Use, and Pleasure of their Princes" (*FT*: no. 156). Filmer's view of human beings entails a denial of their natural freedom and rationality. It assumes that the right to wield political power and the right to property differ only in the objects of control, people on the one hand and animals and things on the other. In contrast, Locke insists that political power and property are essentially different, different in their origin, extent, and purpose as well as in their objects.

Locke develops his distinction between the nature of private property and political power by considering the problem of inheritance. He carefully distinguishes the right of children to inherit the property of their fathers from a right to inherit political power. There is a natural right to inheritance, but this can have nothing to do with political rule. The right of children to inherit the goods of their parents follows from their "right to maintenance and support and comfort from their Parents, and nothing else." This argument cannot support any right to inherit political power.

> But Government being for the benefit of the Governed, and not the sole advantage of the Governors . . . cannot be inherited by the same Title that Children have to the Goods of their Father. . . . He can subsist and receive from him the Portion of good things, and advantages of Education naturally due to him, without *Empire* and *Dominion*. That (if his Father hath any) was vested in him, for the good and behoof of others, and therefore the Son cannot Claim or Inherit it by a Title, which is founded wholly on his own private good and advantage. (*FT*: no. 93)

Locke's argument about inheritance in this case turns on a distinction between the purposes of two qualitatively different rights, the right to property and the right to rule. Property is for the "benefit and sole Advantage of the Proprietor" but government is for the "good of the governed" (*FT*: no. 92).

In the *Second Treatise* Locke provides his well-known account of property. Its origin is in a donation of God, but unlike Filmer he asserts that this donation is to all of mankind: "God, who hath given the World to Men in common, hath also given them reason to make use of it to the best advantage of Life, and convenience" (*ST*: no. 26). He endeavors to show how much a common inheritance could be divided into individual holdings, into private property. The principle of individuation lies in his concept of a person. Men are the property of God since they are his workmanship, but this is not incompatible with men having property in their own person, as Yolton puts it: "*Men* are God's property, *persons* are not" (1985a:69; see also Tully 1980). Locke asserts that

> though the earth, and all inferior Creatures be common to all Men, yet every Man has a *Property* in his own *Person*. This no Body has any Right to but himself. The *Labour* of his Body, and the *Work* of his Hands, we may say, are properly his. Whatsoever then he removed

out of the State that Nature hath provided, and left it in, he hath mixed his Labour with, and joyned to it something that is his own, and thereby makes it his *Property*. (*ST*: no. 27)

There are also two limitations on the right to property that flow from labor: "No Man but he can have a right to what that is once joyned to, at least where there is enough, and as good left in common for others" (*ST*: no. 27); and he points out that the Law of Nature that gives us property also provides a rational limit "as much as any one can make use of to any advantage of life before it spoils; so much he may by his labour fix a Property in. Whatever is beyond this, is more than his share, and belongs to others" (*ST*: no. 31). The spoilage limitation becomes a much less severe restriction on the extent of appropriation with the invention of money.

In an important passage, Locke also notes that since God gave the world to men for their benefit and "the greatest Conveniences of Life they were capable to draw from, it cannot be supposed he meant it should always remain common and uncultivated" (*ST*: no. 34). Thus there is a divine warrant for man to progress beyond a simple subsistence-level economy, which would have been the consequence of an earth that was held in common and not subjected to rational agricultural practices, a condition not unlike that of America populated by Indians. "He gave it to the use of the Industrious and Rational, (and *Labour* was to be *his Title* to it;) not to the Fancy or Covetousness of the Quarrelsom and Contentious" (*ST*: no. 34).

Though Locke's theory of property demonstrates that property is a rational social practice, he also assumes that a process of rationalization occurs in the movement from primitive to more advanced forms of private property, which eventually leads men to prefer legal, conventional titles to property. Private property held under purely natural law has advantages but is appropriate only for very simple conditions of life. At first, the social practice of private property based purely on labor provided no reason for disputes about titles and boundaries: "Right and conveniency went together; for as a Man had a Right to all he could imploy his Labour upon, so he had no temptation to labour for more than he could make use of" (*ST*: no. 51). This simple society provided men with clear titles to their property but did not implant in them any desires to extend their holdings. "The equality of a simple poor way of liveing confineing their desires within the narrow bounds of each mans smal propertie made few controversies and so no need of many laws to decide them" (*ST*: no. 107).

Primitive equality did not last: "As different degrees of Industry were apt to give Men Possessions in different Proportions, so this *Invention of Money* gave them the opportunity to continue to enlarge them" (*ST*: no. 48). With the introduction of a money economy as well as technical advances in agriculture and an increase in human greed and desire, a more sophisticated legal system became necessary. A need grew for "a multiplicity of Laws" to determine titles, boundaries, conveyances, inheritances, and the like, along with legal procedures to adjudicate disputes and to apply sanctions.

It is important that Locke's theory of property sets forth a sphere of social activity that is logically independent of both paternal power and political power. If all property were somehow inherited from Adam, the original owner and father of us all, then fatherhood and property would be linked; but fatherhood has nothing to do with property. Nor is property, as Hobbes claims, the creation of political society. Property and other basic economic activities are logically independent of the state, although as they become more highly developed they require a state. The further rationalization of property relationships cannot occur without the development of law-making institutions, a rational system of legal adjudication, and a means for protecting legal titles from force and violence.

Another aspect of economic activity that is significant for Locke's rational account of economic relationships in the *Two Treatises* is the bond between master and servant. For Filmer there is really no distinction between the power of a husband over a wife, a father over his children, a master over a servant, and a master over a slave. Locke is willing to admit that the family was probably the original locus of all authority. He is even willing to admit that the relationship between a ruler over a subject could have evolved from a primitive family. What he cannot accept is that all of these relationships can be fused into *one*—the relationship of master and slave.

He describes the origin of the family: "The *first Society* was between Man and Wife, which gave beginning to that between Parents and Children; to which, in time, that between Master and Servant came to be added: And though all these might, and commonly did meet together, and make up but one Family, wherein the Master or Mistress of it had some sort of Rule proper to a Family" (*ST*: no. 77). In another passage Locke adds slaves to the types of power relationships existing in families: "A *Master of a Family* with all these subordinate Relations of *Wife, Children, Servants* and *Slaves* united under the Domestic Rule of a Family" (*ST*: no. 86). The concept of "domestic rule" covers these relationships, but they each require a distinct analysis because of their qualitative differences.

For Locke the master/servant relationship is qualitatively distinct from others. For Filmer the servant is under the absolute dominion of the father, and in effect is like a slave, but for Locke the relationship between master and servant, even when they live together with others in a family, is an economic one in the sense that it is a consequence of an economic exchange. Locke distinguishes a servant, in the proper sense of the term, from other frequent members of primitive families, slaves. The relationship between master and servant is easily confused because they are "Names as old as History." Confusion arises because the term *servant* can be used to refer to a person who enters into a voluntary contractual relationship or to a slave who might perform identical services but is in a qualitatively different relationship to the master. Slaves are captives in a just war and are "by the Right of Nature subjected to the Absolute Dominion and Arbitrary Power of their Masters" (*ST*: no. 85). The master/slave relationship exists because of natural right, but the master/servant relationship comes into existence through voluntary consent.

Locke argues that "a Freeman makes himself a Servant to another, by selling him for a certain time, the Service he undertakes to do, in exchange for Wages he is to receive" (*ST*: no. 85). Though this commonly puts him into the family of his master and under his discipline, the master's power is only temporary and is no more than is stipulated by the agreement between them. Locke also acknowledges another type of master/servant relationship that is closer to slavery than a sale of service. He observes that "we find among the *Jews*, as well as other Nations, that Men did sell themselves; but, 'tis plain, this was only to *Drudgery, not to Slavery*" (*ST*: no. 24). It was not slavery because the master did not have absolute arbitrary despotical power. The master's power was limited because he could not kill the servant and was forced to set him free at an appointed time. Locke notes that the master "was so far from having an Arbitrary Power over his Life, that he could not, at pleasure, so much as maim him, but the loss of an Eye, or Tooth, set him free" (*ST*: no. 24). Obviously this is a much stricter interpretation of arbitrary power than we are used to. The master could presumably inflict all sorts of what we would think of as arbitrary punishments so long as they did not cause permanent physical damage.

The context in which Locke discusses the master/servant relationship is exclusively familial, and the master is very far from a capitalist. What is missing is any notion of a firm or a business or a company, that is, of an exclusively economic unit separated from the family that is to employ workers. Even though I agree with Tully (against Macpherson) that it is anachronistic to impute to Locke the assumptions of a capitalist wage-labor concept (Tully 1980:135–44)—if we accept a Marxist definition of capitalist wage-labor—I think it is significant that Locke does provide for an economic relationship that is based on the voluntary exchange of wages for service. This is a relationship that is conceived of in terms of consent and contract, that is private and not dependent upon the state for its legitimacy, that assumes benefits for each party, and that is rational.

THE EVOLUTION OF POLITICAL RATIONALITY

Locke provides a rational account of the origin and purpose of political society, an account demonstrating that the existence of political society is in accord with the values of natural law. He shows how particular political societies are created, given an original situation of one universal community. The state of nature is governed by the Law of Nature, and it is the Law of Nature "by which Law common to them all, he and all the rest of *Mankind are one Community*, make up one Society distinct from all other creatures" (*ST*: no. 128). Just as God has given the world to all men in common, so he has given them a common law and placed them in a common community.

Locke further observes that God has also given men reason to make use of communal property to the best advantage (*ST*: no. 26). The use of reason informs men that there must be a means of appropriating the common stock for it to be of any use. The means are labor, and mixing labor with nature creates a private right that excludes the common right of others, thereby creating private property. Reason also leads men to create private societies; but while man's need to appropriate creates private rights, the need to protect his appropriations—to protect his rights—leads him into political society. If it were not for the "viciousness of degenerate Men" there would be no need to set up any particular communities, "no necessity that Men should separate from this great and natural Community, and by positive agreements combine into smaller and divided associations" (*ST*: no. 128).

Locke not only shows how particular communities could arise from a universal community, but he must also explain how political authority is consistent with natural freedom. That is, he must show that there is a rational reason for man to substitute a condition of juridical equality in which his decisions are not subject to the authority of anyone for a condition in which his liberty is circumscribed by positive laws and political authority. Although a man in the state of nature is "an absolute Lord of his own Person and Possessions," this right is not as valuable to the possessor as it might first appear: "He hath such a Right, yet the Enjoyment of it is very uncertain, and constantly exposed to the Invasion of others" (*ST*: no. 123). Because the greater part of mankind are not "strict Observers of Equity and Justice" he is willing to join with others "for the mutual *Preservation* of their Lives, Liberties and Estates, which I call by the general Name, *Property*" (*ST*: no. 124).

The natural community governed by the Law of Nature lacks three crucial things that, given the propensity of men to violate the law, make it an imperfect society from the point of view of legality. First, it lacks "an *established*, settled, known *Law*, received and allowed by common consent to be the Standard of Right and Wrong" (*ST*: no. 124). It is not the case that the state of nature lacks law since it is governed by natural law, but natural law cannot serve as a secure basis for adjudicating disputes even though it is "plain and intelligible to all rational creatures." The problem is that men are often not willing to refer to it as a common objective standard for either of two reasons: Either they are "ignorant for want of study of it" or they are biased by their interest. By consenting to positive laws the community overcomes the problem of ignorance and self-interest. Individuals cannot so easily plead that there is no applicable law binding on them in a particular dispute.

Second, in the state of nature "there wants a *known and indifferent Judge*, with Authority to determine all differences according to the established Law" (*ST*: no. 125). Every man in a state of nature is both judge and enforcer of natural law. Everyone has (by what Locke calls his *strange doctrine*) the natural right to enforce natural law and punish offenders (*ST*: nos. 8–9). This again raises the problem of bias. When men are judges in their own case "passion and revenge is very apt to carry them too far." The punishments they would inflict might be too harsh and excessive; and since they are more interested in themselves than in others, they would be less than zealous in enforcing the law in respect to other men's cases. Third, in the state of nature men often lack "*Power* to back and support the Sentence when right, and to *give* it due *Execution"* (*ST*: no. 126). Those who commit injustices are often simply not going to submit to their punishments, and this makes it dangerous to enforce justice.

When men agree to overcome these defects in the state of nature and to form political societies, they create political power from two other types of power that they possessed in the state of nature. The first is the power to do anything that a man thinks necessary to preserve himself and others. He gives this power up to be regulated by the laws of society "so far forth as the preservation of himself, and the rest of that Society shall require" (*ST*: no. 129). These positive laws limit the liberty he had under natural law. For Locke, liberty is never absolute; it is always limited by law. Positive law simply adds further restraints to liberty.

The second power is the power to punish, a power that men give up totally to society; in addition, they pledge to assist the executive power in enforcing the law when required. Locke also notes that "he is to part also with as much of his natural liberty in providing for himself, as the good, prosperity, and safety of the Society shall require: which is not only necessary, but just; since the other Members of the Society do the like" (*ST*: no. 130). If man ever had any unlimited rights to accumulation in the state of nature, which, despite Macpherson, Locke never assumes, such liberty is restricted in society.

Though it is certainly true that Locke permits the regulation of property for the common good and acknowledges that property holders exchange the titles to their property that they originally held under natural law for conventional legal titles, I would not agree with Tully that "community ownership of all possessions is the logical consequence of the premises of Locke's theory in the *Two Treatises"* (Tully 1980:165). This would be the case only if, contra Locke, we assume that the common good logically entails the common ownership of property.[7]

The power of society is to extend no further than the common good and to secure everyone's property by providing remedies to the three defects in the state of nature. This entails that the supreme power is "bound to govern by establish'd *standing Laws*, promulgated and known to the People, and not by Extemporary Decrees: by *indifferent* and upright *Judges*, to imploy the force of the Community at home, *only in the Execution of such Laws*, or abroad to prevent or redress Foreign Injuries, and secure the Community from Inroads and Invasions" (*ST*: no. 131).

Locke presents another distinct though not logically inconsistent account of the origin and development of political power. This account is historical and explains and justifies the emergence of an institutional framework to assure what Weber has called legal-rational authority. The rule of law entails the legal limitation of political authority and the development of relatively complex institutional mechanisms to restrain arbitrary power. These rational techniques emerged through historical experience. Though the legitimate ends of political authority always remain the same, the means men use to try to achieve these ends differ throughout recorded history. Certain techniques of rule are appropriate only for simpler times. The people often make mistakes about the effectiveness of political arrangement, sometimes innocently and sometimes as the result of manipulation by rulers and other self-interested individuals.

Locke has a much more sophisticated understanding of the nature of political authority than he is given credit for by those who take a purely philosophical/analytical approach to his political theory. It is interesting to note that his account of the development of government in the *Second Treatise* bears a striking resemblance to Weber's analysis of types of legitimate domination. Locke presents in a rather simple form a movement from charismatic to traditional to legal-rational forms of authority. These three types of authority are all compatible with Locke's rational justification of political power deduced from natural-law premises. It is not the case that legal-rational authority is the only type of legitimate political authority for Locke. The legitimacy of a form of political authority depends, roughly, upon its conformity to the idea of consent and the exercise of political power for the common good. Locke's advocacy of legal-rational authority is justified in terms of its practical rationality in the modern world. Government conducted according to the criteria of legal-rational authority is more likely than any other to assure that power is wielded only for legitimate purposes in a complex society.

In *Economy and Society* Weber defines legitimate domination on charismatic grounds as "resting on devotion to the exceptional sanctity, heroism or exemplary character of an individual person, and of the normative patterns or order revealed or ordained by him (charismatic authority)" (Weber 1968:215). Similarly, Locke says that it is likely that at first "some one good and excellent Man, having got a Preheminency amongst the rest, had this Deference paid to his Goodness and Vertue, as to a kind of Natural Authority, that the chief Rule, with Arbitration of their differences, by a tacit Consent developed into his hands, without any other caution, but the assurance they had of his Uprightness and Wisdom" (*ST*: no. 94).

The emergence of political authority from paternal authority accounts for the fact that the first type of government was monarchical; power was in the hands of one man. This was the simplest and most obvious type, well suited to men who had no previous experience with the advantages and defects of various forms of government (*ST*: no. 107). Locke also notes that this simple form of monarchy was not strictly hereditary: "But when either the Father died, and left his next Heir for want of Age, Wisdom, Courage, or any other Qualities, less fit for Rule: or where several Families met, and consented to continue together: There 'tis not to be doubted, but they used their natural freedom, to set up him, whom they judged the ablest, and most likely to Rule well over them" (*ST*: no. 105). He describes a condition in which heredity was not the sole criterion of succession, although the reference to heirs shows that there was an assumption of hereditary succession barring some significant defect in the heir. Charismatic authority was becoming institutionalized in hereditary monarchies, but it had not yet hardened into a rigid, tradition-bound system of selection. These primitive monarchies did not suffer from the problem of succession that plagues traditional monarchies since the rulers could be chosen on the basis of their personal qualities.

Locke also cites examples from Indian tribes and biblical history to argue that there is another origin of primitive monarchies that has nothing to do with fatherhood. This occurred when several families formed a common society for defense and appointed a ruler. These monarchs were primarily warrior chiefs and "though they command absolutely in War, yet at home and in time of Peace they exercise very little Dominion and have but a very moderate Sovereignty" (*ST*: no. 108). He concludes that almost all monarchies "near their Original" were elective (*ST*: no. 106). That is, political authority depended upon the exceptional personal qualities of the ruler as judged by his followers. Furthermore, this simple form of government, whether it arose from the consent of grown children to acquiesce in the rule of their father or from the consent of families to form defensive alliances, was almost all "prerogative." There were very few established laws (*ST*: no. 162).

Weber defines legitimate domination on traditional grounds as "resting on an established belief in the sanctity of immemorial traditions and the legitimacy of those exercising authority under them (traditional authority)" (Weber 1968:215). The typical constitutional order of a traditional society, as Weber notes, contains two distinct spheres: a sphere of action that is bound to specific traditions and a sphere of action that is free of specific rules. "In the latter sphere, the master is free to do good turns on the basis of his personal pleasure" (Weber 1968:215).

Within the English constitutional tradition these two spheres are, roughly, royal prerogative and common law, which guaranteed the rights of subjects. In the seventeenth century the stability of these two spheres had broken down, and from the parliamentary side the danger was seen in terms of the extension of royal prerogative. Filmer's doctrine was in no sense a traditional theory since it made all government prerogative, but other less absolutist Royalists wished to strengthen, if not extend, prerogative and to resist any attempts by Parliament to define or regulate prerogative by law. The claim that Parliament or the people had a constitutional or extraconstitutional right to limit the royal prerogative grounded on fundamental law or on natural law was considered by Royalists as a direct attack on the ancient constitution, one sanctified by immemorial tradition and custom.

Locke refers to this breakdown in traditional authority when he recounts the transition from a simple monarchy based upon charismatic authority to one based upon custom and tradition, "when time, giving Authority and (as some Men would perswade us) Sacredness to Customs, which the negligent, and unforeseeing Innocence of the First Ages began, had brought in Successors of another Stamp" (*ST*: no. 94). In the Golden Age before men had been corrupted "there was then *no stretching of Prerogative* on the one side to oppress the People; *nor* consequently on the other any *Dispute about Privilege*, to lessen or restrain the Power of the Magistrate; and so no contest between Rulers and People about Governours or Government" (*ST*: no. 111).

Though some commentators see this reference to a golden age as a description of Locke's state of nature (*ST*: no. 111 n. 2) there is nothing to warrant this. It refers to a civil society with legitimate rulers, probably a reference to a situation after the first simple monarchies had become stabilized and custom had delineated two distinct spheres: prerogative rights and popular rights. Locke refers to this golden age as a time before "vain Ambition, and *amor sceleratus habendi*, evil Concupiscence had corrupted Mens minds into a Mistake of true Power and Honor" (*ST*: no. 111). This situation must have arisen after the invention of money. Locke was probably referring to a time after the invention of money and the increase of property, which drove men into civil society, and before they became corrupt.

Notice also that the corruption to which he refers is not a general corruption but one that affects men's understanding of the nature of political power. Ambition and luxury, aided by flattery, drove princes to increase their power and "taught Princes to have distinct and separate

Interest from their People" (*ST*: no. 111). This led men to examine and reflect on the true purposes of government. Rational reflection prompted by the abuse of power caused a crisis in traditional authority.

In the beginning of the seventeeth century, before the constitutional crisis, lawyers and politicians ordinarily conceived of society as a complicated, interlocking arrangement of rights that inhered in various persons, statuses, institutions, and corporate entities. The king had his prerogative, the sphere of *gubernaculum*, or policy, in which he was absolute and above the law; but subjects also had rights that were fundamental to them. Gough refers to this understanding of society as a "semi-feudal network of private rights" (Gough 1961:56). The royal prerogative was conceived of as a private right exercised by the sovereign as he saw fit; its exercise in particular cases was not subject to public scrutiny. It was a legally unreviewable right, a protected sphere of action in which the sovereign acted at his discretion.

The traditional constitution conceived of the sovereign's rights as if they were ordinary property rights. Locke argues in the *First Treatise* that this led to a belief that there was a natural- or divine-right justification for the practice of primogeniture:

> In Countries where their particular Municipal Laws give the whole Possession of Land entirely to the First Born, and Descent of Power has gone so to Men by this Custom, some have been apt to be deceived into an Opinion, that there was a Natural or Divine Right of Primogeniture, so both *Estate* and *Power*; and that the Inheritance of both *Rule* over Men and *Property* in things, sprang from the same Original, and were to descend by the same Rules. (*FT*: no. 91)

More was at stake in this criticism than a confusion about the justification of primogeniture; one of the main props of Royalist ideology was really at issue. The belief that political power was a power that belonged by right to the sovereign was as fundamental a truth as that subjects had their own rights to life, liberty, and property. The birthrights of the sovereign were as sacred as the birthrights of freeborn Englishmen. To conceive of these two categories of rights as both equally fundamental and grounded in immemorial custom led to the belief that they had the same origin and purpose (Resnick 1984). To attack the one was to attack the other: To invade the sovereign's rights was to undermine the very foundation of all rights. Locke's use of natural-law arguments was intended to set aside all such arguments based on tradition and immemorial custom by giving a rational account of these two different types of rights.

According to Locke, it was the conception of prerogative as a private right that was particularly dangerous: "They have a very wrong Notion of Government, who say, that the People have *incroach'd upon the Prerogative* when they have got any part of it to be defined by positive Laws. For in so doing, they have not pulled from the Prince any thing, that of right belong'd to him" (*ST:* no. 163). Prerogative is a power entrusted to the monarch to be used for the public good, and when it is abused it can be modified and restricted. To say that such alterations in prerogative are encroachments is to "speak as if the Prince had a distinct and separate Interest from the good of the Community, and was not made for it, the Root and Source, from which spring almost all those Evils, and Disorders, which happen in Kingly Governments" (*ST:* no. 163). Even individual property rights, which have their origin in the state of nature, may be modified or altered for the common good and with the consent of the governed. Property rights exist for both the individual and the common good, but the right to exercise political power is purely conventional, created only for the common good, and can be altered without the express consent of those who exercise them.

The most fundamental alteration in prerogative rule caused by the corruption of rulers was the establishment of a collective legislative body entrusted with specific lawmaking authority. Locke argues that "the People finding their Properties not secure under the Government, as then it was, (whereas Government has no other end but the preservation of Property) could never be safe nor at rest, *nor think themselves in Civil Society*, till the Legislature was placed in collective Bodies of Men, call them Senate, Parliament, or what you please" (*ST:* no. 94). The result of this fundamental constitutional change was the establishment of the rule of law. "By which means every single person became subject, equally with other the meanest Men, to those Laws, which he himself, as part of the Legislative had established: nor could any one, by his own Authority, avoid the force of the Law, when once made, nor by any pretence of Superiority, plead exemption, thereby to License his own, or the Miscarriages of any of his Dependents" (*ST:* no. 94).

Weber defines rational authority as "resting on a belief in the legality of enacted rules and the right of those elevated to authority under such rules to issue commands (legal authority)" (Weber 1968:215). This entails an impersonal concept of political rule in which obedience is based on legal entitlement rather than on personal loyalty. Locke interprets the oath of allegiance to the sovereign, a hallmark of personal traditional authority, in a way that makes it compatible with legal-rational authority.

> *Allegiance* being nothing but an *Obedience according to Law*, which when he violates, he has no right to Obedience, nor can claim it otherwise than as the publick Person vested with the Power of the Law, and so is to be consider'd as the Image, Phantom, or Representative of the Commonwealth, acted by the will of the Society, declared in its Laws; and thus he has no Will, no Power, but that of the Law. (*ST*: no. 151)

Political obligation is owed only to those who exercise legal power under law.

The idea of the rule of law entails the replacement of political rule as *personal willing* with law understood as *public willing*. Law handed down by a monarch becomes dangerous when the monarch comes to have a separate and distinct interest from society. Though all positive law must be in accord with the common good, Locke argues that it is much more likely to be so when the legislature contains an element of popular representation. In addition to requiring that lawful authority be the only legitimate source of political obligation and that all men must be equally subject to law, the rule of law also entails that law must be applied in a uniform manner, "not to be varied in particular Cases, but to have one Rule for Rich and Poor, for the Favourite at Court, and the Country Man at Plough" (*ST*: no. 142). The rule of law requires the formal rationality of legal norms that come into existence with the consent of the governed and that are enforced only by those authorized to enforce them and only in the manner authorized by law.

The rule of law means more than simply government by the consent of the governed since such a regime does not necessarily operate primarily according to the idea of the rule of law. It is compatible, as Locke says, with simple monarchy, which is practically all prerogative government. A simple patriarchal monarchy lacks those political institutions that have been devised to assure the rule of law and that are characteristic of modern regimes based on legal-rational authority. These include representative bodies, the separation of legislative and executive power, the requirement of consent for taxation, and a fair judiciary, which decides all disputes according to positive laws. These institutions and practices represent the rationalization of the political system. They are the practical means that have been discovered to guarantee as much as possible that political power in the modern world will achieve the ends for which it was created, the preservation of life, liberty, and property.

The rule of law adds stability and predictability to social action. In a very interesting passage, Locke explains why the federative power, the arena of foreign policy, is much less capable than the executive power "to be directed by antecedent, standing, positive Laws" and must be left to the wisdom and prudence of rulers:

> For the *Laws* that concern Subjects one amongst another, being to direct their actions, may well enough *precede* them. But what is to be done in reference to *Foreigners*, depending much upon their actions, and the variation of designs and interests, must be *left* in great part to the *Prudence* of those who have this Power committed to them, to be managed by the best of their Skill, for the advantage of the Commonwealth. (*ST*: no. 148)

The rule of law provides a stable set of expectations to which men can orient their actions. Formal rules with predictable outcomes are less dangerous than an interventionist government's attempting to judge actions on the basis of concrete substantive values. The direction of domestic affairs is not to be left to the prudence and skill of the rulers. Rather, they remain on the whole with the individual citizens who pursue their interests within a legal framework.

There is a significant difference between deciding to perform an action or evaluating an action already performed on the basis of substantive justice or values. In the case of legality the question is whether the action is authorized or required or permitted according to the relevant legal rules. In the case of substantive justice the question is whether the action promotes the common good, the greater glory of God, or whatever values are thought relevant. In the case of establishing legal rules themselves, the comparable notion to legality is the idea of constitutionalism. All legal rules must be in accordance with the basic rules set forth in the constitution. Laws that conflict with the constitution are invalid. Substantive-value considerations certainly enter into framing the purpose of the law, but these considerations cannot make an unconstitutional law constitutional, nor in most cases can the simple argument that it is not for the public good invalidate an otherwise constitutional law.

Such a finding must rest upon a showing that it violates some other more specific constitutional provision.

One problem with a strict interpretation of the idea of the rule of law is that not all types of governmental activities can be rationalized by means of rules. In the case of foreign affairs, as Locke argues, it is not possible to specify a complete system of legal rules that can cover this area. In effect, we must accept a lesser standard. We require a general grant of authority or trust authorized by the constitution. Because of the need for flexibility, we must rely on the wisdom and prudence of those entrusted with such a power and cannot hem them in with a detailed network of rules. Locke provides for contingencies, emergencies, and cases where it is impractical to determine action according to standing rules in domestic affairs under the concept of prerogative: "This Power to act according to discretion, for the publick good, without the prescription of the Law, and sometimes even against it, *is* that which is called *Prerogative*" (*ST*: no. 160). There are cases where formal rationality must yield to substantive rationality. Rules cannot cover all cases; and on rare occasions, following rules entails such dangerous or unjust outcomes that it is necessary to apply substantive-value judgments to override them.

Legal-rational authority is only one way in which political authority can be structured, but its fundamental legitimacy for Locke rests upon natural-law values. Another more significant case in which formal rationality must yield to substantive rationality occurs when there is a fundamental rupture in the legal order itself. The entire constitutional order can be seen as an attempt to enmesh political power in procedure, but Locke's natural-law perspective prevents any attempt to limit legitimate, rational political action to action that can be structured according to constitutional rules and procedures. When the rulers confine themselves to actions authorized by the constitution, then subjects are to obey and exercise their liberty only in ways permitted by law. However, when rulers violate their trust, then the people can and must invoke their more basic political values.

A constitutional crisis arises when there is no common judge between the people and their rulers by which to settle a fundamental dispute about the legitimacy of governmental action. In such a case Locke argues that the people must judge whether their rulers have abused the trust placed in them. When rulers refuse to submit to an adjudication of the dispute and use force upon the people, society is plunged into civil war; and action taken in such cases must conform to natural law (*ST*: no. 240). The people must look toward their fundamental substantive values to guide them when they resort to the appeal to heaven. The appeal to heaven is also an appeal to natural law, which can justify both political obligation and political revolution.

Because of their emphasis on purely philosophical problems, earlier accounts of Locke's rationalism were not able to fully comprehend Locke's contribution to social theory. Once we view Locke as a social theorist we are able to appreciate the complexity of his rationalism. He was able to construct a sophisticated liberal theory of society because he grounded his analysis in natural law and divine providence. Rather than being an obstacle to theory construction, his appeals to natural law and reason provided a stable value system within which to analyze both theoretical and practical problems. This grounding in natural law guaranteed that rational criteria were available for the analysis of human social institutions and practices. Once these were known it was possible to provide the outlines of a theory of society in which such relationships are structured to conform to man's rational nature. The fundamental facts of human nature do not change throughout human history: the fact that we are God's creatures and are all born free, equal, and dependent, and the fact that we must appropriate in order to live. Such fundamental facts provided a moral and rational foundation that Locke used to attack defective theories appealing to reason and revelation and theories attempting to justify social action on the basis of custom and tradition.

Because his theory of justifiable social relationships was deduced from natural law, Locke was able to accommodate the great variety of different social practices without yielding to skepticism or relativism at the level of values. Just as there are innumerable social practices that violate Locke's principles of right, there are also many different social arrangements that conform to his basic ethical standards. That is, although some social practices are always illegitimate, others, while legitimate, are best discarded as a practical matter because they are no longer suitable to changing circumstances. Not only must we realize that as a practical matter different times call for different social arrangements, but we must also be skeptical of those who deny the facts of social change and attempt to preserve outmoded institutions that no longer function as they once did.

Primitive monarchies, which differed little from extended families, cannot serve as a model for modern social relationships because modern society is too complex and unrestrained political power too dangerous. Locke admitted, as a matter of historical fact, that once upon a time all power was concentrated in one man; but the fact that the same man played the roles of father, property owner, priest, master over servants and slaves, and political ruler leads to theoretical confusion about the nature of these various powers and social relationships. Drawing clear theoretical boundaries between different spheres of social action helped lead Locke to an awareness that modern society itself was undergoing a process of social change that necessitated the rationalization of distinct spheres of social life.

Locke participated in the great transformation from a traditional society to a modern liberal society. The theorists of absolute government confronted the social disorganization of a crumbling traditional society by proposing a pseudorational-radical theory of political power that threatened to collapse all distinctions between the spheres of social action. Locke confronted the absolutists with arguments characteristic of classical liberal thought. He condemned absolutist theory as a new form of despotism. Yet he did more than simply reject absolutism; he advocated new principles of social order. He maintained the necessity of distinctions; but rather than accepting the mixture of rational and irrational factors enshrined by custom and tradition, he insisted on a thorough, rational reexamination of the various spheres of social action. Only a society that enshrined rational values and adopted rational techniques to maintain these values would be stable and prosperous.

NOTES

1. I have defended this position and outlined my understanding of the relationship between Locke's rationalism and his views on religion and politics in a recent paper (Resnick 1989).

2. Locke drew upon a great number of different natural-law theorists. For an analysis of his complex relationship to the natural-law tradition see von Leyden's introduction to his edition of Locke's *Essays on the Law of Nature* (1954) and Tully (1980).

3. It is not often noted that Locke believed that the father in the primitive family performed religious functions. This is evident from an argument in the *Second Treatise* against the attempt to set up historical precedent as a normative standard of right. Locke argues that if the de facto exercise of political power by fathers could prove that they have a right to political authority, then by the same argument "it will as strongly prove that all Princes, nay Princes only,

ought to be Priests, since 'tis as certain, that in the Beginning, *The Father of the Family was Priest, as that he was Ruler in his own Household"* (*ST*: no. 75); see also quote from Hooker about priests (*ST*: no. 74).

4. Locke refers to traductionism, the theory used by others to justify paternal right. The theory that Locke himself adopts was called creationism. For a discussion of these two theories see Tully (1980:58).

5. For a penetrating account of the importance of trust in Locke's political thought see Dunn (1985) and Gough (1973).

6. For a discussion of the place of historical and anthropological evidence in Locke's political thought see Grant (1988). This article also convincingly refutes communitarian critics of Locke's liberalism who believe that liberal individualism of Locke's type is grounded in social atomism and is defective because it ignores the social factors in human life.

7. I might also point out that Locke did say that government is established in order to secure men's properties, and "the Prince or Senate, however it may have power to make Laws for the regulating of *Property* between the Subjects one amongst another, yet can never have a Power to take to themselves the whole or any part of the Subjects *Property*, without their own consent. For this would be in effect to leave them no *Property* at all" (*ST*: no. 139). Only if the people consented to community ownership would it be legitimate. If the premises of the *Two Treatises* could lead to socialism it must be democratic socialism, but the entire argument has little merit.

5 / *The Economic Background to Locke's* Two Treatises of Government

KAREN IVERSEN VAUGHN

There are two reasons for examining the economic background to Locke's *Two Treatises of Government*. The first, of interest primarily to economists, is that Locke both presumed and developed economic concepts in his discussion of the "true, original, and extent of civil government," and it is interesting to see if these ideas are part of a coherent economic analysis that advanced the development of economic thought. The second reason, of more general interest, is that Locke's economic presuppositions were important to the development of his argument for limited government. Hence, without understanding the meaning of his economics it is impossible fully to understand his conception of government.

This second claim is controversial, given some of the more well-known critiques of Lockean political thought. In particular, James Tully in *A Discourse on Property* (1980), building on the earlier work of John Dunn (1969a), argues his case as if Locke's economics is totally irrelevant to his grander philosophical system. And though many Locke scholars have noted some economic content to the *Second Treatise*, recent work has tended to emphasize the religious or political motivations of Locke's writings on government to the neglect of the economic (see the essays by Eisenach and Ashcraft in this volume). One can perhaps understand the desire to minimize the economic aspects of the *Second Treatise* as a reaction to the extreme and fundamentally wrong-headed economic interpretation offered by C. B. Macpherson in his famous book, *The Political Theory of Possessive Individualism* (1962). There, through the lens of Marxist economics, he accused Locke of writing the *Treatises* to justify unlimited capitalist accumulation. Yet there is a more moderate position that can be staked out that does not deny the religious and political aspects of Locke's thought, one that finds Locke's economic presuppositions relevant to the interpretation of his political writing.[1] Indeed, the contention of this paper is that Locke's understanding of the principles of economic analysis and of the economic aspects of human nature contributes importantly to his theory of civil government. Locke recognized that in significant areas of their lives, men are economic actors. Men are not exclusively economic actors in Locke's thought, but the rational, calculative aspects of human nature nevertheless are significant to an understanding of their social behavior. Hence, the economic aspects of men's thinking and acting are a major component of Locke's explanation for the formation of civil government, his argument for limited government, and his theory of how a revolution might come about. Indeed, the whole tenor of Locke's arguments is suffused with economic presuppositions.

This claim will seem startling to many noneconomists. To claim that a major work in political philosophy is suffused with economic presuppositions might be regarded as an exercise in economic imperialism. Yet every theory of government contains some set of implicit assumptions about the nature of economic reality, whether the assumptions are articulated or simply taken for granted. At the very least, every theory of government must presume that the economic system embedded in it is efficient enough to generate sufficient wealth for its existence. Further, political theories must assume that the economic activities open to its political actors are consistent with the goals and operations of the polity. Economics is about how people choose, how they trade with each other, how they deal with scarcity, and how they come to know about the opportunities facing them. Economics is about social action and one fundamentally important kind of social order. To neglect to consider the requirements of the economic order would at least call the usefulness of a political theory into question. Locke, however, did not neglect economic concerns in his political theory. An important contributor to the development of economic theory through his writings on interest and money, Locke's understanding of economics also informed his writings on politics. Indeed, what makes Locke's political philosophy so interesting to an economist is that he consciously articulates a theory of economic order in these writings that complements and illuminates the theory of political order that he developed in the *Two Treatises*. His economic system both constrains government and provides a means of evaluating its performance.

THE HISTORICAL CONNECTION BETWEEN LOCKE'S
ECONOMIC AND POLITICAL WRITINGS

Locke's interest in both economics and politics seems to have been ig-
nited by his close association with Anthony Ashley Cooper, first earl of
Shaftesbury, an association that began in earnest in 1667 when Locke
joined the future earl of Shaftesbury's household as physician and aide.[2]
Prior to that time, Locke had lectured in moral philosophy at Oxford, had
written on the *Law of Nature*, and had studied medicine and experimen-
tal philosophy informally with the group surrounding Robert Boyle.
Under Shaftesbury's tutelage, Locke soon shifted his interest in medicine
to an interest in the affairs of the day. In 1667 Locke drafted his first *Essay
on Toleration*, which included the argument that religious toleration was
good policy because it enhanced the wealth and power of the nation, an
idea that Locke seems to have learned from Shaftesbury. In the following
year Locke made his first attempt to analyze a problem of economic
policy, a short essay entitled *Some of the Consequences that are like to
follow upon Lessening of Interest to 4 percent*.[3] It was written, probably at
Shaftesbury's behest, to answer a proposal made by Josiah Child to reduce
the legal rate of interest to 4 percent in an effort to reduce the cost of trade.

Locke's first attempt to analyze an economic problem was halting and
incomplete. It was never published, and the issues raised by the problem
of setting a legal interest rate must have continued to puzzle him for a
number of years since he continued to revise his essay until about 1674.[4]
His commonplace book is full of notes about exchange rates and trade
issues over the next twenty years. In 1692, when Locke had become something of a gray eminence and a respected public adviser, he set about again
to unravel the problem of interest. Once more a bill was before Parliament
to lower the legal rate of interest to 4 percent, and Locke revised his 1674
essay to meet the arguments of the day. This time, however, the rather
stark analysis of potential gainers and losers from the proposed legislation
that marked his early effort was folded into a much more comprehensive
and sophisticated general economic analysis. His policy conclusions had
remained the same over the twenty-four-year period from when he began
writing the economic essay until the time of its publication, but his
supporting analysis got better and better. Although the final published
product, *Some Considerations of the Consequences of Lowering of Interest and Raising the Value of Money*, does seem a bit disjointed in its

exposition, probably because Locke incorporated sheets of his 1674 revision into the 1692 text (Letwin 1965), it nevertheless presents a coherent and largely consistent economic analysis from which to derive recommendations for economic policy.

My contention here is that a close concordance exists between Locke's economic essay and the *Treatises*. If one considers the history of Locke's publications, my contention gains force. Locke spent the years from 1683 to 1689 in Holland living in exile. During that time he wrote his *Essay Concerning Human Understanding* and *Thoughts Concerning Education*. At the end of his exile, close upon his return to England, he completed and published both these works and in addition the *Two Treatises of Government*, the *Letter Concerning Toleration*, and *Some Considerations*. Although these works were not exactly written simultaneously, they were thought about and written upon during the same phase of his life. It is not unusual for scholars to change their minds about problems over the years as they grow and mature, but it would be surprising if there were major inconsistencies in the basic presuppositions undergirding these important works. More specifically, it would be astonishing if the *Treatises* and the *Considerations* (published within two years of each other) did not presuppose the same basic assumptions about human nature and human action since the first was a work about the legitimacy and limits of political authority and the second was a work about the limits of political efficacy in public policy.

LOCKE'S ECONOMIC SYSTEM

Locke begins his economic essay with the question "Can the price of the hire of money be regulated by law?" and answers with a resounding " 'tis manifest it cannot" (*SC*:1). The rest of the essay is an increasingly complex elaboration of the reasons why government cannot regulate certain economic activities and hence why it would be imprudent for it to try. The crux of his argument is that economic values are the consequence of bargains that individuals strike with one another to pursue their own advantage. Government's attempts to interfere with those bargains will set off a chain of consequences that are unexpected and undesirable (*SC*:6–7). The reasons that individuals borrow and lend at particular rates of interest have to do with the profitability of investment and trade

(SC:14). In fact, the resultant of the interaction between borrowers and lenders in the marketplace is the establishment of a natural rate of interest (SC:18). A price ceiling on interest rates will do nothing to affect that natural rate. Political attempts to govern the terms of trade of voluntary bargains will only cause individual borrowers and lenders to find ways around the law and will lead to great inconvenience and loss to those who are not wiley enough to thwart the law to their own advantage (SC:12). From that beginning Locke goes on to explain how money commands a price for its use, how that differs from the value of money in exchange, how money functions in the economy, how the value of things in general is determined, and what the proper concerns of England should be in the conduct of world trade.[5]

Locke's economic analysis is interesting for an economist because he developed a model to explain market value that he applied to all the problems he set himself in his essay. The intrinsic value of goods depends upon their "fitness to supply the necessities or serve the conveniences of human life" (SC:66), but intrinsic value is only indirectly related to market value. "There is no such intrinsic natural settled value in anything, as to make any assigned quantity of it, constantly worth any assigned quantity of another" (SC:66). Markets are concerned with establishing the relative values of things only. Relative values in turn depend upon the proportion between quantity and vent (roughly the equivalent of supply and demand). Quantity offered for sale is directly related to price, and vent or demand is inversely proportional to price. Price varies according to those proportions, and the proportions depend upon such things as tastes and the size of the harvest. Money is a special case of goods in general in that it has two values, a value in use (interest) and a value in exchange (as a medium of exchange). Its value in use is the interest rate, and its value in exchange depends upon its purchasing power. Money is needed both as money capital and as a medium of exchange to drive the "wheels of trade" (SC:30).

Locke's value theory is simple and even crude, but it is also surprisingly powerful as a means of predicting the direction of change of price in response to parametric changes. Moreover, Locke's theory enabled him to penetrate to the heart of market phenomena. He understood markets, trade, and money. Even Locke's "macro" theory, which has been accused of being backward for his time because he advocated that England should have a net-positive flow of gold into the country, makes sense within the context of his argument.[6] His major goal throughout his essay was to advocate policies that would make England's trade vigorous and her people prosperous.

An economist can find much that is interesting in Locke's economic analysis, but for our purposes here the particulars of his model are not as important as is the tenor of his overall approach. William Letwin (1965) has called Locke one of the originators of scientific economics. His approach was scientific in the sense of concentrating on causal arguments to explain a social phenomenon according to regular abstract principles of behavior. Joyce Appleby (1978) has argued that the whole history of seventeenth-century economic thought was characterized by a growing perception that there were laws of economics and that economic policy had to be consistent with those laws. Economic phenomena increasingly were explained as the predictable outcomes of comprehensible systems rather than as the consequences of the perverse behavior of individuals. That is, the fact that there are predictable, unintended consequences of human action was becoming more and more taken for granted in the economic writings of the seventeenth century. Yet even within that context, Locke's system was striking.

Locke's "scientific economics" was based on a very modern assumption about human nature, that humans interact in the marketplace to pursue their own gain. By calling that modern, I do not mean to imply that Locke was the first ever to notice this. Indeed, that has been the underlying notion behind all economic analysis from the Scholastics to the present.[7] Yet it is modern in the sense that Locke believed that government could not easily override the aims and projects of people trading in the marketplace. In *Some Considerations*, the message was for government to work within the confines of human nature and to take into account the likely response people will make to legislation. There is simply no point in enacting a law that will decree all interest rates above 4 percent to be illegal. As long as there is no increase in the supply of loanable funds (and in fact there will be a decrease because of the reduction in the return a lender can expect from his risk), those who want to borrow at 6 percent but cannot find a lender will not stick at offering a higher price for the money that they need for their ventures (*SC*:11). Where there is profit to be made, a mere law controlling price will be heartily ignored (*SC*:2). For Locke, men's actions in the marketplace gave rise to an economic system that was at least in principle separable from the polity. This systematic outcome of individual, purposeful action could not be ignored in the formation of economic policy.

ECONOMIC MAN IN THE *SECOND TREATISE OF GOVERNMENT*

It is my contention here that *Some Considerations* must be read as something of a companion piece to the *Second Treatise of Government* if Locke's understanding of the relationship between the individual and the polity is to be fully understood. As we have seen, both books were written during the same period in Locke's life and published at about the same time. Both were reflections of Shaftesbury's concerns, and both were written as pieces of advocacy whose importance went beyond the issues of the day. Interestingly, both were written to comment upon some aspect of the relationship of government to its citizens. Even though Locke actively worked on the economic essay about eight years before he wrote the *Two Treatises*, I think it is fair to say that when Locke was originally in the throes of composing his political essays he had not forgotten or repudiated his economic ideas. Considering that he published both pieces so close to each other, any major inconsistencies in the underlying premises of the two essays certainly would have become obvious to him. Clearly, he stood by the ideas expressed in both publications to the end of his life. Certainly if we consider both in their role as pieces of social analysis, important arguments in the *Treatises* are dependent on the analysis in *Some Considerations*.

In particular, one should read the *Treatises* keeping in mind the kind of world Locke was writing about in *Some Considerations*. In the economic essay Locke describes how people will behave in the everyday business of making a living in political society. He gives us strong clues as to the kind of people he thinks live in this world, and he also gives us clues as to his moral judgments about these people. As I have already argued, these people are concerned with their economic well-being. They pursue profits even if that entails evading laws, and they alter their behavior in response to perceived pay offs. Workers, for instance, move to the highest paying jobs they can get, and skilled artisans emigrate to whatever country has an economy that promises them the best living (*SC*:79). They live in a world that is changeable and hence uncertain (*SC*:51−52). Some of them have noble occupations like farming; others are wretched middlemen (*SC*:42). Some are frugal and build fortunes; others are profligate and lose them. There are those who injure the nation through their taste for foreign luxuries and those who enrich the nation through their skills and talents (*SC*:94). Throughout his essay, Locke gives the reader a sense of what is important to the nation and of the limits to what government can do to achieve the economic well-being of the nation. Though his recommendations for governmental policy tend to be more negative than positive, the underlying presumption seems to be that it is the responsibility of government to protect and enhance the prosperity of its citizens.

One gets no sense of asceticism from the pages of *Some Considerations*, nor does one perceive an underlying despair with the materialism of Englishmen.[8] In fact, Locke seems to have a robust appreciation of the challenges of economic life and of economic policy. Prosperity is good, and the free exercise of economic activity benefits everyone, especially "widows and orphans"—the weakest members of society.[9]

Now, what does a man who writes thus about the actual economic life of England around him believe about the origin, limits, and purposes of civil government? It seems likely to me that the kind of people who live in the pages of *Some Considerations* are the same people who roam around Locke's state of nature and who eventually come to create a civil society. The same people who are capable of contracting to sell grain, to lend money at interest, to sell their labor services to the highest bidder, and to avoid the ill-thought-out economic regulations of a misguided sovereign are the same people who are capable of perceiving that there is a better alternative to the state of nature and who can enter into a contract to form civil society. In other words, they are economic men in the eighteenth-century meaning of the term, men who are reasonable within the limits of their knowledge and of the surrounding circumstances. They are what the late Scholastics referred to as men of prudent reason.

Not only are Locke's people economic men in the broad sense of the term, but they are also men who specifically produce for and trade in organized markets. When C. B. Macpherson claimed that Locke's argument in the *Second Treatise* was at base an economic one, he was partially correct. His mistake was in using a Marxist framework for trying to understand Locke's economic premises. There have been many refutations of Macpherson's interpretation of Locke as a "possessive individualist," most of which focus on the claims Macpherson made about the moral interpretation of Locke's system (See Ryan 1965; Vaughn 1980; Wood 1984). Was Locke really trying to justify unlimited accumulation? Was he really an apologist for capitalism? Did he really think workers belonged to an inferior class possessing limited rationality? The answers to these questions are interesting, but they are beside the point of the economics of Locke's *Treatises*. Locke was writing a defense of limited government in order to justify a revolution.[10] The *Two Treatises* presupposed an understanding of human action and a market order that made the arguments intelligible.

The foundation of a market economy is the act of exchange between two purposeful human beings. An exchange is a kind of contract between individuals that implies a set of rights and responsibilities. As Adam Smith (1981, 26) points out, it is a particularly human activity in that "nobody ever saw a dog make a fair and deliberate exchange of one bone for another with another dog. Nobody ever saw one animal by its gestures and natural cries signify to another, this is mine, that is yours; I am willing to give this for that."

Smith accounts for this difference between humans and dogs by invoking a propensity to "truck, barter and exchange one thing for another." He does not regard this propensity as some sort of extra attribute of humans equivalent to opposable thumbs or upright stance. The propensity to truck, barter, and exchange is better thought of as a by-product of the same human intelligence that indulges in creativity, imagination, calculation, that can plan a course of action and can carry it out according to internalized constraints, and that can communicate its wants, observations, and plans through language. Human society is possible at all only because of all of these particularly human traits, and human society above the most primitive level is possible only because of the phenomenon of exchange.

Although human society, almost by definition, requires some form of exchange to take place, people cannot enter into exchanges with each other in the absence of some minimal amount of trust between the parties to the exchange. Even in the simplest of trades there is always the possibility that one party to the agreement will renege; exact simultaneity of a swap is almost impossible. The more complex the exchange, the greater the opportunity for cheating. Hence, a complex system of trades requires at a minimum the expectation that people will stick to their agreements. Even though cheating on contracts does occur, no market could function if cheating were the norm rather than the exception. Informal mechanisms have evolved to guard against cheating, such as knowledge of the trading partner's past performance or the promise of potential future trades within a group to provide an incentive for honesty, but defection is always a possibility. Even in a system where contracts are upheld in a court of law, one can never fully specify every contingency in a contract to eliminate all possibility of cheating. If most people in most trades were not cooperators, trade and markets could never flourish. Hence, some level of shared moral values is necessary in order for contracts to be possible.

Locke perceives both the importance of contract in human society and the necessary prerequisite of some minimal level of shared moral values to make contract possible. Indeed, contract is both the foundation of a market economy and the foundation of Locke's political system. All through the *Second Treatise*, contract is a pervasive element. Locke refers to contracts between servant and employer (*ST*: no. 85), to marriage as a compact between man and woman entailing mutual benefits and obligations (*ST*: nos. 78–83), to money as the product of mutual consent (*ST*: no. 47), to barter contracts and, of course, to the contract of all contracts, the community formed by agreement among its members (*ST*: no. 95).[11]

Further, it is clear that Locke believed the ability to enter into contracts and to make exchanges was prerequisite to the formation of civil order since contract predated the establishment of government both analytically and historically. In the property chapter Locke observes, "For truth and keeping of faith belong to Men, as Men, and not as members of society" (*ST*: no. 14). Indeed, if truth and keeping of faith did not belong to men as men, there would be no way for Locke to explain how they could escape from the state of nature and contract to form civil society in the first place. In order for the social contract to work, there must have been at the very least some expectation on the part of each man that the others would keep their political bargains. Not only are men presumed to keep their bargains, however, but in Locke's system the social contract is so binding that once made it can never be broken—although it can be renegotiated.

The whole notion that men in a state of nature could enter into such a complex and binding contract is bold indeed. From where did the shared moral values necessary to make his model work come while men were still in the state of nature with one another? Hobbes had avoided this problem by treating men as amoral defectors who needed government to provide any order at all. Locke, however, did not take this route. For Locke, men are already part of a moral community in the state of nature before they enter into the agreement to form civil government. This is so because men all have access to the Law of Nature through their reason.[12]

The Law of Nature was the necessary foundation to Locke's conception of the state of nature. Men could enter into economic contracts in the state of nature and have some presumption that the contracts would be upheld because all men had only to consult their reason to know what was right behavior. Even more to the point, men could exit the state of nature and enter into the compact to form civil society because they were morally capable of agreeing with one another and of sticking to the agreement. Hence, there is a necessary connection between Locke's presumption of an accessible natural law that guaranteed the set of shared moral values and the possibility of contract in general and in particular the contract that forms the state.[13]

Another requirement for contract to be possible to which I have already called attention is that the participants be imaginative. Before they can agree to an exchange, they must be able to imagine a state of affairs that does not yet exist—the state of the world after the exchange takes place. Further, they must be able to calculate potential costs and benefits of the change in the state of the world to be brought about by their trade. Evidence of men's ability to calculate costs and benefits abounds in Locke's economic writings as one would expect, and evidence is also available that he believed men calculated in nonmarket contexts as well. For instance, in chapter 2 of the *Second Treatise* Locke explains that men have the right to punish transgressions in the state of nature, but the question of the acceptable degree of punishment is raised. He maintains that in setting punishment, "each transgression may be punished to that degree, and with so much severity as will suffice to make it an ill-bargain to the offender, give him cause to repent, and terrifie others from doing the like" (*ST*: no. 12). Locke's implicit assumption here is that criminals weigh the costs and benefits of a potential crime and commit the crime only if they stand to have a net gain. The same assumption, by the way, underlies the modern study of the economics of crime. A man who could so casually draw out the calculative dimension of supposedly irrational criminal behavior, it seems to me, would surely understand the calculative abilities of everyday human beings.[14] In fact, the crux of his argument for limited government is that men agree to leave the state of nature when the inconvenience of each man's being his own judge outweighs the benefits of unlimited political freedom in the state of nature.[15] Further, when the costs of any particular government become so onerous that they outweigh the benefits garnered from political stability, men will resort to revolution. The beginning of civil society and the dissolution of any particular government are decisions made primarily by cost/benefit analysis broadly conceived.

PROPERTY IN THE STATE OF NATURE

The most fundamental requirement for an exchange to take place is that both parties to the exchange own something. One cannot trade without possessions, so it is not surprising that Locke devotes a central chapter in the *Second Treatise* to an explanation of how men came to own property in the state of nature.

Locke's theory of property is generally, and properly, read as a justification of private property. The debates that rage over this chapter center on such questions as whether Locke believed that men had a right to unlimited amounts of property, whether he really believed inequality of possessions was morally justified, and whether he believed his labor theory of property also applied to civil society. I shall have some comments on what I think the moral presuppositions are later, but I shall first focus on the analytic nature of this chapter. What does this chapter tell us about Locke's economic understanding, and how does that relate to his analytic explanation for the origin of civil society? Chapter 5 should be read partly as an exercise in conjectural history,[16] the analysis of an institution by explaining how that institution could have come about as the product of human action. Locke uses this chapter to explain how property could have emerged, how money might have evolved, and how economic development could lead to the formation of organized polities. Although conjectural histories are generally wrong—or at least incomplete—as factual accounts, they can lay bare the meaning and function of a particular institution.

The basis for Locke's justification of private property in the state of nature is his labor theory of property. God gave the world to men in common for their use. Men own themselves, and by extension they own their own labor. They create property by mixing their own labor, which is unconditionally their property, with unowned common resources, thereby creating something new, which becomes their property as well (*ST*: no. 27). The details of Locke's labor theory of property are so familiar that they need not be repeated once again. For the purposes of this paper, I want to call attention to some characteristics of labor in the property chapter that illuminate my argument.

It is important first to recognize that the labor that creates property in Locke's system is not limited to some kind of brute force or physical exertion. Labor is better described as a purposeful and creative act that may be mental as well as physical. Men labor by picking berries, gathering acorns from the ground, and, significantly, by tracking wild animals: "Even amongst us the Hare that anyone is Hunting, is thought his who pursues her during the Chase. For being a Beast that is still looked upon as common, and no Man's private possession; whoever has imploy'd so much labour about any of that kind, as to find and pursue her, has thereby removed her from the state of Nature, wherein she was common, and hath begun a Property" (ST: no. 30). During the tracking there is no physical contact with the animal, yet it is carved out of the common by the hunter's intention to kill the animal. The labor is both a mental act of planning and a physical act of pursuing. This reading is further supported later on in the chapter where Locke refers to "invention and arts" improving the "conveniences of life" (ST: no. 44).

Labor also includes the work of a supervisor. In a much commented-upon passage Locke argues that "the Grass my Horse has bit; the Turfs my Servant has cut; and the Ore I have digg'd in any place where I have a right to them in common with others, become my Property" (ST: no. 28). I create property not only through my own labor (digging ore) but also by owning and employing a piece of capital equipment (my horse) and by hiring an employee for a fixed return to work for me (my servant). This kind of understanding of labor is especially difficult for Marxists because they define labor solely as the action of the laborer directly and physically involved in the final production of commodities, excluding actions taken by the owners of the means of production. The more modern view, of course, is that productive activity includes the efforts of all those who provide some service to the final production of output, including hired laborers, managers, entrepreneurs, and owners of money capital who lend it out for productive purposes. Given this distinction, Locke surely is ancestor to the modern analysis of productive factors in the economy.

The issue of what constitutes labor in the *Second Treatise* is important to an understanding of Locke's justification of private property. Locke's purpose is to show how "Men might come to have a property in several parts of that which God gave to Mankind in common, and that without any express Compact of all the Commoners" (ST: no. 25). The right to own property in the state of nature is a direct implication of self-ownership that requires no agreement from others. Labor gives men title to property in the state of nature, that is, *all* labor and not just some subset of manual labor. Though the moral justification of property is complete in itself, Locke does not leave his argument there. He carefully and emphatically also points out that there are practical advantages to the institution of private property that makes it serve everyone's self-interest.

It is not so strange, Locke argues, that "the Property of labour should be able to over-balance the Community of Land" because "tis Labour indeed that puts the difference of value on every thing; and let any one consider, what the difference is between an Acre of Land planted with Tobacco or Sugar, sown with Wheat or Barley; and an Acre of the same Land lying in common, without any Husbandry upon it, and he will find, that the improvement of labour makes the far greater part of the value" (*ST*: no. 40). In other words, by laboring men improve upon nature and create valuable things. Nor is the increment to the value of unimproved nature trivial. "I think it will be but a very modest Computation to say, that of the Products of the Earth useful to the Life of Man 9/10 are the effect of labour: Nay, if we will rightly estimate things as they come to our use, and cast up the several Expences about them, what in them is purely owing to Nature, and what to labour, we shall find, that in most of them 99/100 are wholly to be put on the account of labor" (*ST*: no. 40).

What are we to make of these claims about the value of labor? One thing we are emphatically not to make of them is that Locke is espousing some primitive labor theory of value. He is clearly identifying labor as a major source of value, but there is no textual evidence that he is alluding to any quantitative or causal relationship between quantities of labor input and the value of output such as David Ricardo and Karl Marx develop in their own various ways two centuries later. Indeed, in Locke's economic writings, as we have seen, he develops a theory of market value based on a close analog to supply and demand.[17]

Market value is relative value—how much of one thing will trade for another—and market values depend on the proportion between the quantity of a thing offered for sale and the amount people are willing to buy. So when Locke talks about labor putting the difference of value on all things or when he suggests that ninety-nine one hundredths of the value of anything is owing to labor, he is simply stating in an emphatic way that most of the goods we value do not come directly from nature but require a great deal of labor effort to bring them to their consumable state. He is not proposing an alternative theory of value. In fact, when Locke compares the value of land planted with tobacco with land left fallow (*ST*: no. 40) or when he claims that "whatever Bread is more worth than Acorns, wine than Water, and Cloth or Silk than Leaves, Skins, or Moss, that is wholly owing to labour and industry" (*ST*: no. 42), it is clear that he intends to use the market values of those goods as the mode of comparison. For instance, in his next paragraph he evaluates the "benefit mankind receives" from land overtly in terms of market prices.

An Acre of Land that bears here Twenty Bushels of Wheat, and another in America, which, with the same Husbandry, would do the like, are without doubt, of the same natural, intrinsick Value. But yet the Benefit Mankind receives from the one, in a Year, is worth 5 £ and from the other possibly not worth a Penny, if all the Profit an Indian received from it were to be valued, and sold here; at least, I may truly say, not 1/1000. (*ST*: no. 43)

Clearly, labor creates value, but value is measured by the marketplace.

Locke claims not only that labor creates value as a by-product of the creation of property but also that everyone is better off as a result of the creation of private property. He has two arguments to back up this claim; the first holds even in the most primitive stage of the state of nature, and the second requires the functioning of a market economy.

The first argument is straightforward. "He, that incloses Land and has a greater plenty of the conveniencys of life from ten acres, than he could have from an hundred left to Nature, may truly be said, to give ninety acres to Mankind. For his labour now supplys him with provisions out of ten acres, which were but the product of an hundred lying in common" (*ST*: no. 37). This, of course, assumes that the man's level of consumption remains constant over the two states. However, as long as he uses fewer acres to sustain himself than he would have without enclosure, the point holds. This situation requires no exchange for mankind to benefit from one person's labor; all benefit because resources have been freed for the use of others.

The second example Locke gives of mankind benefiting from private property is less obvious. He argues that the native peoples of America "who are rich in Land, and poor in all the Comforts of Life; whom Nature having furnished as liberally as any other people, with the materials of Plenty . . . yet for want of improving it by labour, have not one hundreth part of the Conveniencies we enjoy: and a King of a large and fruitful

Territory there feed, lodges, and is clad worse than a day Labourer in England" (*ST*: no. 41). Day laborers are contract workers in a market economy. By claiming that these laborers are better off in England than a king in America, he is obviously claiming that the value created in a private-property market economy is so great that everyone including the lowest-paid worker is far better off than even the most privileged would be in a state of nature without private property. Now how can this be true? It might be the case that Locke believed the day laborer in himself was more productive of value than the king of a large and fruitful territory in America. But if the land is of equal "intrinsic" value as Locke earlier claimed, why would any one man (a day laborer in England) be more productive than any other man (a king in America)? The only plausible answer is that the day laborer in England functions with a capital stock and/or benefits from the productive capacity of other workers in an economy characterized by the division of labor, and the king in America labors in isolation on unimproved land.

Unlike Adam Smith, Locke does not specifically say that the wealth of the nation depends on the division of labor. Yet it is clear that Locke understood the English economy to be characterized by a complex division of labor:

> For 'tis not barely the Plough-man's Pains, counted into the Bread we eat; the Labour of those who broke the Oxen, who digged and wrought the Iron and Stones, who felled and framed the Timber imployed about the Plough, Mill, Oven, or any other Utensils, which are a vast Number, requisite to this Corn, from its being seed to be sown to its being made Bread, must all be charged on the account of Labour, and received as an effect of that. (*ST*: no. 43)

As Adam Smith was to argue one century later (probably with Locke's essay in mind), if a laborer in Europe is better off than a king in a primitive land, it is because of the productive benefits of the division of labor.[18] Further, in a system characterized by private property and the division of labor, people must exchange goods with one another to meet the variety and complexity of their wants; and exchange leads to the emergence of market prices that reflect the relative values of the goods that meet these wants. People were better off with private property largely because they were wealthier with the division of labor and trade in markets.[19]

THE THEORY OF MONEY

From the point of view of an economist, one of the most interesting aspects of chapter 5 of the *Second Treatise* is Locke's account of the origin and consequences of money. Locke's theory of money should be seen as part of a long-standing debate in the history of economic thought concerning the nature of money. At least from the time of Aristotle, thinkers debated whether money was a natural phenomenon that could exist apart from the state or whether it was purely a creation of the state. Closely aligned with this debate was the controversy over whether the value of money was real in some sense or artificially attached to the money commodity. The commodity theorists tended to believe that the money commodity had value in itself and was the property of individuals; the fiat theorists tended to believe that money had an artificial value that was attributable to its being issued by the state. In his economic writings, especially his second major economic essay, *Further Considerations Concerning Raising the Value of Money*, Locke treats money as a commodity that was the lawful property of the citizens of a state but whose value was determined in the marketplace, much like any other commodity. The only difference between money and other commodities is that money is valued solely because it can be exchanged for other goods and not because of any inherent properties in the money commodity. In that sense, and in only that sense, its value is imaginary—based on a quality that does not inhere in the money commodity itself. Locke strongly argues that the value of money should not be interfered with by the government, a practice he places on the level of fraud.[20] It is interesting to see the basis for his attitudes toward money spelled out in the *Second Treatise*.

In this work, Locke addresses the problem of the origin of money. Since money is not valued for its own sake, how did any commodity ever emerge as a medium of exchange? Locke's account of the origin of money is in the form of what has lately come to be called an invisible-hand explanation.[21]

Locke's explanation for what limits the accumulation of property in the state of nature is generally read for its moral content. Locke argues that although God gave the world to men for their use and enjoined them to be fruitful and multiply, there was a limit to how much men could lawfully accumulate in the state of nature: "God has given us all things richly, 1

Tim. vi. 17. is the voice of Reason confirmed by Inspiration. But how far has he given it us? *To enjoy.* As much as any one can make use to any advantage of life before it spoils; so much he may by his labour fix a Property in. Whatever is beyond this, is more than his share, and belongs to others, Nothing was made by God for Man to spoil or destroy" (*ST*: no. 31).

Notice here that Locke does not say that men can accumulate as much as is necessary for their lives or as much as they can use to a noble purpose. His limitation is far less restrictive than that: as much as anyone can make use of *to any advantage*. God has given us things *to enjoy*. The subjective aspects of this are unmistakable. Apparently, the only case in which property would be forbidden is in the instance of someone's allowing goods to decay or spoil, say, by letting corn rot in the field or by permitting a house to fall into ruin. One is tempted to see in this the idea that it is the destruction of capital rather than its accumulation that Locke would find morally offensive.[22]

Locke argues that in the state of nature it is not only immoral to permit resources to go to waste, but it is also imprudent. However, people face a dilemma since they are capable of creating more property than they can use in the short run. The way out of this dilemma is a tribute to the resourcefulness of human beings. Locke argues that if a man were to produce more than he could consume in the short run, there would be no sin involved if he traded his perishable goods for more durable ones in an effort to avoid waste. If, for instance, he

bartered away Plumbs that would have rotted in a Week, for Nuts that would last good for his eating a whole Year, he did no injury; he wasted not the common Stock; destroyed no part of the portion of Goods that belonged to others, so long as nothing perished uselessly in his hands, Again, if he would give his Nuts for a piece of Metal, for a sparkling Pebble or a Diamond, and keep those by him all his Life, he invaded not the Right of others, he might heap up as much of these durable things as he pleased; the exceeding of the bounds of his just Property not lying in the largeness of his Possession, but the perishing of any thing uselessly in it. And thus came in the use of Money, some lasting thing that Men might keep without spoiling, and that by mutual consent Men would take in exchange for the truly useful, but perishable Supports of Life. (*ST*: nos. 47, 48)

Most commentators have pointed out that in these passages Locke explains how men can circumvent the primary limitation to just property ownership in the state of nature so that nothing should spoil in their possession. Though that is the important implication for his account of the move into civil society—which I shall discuss further—the importance of this passage for the history of economic thought has generally been overlooked. This was probably the first evolutionary account of the origin of money in the literature of economic thought. It undoubtedly influenced Carl Menger, who in the nineteenth century provided a much more detailed and convincing account of the origin of money that nevertheless had the same Lockean elements in it.[23]

MONEY AND THE MOVE INTO CIVIL SOCIETY

Locke's evolutionary account of the origin of money is part of a more general account of how it ever came about that men could agree to enter into civil society. The connection here between Locke's economics and his politics is most interesting.

Locke's state of nature is not simply an analytic construct, nor is it a static model of an equilibrium state that exists without government. The purpose of Locke's state of nature is designed to show why men would choose to be subject to government and why government must be limited in its powers. However, the method he uses to achieve his purpose is to show a process of development in the state of nature that makes government a reasonable, profitable institution for his reasonable, profit-seeking men.

Locke seems to have imagined the original state of the world as one with low population density and abundant natural resources. In economic jargon, it was a time of no resource scarcity. Humans could take whatever they wanted from the earth without limiting equivalent supplies of resources to anyone else. It seems that Locke did not believe this was a particularly wealthy state for men to live in. His many comparisons of America to the original state of the world suggest that he thought people were then much poorer than in bustling seventeenth-century England (ST: no. 36). They seemed to live a hunter-gatherer existence or a nomadic one. If conditions began to get crowded in this early world, people could simply pick up and move to a place of equivalent fertility (ST: no. 38). Even when men took up agriculture and stopped moving around, resource scarcity was not a problem. In these early days, agriculture served only to increase the amount of land available for the support of others (*ST*: no. 37).

However, men have certain character traits that made it inevitable that this early state would give way to a more complicated stage of human existence. Although all men can create property, some will be more productive than others. Further, some men are also covetous, "quarrelsome and contentious" (*ST*: no. 34), and given to disputing the lawful property of others. In the earliest state, Locke believed, there would be "little room for quarrels or contentions about property" because of the scarcity of people and the abundance of natural resources and because men would have very little property about which to argue (*ST*: no. 31). (One might also add that property would tend to be of the immediately consumable kind—acorns, apples, or hares—so there would not be much visible property for anyone to covet.) However, populations grew, and so did the gap in wealth between the more productive, and the less productive, leading to more disputes over property. Locke argues that even in this case there still would have been an abundance of natural resources had it not been for the introduction of money into the state of nature.

We have already seen that money in Locke's state of nature emerges as the by-product of men's attempts to store their wealth in durable form. The introduction of money into any society has enormous implications for its potential size and wealth. In a barter economy, the division of labor is severely restricted by the inconvenience of trying to satisfy the double coincidence of wants. This puts a limit on the total wealth of a community and also on its size. However, once money enters into the picture, specialization and the division of labor are limited only by the extent of the market, as Adam Smith tells us. Not only does money make possible increased wealth through enabling specialization and the division of labor, but money also enables people to save and accumulate wealth, Locke's point in the *Second Treatise*. Money in effect allows people to trade immediate consumption for future consumption, thereby freeing current goods for use by others. Saving permits productive investment and thereby allows total wealth to grow.

In the *Second Treatise* the only direct consequence of the emergence of money that Locke mentions is that men can thereby enlarge their possessions. Without money, he argues, there would be no point in cultivating more land than was sufficient to provide ample consumption for one's family and for occasional barter with neighbors. "What would a Man value Ten thousand, or an Hundred Thousand Acres of excellent Land, ready cultivated, and well stocked too with Cattle, in the middle of the in-land Parts of America, where he had no hopes of Commerce with other Parts of the World, to draw Money to him by the Sale of the Product? It would not be worth the inclosing"(*ST*: no. 48). Is there any evidence that Locke saw more than mere hoarding as an outcome of the use of money? Did he understand the productive implications of money in an economy?

In the *Considerations*, the whole basis for Locke's argument opposing interest-rate regulation is that money is valuable largely because of its role in productive investment. Money capital (or stock) is used to buy the goods necessary to finance remunerative enterprises, which is the reason borrowers are willing to pay interest for its use. In fact, in both of Locke's major economic essays, he emphasizes the central importance of money to a healthy, smoothly functioning economic system.[24] With this as background, his description of the implications of the introduction of money into the state of nature becomes more intelligible.

The argument can be reconstructed as follows. At some point in the distant past, hunting-gathering and pastorage gave way to agriculture. As a result, both wealth and population started to grow. The growth in wealth led to a desire to store surplus output that in turn led to the emergence of money, which permitted further growth in population and wealth. However, it also led to increasing resource scarcity and eventually to increasing disputes about property in the state of nature. Although natural law could still in principle permit people to resolve their disputes, in fact, the majority of men were "no strict observers of equity and justice" (*ST*: no. 123). The increase in population, increasing scarcity of land, and resultant increase in disputes in the state of nature eventually led to a point where the advantages of living in perfect freedom were outweighed by the disadvantages of living without a common judge and a common set of laws and attached penalties (*ST*: no. 127). At this point it makes sense for Locke's rational, sensible men to agree to form civil society.

THE ECONOMICS OF CIVIL SOCIETY

There is a great deal of controversy over what Locke thought the role of government was vis-à-vis private property. Nothing in Locke is ever perfectly clear, but the weight of textual evidence seems to rest with those who argue that the labor theory of property does not apply in civil government. The labor theory of property applies unambiguously only when resources are abundant and when it is therefore possible for men to find unowned land with which to mix their labor (*ST*: no. 33). Yet one of the hallmarks of civil society is land scarcity since in civil society no more equally good land is left lying waste, waiting for productive labor to claim it for private property. The ownership of land must be regulated by positive constitutions (*ST*: no. 50). Even the commons of seventeenth-century England are not oases of the original state in the midst of civil society; they are plots of land left common by compact, and their use is bounded by civil rules (*ST*: no. 37).

Although property is to be regulated by civil laws, Locke says very little about the exact nature of such regulation in the *Second Treatise*. He does, however, make repeated and emphatic comments that make it clear that the duty of government is to protect property "that labor and industry began" (*ST*: no. 45).

In chapter 9 Locke tells us that men are willing to give up the freedom of the state of nature, which is fraught with "fears and continual dangers," in order to ensure "the mutual Preservation of their Lives, Liberties and Estate, which I call by the general Name, Property" (*ST*: no. 123). He follows this up with "the great and chief end . . . of Mens uniting into Commonwealths, and putting themselves under Government, is *the Preservation of the Property* (*ST*: no. 124). He repeats this sentiment on the next page when he observes that men rarely stay in the state of nature because "the inconveniences, that they are therein exposed to, by the irregular and uncertain exercise of the Power every Man has of punishing the transgression of others, make them take Sanctuary under the establish'd Laws of Government, and therein seek the preservation of their Property" (*ST*: no. 127). In chapter 11 he writes, "the great end of men's entering into society being the enjoyment of their properties in peace and safety, and the great instrument and means of that being the laws established in that society" (ST:134). Later he reiterates, "To avoid . . . inconveniences which disorder mens properties in the state of nature, men unite into societies, that they may have the united strength of the whole society to secure and defend their properties" (*ST*: no. 136), and "Men would not quit the freedom of the state of Nature for, and tie themselves up under [government], were it not to preserve their Lives, liberties and fortunes" (*ST*: no. 137).

The context of all of these statements is to oppose arbitrary power in the hands of an absolute monarch. The gist of Locke's observations is that men enter into civil society only to make themselves better off and more secure than they would have been in the state of nature. Being better off and more secure largely concerns the preservation and protection of their properties—life, liberty, and estate. It would be foolish for men to enter into civil society only to find themselves at the mercy of an absolute sovereign who could make a mockery of the protections of civil society.

It is true that Locke gives a broad interpretation to the word "property" in the beginning of chapter 9, where he defines it as life, liberty, and estate, but there is reason to believe that he thinks the protection of estate is of special importance. Consider, for instance, his specific examples at the end of chapter 11, where his use of the term "property" is largely confined to the narrow meaning of estate. He says emphatically:

> The supreme power cannot take from any man any part of his property without his own consent. For the preservation of property being the end of government, and that for which men enter into society, it necessarily supposes and requires, that the People should *have property*, without which they must be supposed to lose that by entering into Society, which was the end for which they entered into it, too gross an absurdity for any man to own. Men therefore in society having property, they have such a right to the goods, which by the Law of the Community are theirs, that no body hath a right to take their substance, or any part of it from them, without their own consent; without this, they have no property at all, for I have truly no Property in that, which another can by right take from me, when he pleases, against my consent. (*ST*: no. 138)

> But government into whatsoever hands it is put, being . . . intrusted with this condition and for this end that men might have and secure their properties, the Prince or Senate, however it may have power to make laws for the regulating of Property between the subjects one amongst another, yet can never have a power to take to themselves the whole or any part of the subjects property, without their own consent. (*ST*: no. 139)

People should have property; government should make laws for the regulation of property between the subjects; it should not engage in any kind of arbitrary confiscation, including the levying of taxes upon the people without their consent (*ST*: no. 140). Locke says very little about the proper content of the laws to regulate property. He maintains merely that the government is "to govern by promulgated established laws, not to be varied in particular cases, but to have one Rule for Rich and Poor, for the Favourite at Court, and the country man at Plough" (*ST*: no. 142).[25]

This attitude that "people should have property" is also an underlying premise of the economic writings. His major objection to devaluation of the coinage in 1696 was that money belonged to the people of England and not to the sovereign. To devalue the coinage was to steal money from the populace. Moreover, to lower the legal rate of interest would "void bargains lawfully made" (*SC*:12), redistribute to debtors at the expense of creditors "and that without any merit in the one, or transgression in the other" (*SC*:13). He continues with a basic precept for government: "Private men's interest ought not thus to be neglected, nor sacrificed to any thing but the manifest advantage of the publick." Certainly, governmental policy should not be to "give to Richard what is Peter's due" (*SC*:12) when both are citizens.[26] Further, property is the consequence of market activity and people have a right to whatever price they can get for their products (as long as it is not a monopoly price—a judgment Locke shared with the late Scholastic thinkers). Market prices have moral force in Locke's economy because they are the outcome of "consent" (*SC*:111), a voluntary system of exchange among buyers and sellers. Market prices are natural prices, and they are just prices because they are the outcome of consent.[27]

I have argued that the same understanding of human action undergirds both the *Treatises* and Locke's economic essays, an understanding that takes account of the rational, calculating aspect of men. Further, Locke employs the same model of how an economy functions and the relationship between the economy and the polity in these writings. The economy is a market system that is productive of wealth and well-being. Citizens value government largely to make their lives, their liberties, and their properties secure. The means to achieving security is to create an authoritative but also a limited government. Locke's complaint against Charles II was that he had placed himself in a state of war with his people. Ultimately, the dissolution of government comes about because of a broken contract.

Locke's *Two Treatises* is a sustained attack on the notion of unlimited government. One final point that should be noted is Locke's primary reason for wanting to limit the powers of the sovereign. Locke argues, in good public-choice fashion, that the sovereign was a flawed and biased human being like every other human being:

> Absolute monarchs are but men, and if government is to be the remedy of those evils, which necessarily follow from mens being judges in their own cases, and the state of nature is therefore not to be endured, I desire to know what kind of government that is, and how much better it is than the state of nature, where one man commanding a multitude has the liberty to be judge in his own case, and may do to all his subjects whatever he pleases, without the least liberty to any one to question or controle those who execute his pleasure? . . . Much better it is in the state of nature wherein men are not bound to submit to the unjust will of another: and if he that judges, judges amiss in his own case, he is answerable for it to the rest of mankind. (*ST*: no. 13)

Perhaps a saintly sovereign could use absolute power for unlimited good, but there was no reason to presume that any one sovereign was likely to be saintly. The probability was greater that sovereigns would be as human as everyone else, and a throne would do little to improve their character. "He that would have been insolent and injurious in the woods of America would not probably be much better in a throne" (*ST*: no. 92).

The prince, being a man like other men, has interests of his own that are often opposed to those of his subjects. Locke did not conceive of society in general as having one common interest. He did not place the will of the sovereign in opposition to a general will of the population. Rather, he saw political life as consisting of a "variety of opinions and contrariety of interests" (*ST*: no. 99). (This was the reason he gave for the necessity of a majority-decision rule in setting policy.) Locke thought it obvious that it would be to no one's advantage to permit one person's interests to prevail over those of the rest of society. Hence, the sovereign had to be limited in his powers to prevent him from exploiting his subjects.

What better evidence of Locke's assumption that the economic aspects of man's behavior permeated all aspects of life? All men, including the sovereign, have interests that they pursue in a social context. Hence, civil society requires enforceable rules to contain the self-seeking actions of all men so that life, liberty, and property can be protected. Although it is an exaggeration to say that Locke's theory of government was *primarily* an economic one, it is certainly not an exaggeration to say that Locke's theory of government was crafted in light of his deep knowledge and interest in economic theory and contemporary economic practice. Locke surely did not write the *Two Treatises* to justify any particular economic system (indeed, in the 1690s the very idea of an economic system was just beginning to emerge). Nevertheless, his political theory clearly did presuppose that the people to whom his political writings were addressed were engaged in economic activity within the context of markets and a money economy, an economy that Locke recognized as the source of the wealth and well-being of England.

NOTES

1. I myself developed a more moderate economic interpretation of the *Second Treatise* in my 1980 book, *John Locke: Economist and Social Scientist*, although my argument here will be even more moderate than that earlier effort.
2. For biographical material on Locke, I have relied primarily on Cranston (1957).
3. The history of the successive publications of the economic essay as well as a copy of the 1674 draft are found in Letwin (1965:295–323).
4. In 1673 Locke became secretary of the newly formed Council of Trade and Plantations of which Shaftesbury was president. During the two years that Locke was associated with the council, part of his responsibility was to study matters of foreign and domestic trade. It was probably for this reason that he continued to work on his economic essay until 1674.
5. For a detailed exposition and analysis of Locke's economic theories, see Vaughn (1978; 1980, especially chaps. 2 and 3). See also Letwin (1965: chap. 6) and Harpham (1984b, 1985).
6. In *Some Considerations*, Locke asks the typical mercantilist question: How much money is needed to drive the trade of the country? His answer is that for an isolated kingdom, the amount of money in circulation is unimportant since prices will simply adjust to the needs of trade, thereby displaying a familiarity with the emerging quantity theory of money. However, Locke confuses his critics by continuing that a country like England actively involved in world trade in fact requires enough money to keep its price level consistent with world prices. Historians of economic thought have often puzzled over this apparent mistake in Locke's reasoning. Why couldn't he see that prices would always adjust to world levels through the import or export of specie? Why did he not articulate the price-specie-flow mechanism inherent in his quantity theory of money and stated half a century later by David Hume? The answer is that Locke believed that outflows of gold would depress both price and output, resulting in unemployment and reduced wealth. Although the only policy measure he seemed to advocate to avoid this problem was moral condemnation of spending on foreign luxuries, it was clear that he thought that having too little gold in

proportion to England's trade was a problem the government should be concerned about.

7. Augustine, for example, said that all men had in their hearts the desire to buy cheap and sell dear. See Dempsey (1965):10.

8. Locke does criticize certain kinds of luxurious tastes and patterns of spending. In particular, in *Some Considerations* he rails against those who must have foreign luxuries rather than domestic products and implies that they are engaging in display for others rather than satisfying some genuine desire for the goods themselves (94–95). It should also be noted that his attitude toward money is ambiguous. In the *Second Treatise* he complains that the "desire for having more than men needed" led to the emergence of money (no. 37). Although there was no sustained sense of asceticism in Locke's writings, that is not to say that he approved of all of the tastes and behaviors of economic men.

9. Locke argues that a law to reduce the legal rate of interest in addition to making borrowing more difficult and thereby obstructing trade "will be a prejudice to none but those who most need assistance and help, . . . widows and orphans, and others uninstructed in the arts and managements of more skillful men; whose estate lying in money, they will be sure, especially orphans, to have no more profit of their money, than what interest the law barely allows" (SC:2). The skillful trader will continue to borrow by circumventing the law while the guileless and law-abiding will suffer from the losses the law imposes on all lenders.

Interestingly, Locke also worries that passing a law that will be roundly ignored will weaken the moral fiber of the country. People will increase the number of false oaths they take, which will surely undercut the moral basis for society. This further supports my argument that Locke understood that an exchange economy requires a set of shared moral values to function.

10. Richard Ashcraft (1980b) has shown convincingly that the *Two Treatises* was indeed a highly radical tract that was intended to support a revolution planned by Shaftesbury in 1681–1682.

11. If this is not enough to convince us of the importance of contract and agreement in Locke's thought, consider how he poses the question of what was lost by Adam at the Fall and hence, what was restored by Christ at the Resurrection in *The Reasonableness of Christianity*. According to Locke, "some men would have all Adam's posterity doomed to eternal, infinite punishment, for the transgression of Adam, whom millions had never heard of, and no one had authorized to transact for him, or be his representative; this seemed to others so little consistent with the justice or goodness of the great and infinite God, that they thought there was no redemption necessary, and consequently, that there was none; rather than to admit of it upon a supposition so derogatory to the honor and attributes of that infinite being" (RC: no. 1).

12. In the *Reasonableness of Christianity* Locke argues that though the Law of Nature is discoverable by reason alone, men differ in their reasoning ability. Hence, for many, revelation is necessary to supplement reason in learning the law. "Some parts of that truth lie too deep for our natural powers easily to reach, and make plain and visible to mankind; without some light from above to direct them" (RC: no. 243). For Locke, however, revelation is always confirmed by reason (RC: no. 241).

13. Hobbes's state of nature is peopled by short-sighted defectors with no natural restraints on their behavior. Such people could never be presumed to have the moral equipment to enable them to enter into such a complicated and binding contract as that which creates society. Locke's people not only can create civil society, but they also can participate in running it, they can judge it, and they can find it wanting.

14. Note also that Locke's explanation for why Jesus could not proclaim his identity at the beginning of his ministry shows God to be a rational, calculating entity. Given the political situation of the day, if Jesus had declared himself the Son of God right away, he would have been arrested immediately and thereby would have been prevented from preaching his message to the multitudes. God would have prevented this by making the Pharisees behave contrary to their natures, but he chose not to in order to save miracles for times when they were really needed to convince men of his intervention.

> For though it be as easy to omnipotent power to do all things by an immediate over-ruling will, and so to make any instruments work, even contrary to their nature, in subserviency to his ends; yet his wisdom is not usually at the expense of miracles, . . . but only in cases that require them, for the evidencing of some revelation or mission to be from him. He does constantly (unless where the confirmation of some truth requires it otherwise) bring about his purposes by means operating according to their natures. (*RC*: no. 143)

15. Men also enter into civil society because God "put him under strong obligations of necessity, convenience, and inclination to drive him into society, as well as fitted him with understanding and language to continue and enjoy it" (*ST*: no. 77). However, Locke continually emphasized the prudential reason for joining society.

16. By calling Locke's state of nature "conjectural history," I am not disagreeing very much with Ashcraft (1968). I agree that the state of nature functions as a "moral fiction" in that it provides a definition of a circumstance without government in order to penetrate the meaning of and reasons for government in human life. However, I believe that in order for Locke to carry out his program, he had to describe a conjectural historical process that carried men out of the state of nature.

17. To clarify Locke's use of the term "value" in these important passages from the Property chapter, it is worth taking a closer look at his discussion of value in his economic writings. In *Some Considerations* (66–67) he writes:

> 1. The intrinsick natural worth of anything, consists in its fitness to supply the necessities or serve the conveniences of human life; and the more necessary it is to our being, or the more it contributes to our well-being the greater is its worth; but yet,
> 2. That there is no such intrinsick natural settled value of anything as to make any assigned quantity of it constantly worth any assigned quantity of another.
> 3. The marketable value of any assigned quantity of two or more commodities are pro hic et nunc, equal, when they will exchange one for another.

4. The change of this marketable value of any commodity in respect of another commodity or in respect of a standing common measure, is not the altering of any intrinsick value or quantity in the commodity . . . but the alteration of some proportion, which the commodity bears to something else.

5. This proportion in all commodities . . . is the proportion of their quantity to their vent.

His main point here is that value is changeable in a market and that the changes can be explained according to a predictable theory.

18. "It may be true, perhaps, that the accommodation of a European prince does not always so much exceed that of an industrious and frugal peasant, as the accommodation of the latter exceeds that of many an African King, the absolute master of the lives and liberties of ten thousand naked savages" (Smith 1981:11).

19. This is distinct from the argument that wealth is a function of capital accumulation per se. Locke, however, argued that capital accumulation did not take place before the introduction of money into society.

Neal Wood (1984) has shown convincingly that Locke was part of a group of intellectuals who were enthusiasts for the Baconian method and who were great advocates of agricultural capitalism. These "improvers" were for enclosures, eliminating waste lands, and using capitalist methods for farming.

20. Locke based his argument on the presumption that men contract for specific quantities of gold and silver and not for an extrinsic title like pounds or pence.

21. Invisible-hand explanations are of course named after Adam Smith's famous metaphor that he used in both the *Theory of Moral Sentiments* and in the *Wealth of Nations*. In the latter Smith argued that there was no need for government to control investments of individuals engaged in world trade because each person in pursuing his own interest would be led by an invisible hand to achieve the interests of all (1981:456). The notion is that because in a market people have to engage each other in voluntary trades, my pursuit of my interest means that I must engage your interests in order to obtain your cooperation. My intention is to further my own well-being, but the incentives are such that I unintentionally further your well-being in the process. An invisible-hand explanation, then, is one where a systematic outcome to individual actions is an unintended by-product of those actions. In the *Second Treatise* money emerged as the unintended by-product of individuals' self-interested attempts to preserve their wealth. The term "invisible-hand explanation," I think, was coined by Robert Nozick (1974). Another way of stating the same thing is to speak of a process that is the product of human action but not of human design, as did Adam Ferguson and, later, Friedrich Hayek (1967).

22. Given Locke's emphasis on enjoyment as the test for lawful property, a modern economist could argue that if a miser enjoys his hoard of gold, he is using it to his advantage. However, I do not think that this is an appropriate reading of Locke. Locke did seem to have a more interpersonal definition of advantage; his was not the subjectivism that eschews moral judgments on the enjoyment of others.

23. Carl Menger (1981), in his famous account in the *Principles of Economics*, chose to emphasize the difficulties of barter rather than the difficulties of storing

surplus to explain the actions that led to the origin of money. He argued that in order to make barter more successful, people would naturally choose to exchange less marketable goods for more marketable goods that they acquired solely for the purpose of effecting exchanges for what they really wanted in the first place. Eventually, one or a few goods would emerge as the most marketable commodity, which would take on the characteristics of money.

24. "Trade, then, is necessary to the producing of riches, and money necessary to the carrying out of trade" (*SC*:17).

25. James Tully (1980) argues that Locke's theory of property was not a natural-rights justification of individual private property in the modern sense but rather was an argument for the essentially social nature of property in civil society. Tully claims that Locke thought property belongs to the commonwealth and that individuals acquire the right to use part of the common contingent only upon their performance of their duties to society. He also claims that Locke regarded acquisitive behavior as essentially immoral.

Among the many weaknesses I find in Tully's reading of Locke, Tully's complete unfamiliarity with Locke's economics is the most egregious. A reading of the *Considerations* and *Further Considerations* simply belies his interpretation. See Vaughn (1982) and Wood (1984), especially chap. 5.

26. Of course, the whole question of what any man is due is really the crux of some of the recent Lockean scholarship. This is not the place for me to comment upon that large and complex question, except to note that Locke really says almost nothing directly on that issue. In order to make the case that Locke was really an egalitarian of sorts (or even to make the opposite case that he definitely believed income should be unequally distributed) requires textual gymnastics that can never be completely convincing. Here, I simply take the position that Locke, by saying little on the matter, probably more or less accepted the economic status quo with a few reservations about monopoly bankers and middlemen.

27. In 1695 Locke made an entry into his commonplace book that he entitled "Venditio." It is a discussion of the just price, wherein he comes to the eventual conclusion that the market provides a rough-and-ready justice. He concludes with the observation that in the long run, the question of just profit is irrelevant to the market economy. According to Locke, "The measure that is common to buyer and seller is just that if one should buy as cheap as he could in the market the other should sell as dear as he could there, everyone running his venture and taking his chances which by the mutual and perpetually changing wants of money and commodities in buyer and seller comes to a pretty equal and fair account." See Vaughn (1980:123–31).

6 / Cato's Letters, *John Locke,* and the Republican Paradigm

RONALD HAMOWY

Few historians today have not reshaped their interpretation of eighteenth-century Anglo-American thought in light of the work of J. G. A. Pocock and others, who have argued that political theory during this period can best be analyzed not in terms of a concern for natural rights but rather as a product of Renaissance civic humanism. The political principles that formed the foundation of Whig politics during the period 1689–1776 are no longer regarded as Lockean but as neo-Machiavellian.

The substance of this reinterpretation is easily summarized. The radical Whig, or Lockean, paradigm, previously thought to dominate eighteenth-century political discourse, rests on the following principles: that all men in the state of nature are equal; that the basis of all legitimate government is the consent of the governed; that all men are possessed of certain natural, inalienable rights; and that the civil magistrate is bound by the terms of the original contract by which he holds authority to govern and should he violate this contract, men have a right to resist him. The language of classical republicanism, on the other hand, stresses the singular importance of the civic virtues and of active participation in public life. It is associated with a distrust of commerce and an aversion to the marketplace, a preference for landed wealth and for agrarian values, a preoccupation with questions of political morality and corruption, and a propensity to couch political debate in the language of the ancient constitution rather than in terms of abstract rights.

In a series of essays of varying lengths, John Pocock has argued with great force and erudition that Italian Renaissance political philosophy, and particularly Machiavelli's *Discourses,* structured many of the concerns of eighteenth-century Anglo-American thought (see Pocock 1975b, 1972, 1971a, 1971b). Civic humanism, whose roots extended back to classical political philosophy, entered British thought primarily through the writings of James Harrington, the quintessential seventeenth-century Machiavellian, whose foremost accomplishment, Pocock writes (1977:15), was to offer "a paradigmatic restatement of English political understanding in the language and world-view inherited through Machiavelli."[1] The influence of Harrington's classical republicanism on British political thought, we are told, was both profound and far reaching. This "neo-Harringtonianism," like its Florentine predecessor, was preoccupied with preserving a virtuous freeholding citizenry, independent of governmental patronage and immune to the blandishments of the court. It thus strongly opposed standing armies as a substitute for citizen militias and viewed the instrumentalities of finance with grave misgiving. This ideology lay at the heart of the eighteenth-century Country opposition to Court politics and gave shape and direction to the writings of a host of Augustan writers, among them Henry Neville, Andrew Fletcher, Henry St. John, Viscount Bolingbroke, and John Trenchard and Thomas Gordon, the authors of *Cato's Letters*.

Nor was the language of civic humanism confined to Great Britain.[2] In his study of early American politics, Lance Banning (1978) has contended that Jeffersonian republicanism can be understood best as a restatement of the Country party's preoccupation with the mixed constitution, civic virtue, and corruption. And Drew McCoy (1980) has extended this application of the civic-humanist paradigm to the political economy of Jeffersonian America where, he maintains, the ethical implications of financial and commercial policies were of no less concern to Americans than were the purely economic effects of the arrangements that grew out of them. Forrest McDonald (1976), in his study of Jefferson, has concluded that Jeffersonian ideology follows Bolingbroke in almost every particular;[3] and John Murrin (1980), in addition to finding that the Jeffersonian canon constituted a repetition of Country doctrine, has also identified Court ideology with the views of Alexander Hamilton and his supporters.

Indeed, the influence of neo-Harringtonianism in the eighteenth century appears to be everywhere. Where once it was thought that the issues that dominated eighteenth-century Scottish political philosophy were those touching on the notion of individual rights and the proper limits of government, it is now assumed that questions revolving around a neoclassical conception of the public good were of equal or greater concern. Thus, the major figures of the Scottish Enlightenment have been assimilated into the republican tradition. Pocock has characterized Scottish conjectural history as preoccupied with notions of virtue and corruption,[4] and Hont and Ignatieff (1983a:44) have argued that the language of civic humanism "exerted a profound hold on the imagination of the Scottish Enlightenment."[5] Not only has the thought of David Hume, Adam Ferguson, and Lord Kames been shown to bear the imprint of classical republicanism, but Donald Winch (1978) has also attempted a thorough reinterpretation of the social and political philosophy of Adam Smith in terms of republican concerns.[6]

This civic-humanist paradigm has all but dispossessed Locke's political philosophy from the position of preeminence it had earlier been thought to occupy.[7] Far from being a major factor in structuring eighteenth-century political language, Locke's Treatises is now considered "of strictly limited significance to many of the most lively as well as profound developments in Anglo-American political thought" until after the American Revolution (Winch 1978:29).

No writer is more forceful in taking issue with the notion that Lockean ideas played a crucial role in shaping the vocabulary of eighteenth-century politics than is Pocock, who at one point writes:

> The time for a reassessment of Locke's reputation and authority in the age between the Revolutions may be at hand, for at any rate it is clear that the image of a monolithically Lockean eighteenth century has gone forever. The rejection of virtue as (in Montesquieu's phrase) the principle of republics emerged slowly and painfully from an intellectual scene dominated to the point of obsessiveness by concepts of virtue, patriotism, and corruption, in whose making and transmission Locke played little part. Aristotle, Polybius, Machiavelli, Harrington, Sidney, Toland, John Trenchard, Thomas Gordon, Bolingbroke, and Burgh were its lineage; and the extent to which our thought is dominated by a fiction of Locke is shown by our uncertainty whether the later figures in this tradition were Lockeans under the skin or that they found in Locke their chief dialectical adversary. (Pocock 1972:127)

If we are to accept the entirety of this revisionist interpretation, we must conclude that not only were British concerns during the eighteenth century centered on the ideas of corruption and a virtuous citizenry but that the language to which American Whigs had recourse in their struggle with the Crown, which came to form the ideological underpinnings of the American Revolution and of the Founding, had far more to do with James

Harrington than with John Locke. A claim so radical, one so sharply in conflict with earlier orthodoxy,[8] cannot help but have its critics. For example, John Diggins (1985:631) has concluded that the classical idea of political virtue was of no central importance in four of the most influential works of the Revolutionary and Constitutional eras: Paine's *Common Sense*, the Declaration of Independence, Hamilton, Jay, and Madison's *Federalist*, and John Adams's *Defence of the Constitutions of Government of the United States of America*. Nor is Diggins alone in taking issue with the revisionists' claim. Joyce Appleby has recently argued against the view that Jefferson and those who identified with him adopted the language and concerns of classical republicanism.

> In espousing limited government the Jeffersonians endorsed a redrawing of the lines between the public and private spheres, and this meant reordering their significance for the whole human enterprise. Old and well-documented abuses rendered government suspect because it relied on coercion. The new realm of voluntary associations—for worship, for study, for enterprise—held out the wonderful promise of shedding past oppression. The virtue whose fragility required a carefully balanced constitution grew robust when freed from old systems. (Appleby 1986:25; see also Appleby 1982)

There is nothing here of the civic-humanist emphasis on active involvement in public life. Rather, this is the language of Locke and the radical Whigs.

Isaac Kramnick has arrived at similar conclusions respecting the parliamentary reform movement in Britain after 1760. His earlier analysis (1968) of the political and social philosophy of Viscount Bolingbroke had placed Bolingbroke squarely among the civic humanists, and Kramnick (1982:630) continues to maintain that the concerns that sprang out of this tradition, at such variance with those of Lockean theory, determined the political preoccupations of the early eighteenth century. "Locke deserves the de-emphasis he has received for the early part of the century," he writes. More recently, however, Kramnick (1982:635) has shown that classical republican ideology played little if any role in animating British and American radicals after 1760, who were "much more likely to base their arguments on natural rights than on historical rights." These writers "were preoccupied less with nostalgic country concerns than with very modern socioeconomic grievances."

It is not surprising that Pocock's conclusions have occasioned criticism inasmuch as his interpretation of the nature of political discourse in the eighteenth century has subverted the traditional Marxist categories. Notions of class and class-based ideology play no role in the republican paradigm,[9] while, as C. B. Macpherson (1962) has shown, Locke's language—or, more broadly, the language of the radical Whigs—provides a possible reading of eighteenth-century political thought consistent with Marxist theory. I would suggest, however, that even if one had serious reservations about the applicability of the Marxist schema to Augustan social theory, good grounds exist for questioning Pocock's placement of certain writers in the civic-humanist camp. I have in mind specifically John Trenchard and Thomas Gordon's *Cato's Letters*, which has been singled out by both Pocock and Kramnick as a particularly apt instance of a work written in the language of classical republicanism expressing appropriate civic-humanist concerns and which appears to be almost universally regarded as such by current scholars.[10]

Cato's Letters is a singularly profitable text to examine, both because it is an especially important instance of the literature of political opposition during the Augustan age and because of the position of preeminence the letters were to have over the next half century as revolutionary tracts in the colonial struggle against the Crown. The *Letters*, which appeared in the *London Journal* from autumn 1720 to summer 1723,[11] were originally inspired by the bursting of the South Sea Bubble in September 1720. They are the work of John Trenchard, an impassioned supporter of the Glorious Revolution and a man of substantial wealth, and Thomas Gordon, a Scots pamphleteer and journalist who had earlier cooperated with Trenchard in publishing and writing the weekly *Independent Whig*. Of the one hundred thirty-eight letters that constitute *Cato's Letters*,[12] approximately a dozen are devoted to a discussion of the South Sea crisis and the dangers inherent in such financial enterprises; the remainder range over a wide variety of topics of public concern, including the idea of liberty, the nature of tyranny, the danger posed to Britain by Jacobites and papists of all stripes, and general questions of public morality. One historian has noted that the *London Journal* was the most influential paper to appear during the period 1720–1723 and, with the possible exception of Bolingbroke's *Craftsman*, probably of far greater political significance than any other journal published during Walpole's administration (Realey 1935:1). The letters themselves were immensely popular, generating a huge amount of applause and criticism and "were to prove for nearly three years among the most troublesome thorns that pricked the vulnerable sides of the British ministry" (Realey 1935:1).

The South Sea crisis, which had occasioned the earliest of the letters, had come to a head in early autumn 1720 when, between 1 September and 14 October, the stock of the South Sea Company fell from 775 to 170 (Sperling 1962:31).[13] The effects of this sudden collapse were extensive; large numbers of people, including some of the leading families in England and Scotland, were wiped out or brought to the brink of bankruptcy. More important, disclosures concerning the manipulation of stock, of bribery, and of other corrupt practices by the officers and directors of the company implicated not only government ministers and members of Parliament but of the royal family itself. When in 1719 the South Sea Company was chosen over its rival, the Bank of England, as the instrument whereby the national debt would be consolidated,[14] its selection was largely the result of wholesale bribery. The directors of the South Sea Company could, and regularly did, create stock in the company on its books, which it then sold back to the company at inflated prices; this method, by which large profits could be made from nonexistent stock, was employed as a means of distributing bribes among the Lords, the Commons, and the royal household.

Clearly, government creditors chose to surrender their government annuities for South Sea stock because they expected to make large capital gains. The company itself had nothing to recommend it; it produced nothing and possessed no tangible assets.[15] Its capital consisted of debts owed the company, the greatest part of which were government IOUs. Indeed, its only secure asset was the government annuity it was to receive for assuming the £31 million national debt, but the company simply did not possess the £7.5 million it had promised the government for the right to assume its debt. This amount could be raised only if newly issued stock could be exchanged for the public's government obligations at prices far above the par value of South Sea stock. So long as the market for its stock continued to rise, the company was able to pay off its obligations, meet the substantial costs of its bribes, and handsomely reward those who had the foresight to sell before the market finally collapsed. The company, severely overextended, could maintain itself only by selling its surplus stock at higher and higher prices. But the moment the expectation of further advances ceased, a precipitous fall in the price of South Sea stock was inevitable.

The pervasive air of speculation that had sustained not only the price of

South Sea stock but also a host of other questionable ventures that had sought to raise capital during spring and summer 1720 was finally dissipated in late August.[16] An outflow of foreign money, which had earlier helped sustain the market, and the government's issuance of writs against four smaller companies suspected of contravening the recently passed Bubble Act contributed to the pressures that soon led to a frenzy of selling throughout the market.[17]

There can be little doubt that the machinations of the officers and directors of the South Sea Company and of the large number of ministers and public officials who were later implicated in the scandal were at least partially responsible for the speculative mania that seized the London Exchange in 1720 and that eventuated in the collapse of the market. The London Exchange had at least a thirty-year history of extensive dealings in the shares and bonds of private companies, and it had served as a center of public credit for far longer.[18] Yet it had never experienced anything like the events of 1720. A group of unscrupulous financiers had combined with a government riddled with corrupt ministers to defraud large numbers of investors in a company whose solidity appeared guaranteed by the fact that the company's chief asset was the credit of the government itself.

It was this alliance between the manipulators of credit and a corrupt Court that was the object of censure in *Cato's Letters* and not, as Kramnick (1968:246) has it, "the new economic order." In assailing the South Sea scheme with such intensity, Trenchard and Gordon were not, as has been suggested, opposing the newly developed instruments of finance that were dictated by an advanced commercial society. They were taking issue with those financial arrangements that were nothing more than extensions of the Court; that is, they opposed the intervention of the government into the marketplace on the grounds that such intrusions by the Court provided an almost unlimited opportunity for political corruption. Their distrust was not of commerce but of the political mechanism.

Pocock attempts to assimilate the many favorable references that Trenchard and Gordon make to commerce and trade into the language of civic humanism by arguing that the dominant theme of the *Letters* is the accommodation of commercial activity to virtue. According to Pocock, Cato equates the unbridled embrace of commerce with an unrestrained surrender to private passions. The function of civic virtue in this schema is to moderate these passions and to direct them, at least in part, toward a passion for the public good. Corruption, on the other hand, is the failure to effect this transformation. In keeping with this civic-humanist worldview, Pocock (1975b:472) notes, Cato regarded government as the mechanism by which men would be required "to take long views instead of short, to identify their private interests with the general good, [and] to erect an edifice of reason and virtue on a foundation of passion."

This notion of government is incompatible with the Lockean conception of political society as above all the instrument through which inalienable rights are protected—and it is of inalienable rights that Cato speaks when he discusses the nature of government. Indeed, natural law and natural rights play a critical role in the structure of Cato's argument. When read within the context of Lockean theory, Cato's reservations about commerce emerge as an elaborate critique of governmental intrusion into the world of trade. Political corruption is not the result of a failure to constrain our private passions. Rather, it arises when our rights are either ignored or unprotected by law, conditions that occur as consequences of the dishonesty or lack of diligence of our magistrates. Indeed, Cato argues that the corruption of a people can originate only in the deceit and chicanery of a duplicitous court and not in the actions of men in their capacity as private individuals. It is in the nature of corrupt courts, writes Cato (Trenchard and Gordon 1969: Letter 94, 3:238–39),

> to blame the poor People for the Misery which they bring upon them. They say that they are extremely corrupt, and so keep them starving and enslaved by Way of Protection. They corrupt them by all manner of Ways and Inventions, and then reproach them for being corrupt. A whole nation cannot be bribed, and if its Representatives are, it is not the Fault, but the Misfortune, of the Nation: And if the Corrupt save themselves by corrupting others, the People who suffer by the Corruption of both, are to be pitied, and not abused.[19]

The purposes that motivate men originally to enter into civil society dictate that when our rights have been violated, justice demands that the trespasser be punished. In calling for the punishment of the malefactors responsible for the South Sea swindle, Cato argues this view in clearly Lockean terms:

> That the Benefit and Safety of the People constitutes the Supreme Law, is a universal and everlasting Maxim in Government: It can never be altered by municipal Statutes: No Customs can change, no positive Institutions can abrogate, no Time can efface this primary

Law of Nature and Nations. The sole End of Mens entering into political Societies, was mutual Protection and Defence; and whatever Power does not contribute to those Purposes, is not Government, but Usurpation.

Every Man in the State of Nature, had a Right to repel Injuries, and to revenge them; that is, he had a Right to punish the Authors of those Injuries, and to prevent their being again committed; . . . Seeing therefore, that this Right was inherent in every private Man, it is absurd to suppose that National Legislatures, to whom every Man's private Power is committed, have not the same Right, and ought not to exercise it upon proper Occasions. (Letter 11, 1:66)

Cato is here demanding not vengeance against those who wronged the republic (Pocock 1975b:468) but justice in the name of the individuals who have been injured. The laws of nature dictate that just as we may not take the life of another except in self-defense so we may not violate another's property. And what we do not originally possess, we cannot transfer, either to another or to the civil magistrate.

Nor has any Man in the State of Nature, Power over his own Life, or to take away the Life of another, unless to defend his own, or what is as much his own, namely his Property. This Power therefore, which no Man has, no Man can transfer to another.

  Nor could any Man, in the State of Nature, have a Right to violate the Property of another; that is, what another had acquired by his Art or Labour; or to interrupt him in his Industry and Enjoyments, as long as he himself was not injured by that Industry and those Enjoyments. No Man therefore could transfer to the Magistrate that Right which he had not himself. (Letter 60, 2:228)

The anatomy of Cato's argument closely echoes Locke's in defining political authority in terms of inalienable rights. Our liberty is not the product of a delicate balance of social forces but ours by virtue of our nature. "All Men are born free," writes Cato. "Liberty is a Gift from God himself; nor can they alienate the same by Consent, though possibly they may forfeit it by Crimes" (Letter 59, 2:216). The authority and compass of government rest on no foundation other than our inherent right to defend ourselves against those who would trespass against our lives, liberty, or property.

The Right of the Magistrate arises only from the Right of private Men to defend themselves, or repel Injuries, and to punish those who commit them: That Right being conveyed by the Society to their publick Representative, he can execute the same no further than the Benefit and Security of that Society requires he should. When he exceeds his Commission, his Acts are as extrajudicial as are those of any private Officer usurping an unlawful Authority, that is, they are void. (Letter 59, 2:216–17)

The gulf between civic humanism and Cato's politics is no less great when we examine how liberty is conceived. Civic humanism, Pocock has shown, anchors the freedom of the citizen in his active participation in political life and ultimately in his possession of real property, which assures his independence. The liberating aspects of property do not, however, extend to mobile property, which in the civic-humanist paradigm, is regarded as a corrupting force, depriving men of their autonomy (Pocock 1975b:461). No such distinction between real and mobile property appears in Cato's conception of liberty. Liberty, as it is defined in the *Letters*, is the right we have both over our actions and over all of our property of whatever sort, a right circumscribed only to the extent that we are precluded from infringing upon a similar right in others.

By Liberty I understand the Power which every Man has over his own Actions, and his Right to enjoy the Fruits of his Labour, Art, and Industry, as far as by it he hurts not the Society, or any Members of it, by taking from any Member, or by hindering him from enjoying what he himself enjoys. The Fruits of a Man's honest Industry are the just Rewards of it, ascertained to him by natural and eternal Equity, as is his Title to use them in the Manner which he thinks fit: And thus, with the above Limitations, every Man is sole Lord and Arbiter of his own private Actions and Property. (Letter 62, 2:244–45).[20]

The relation between liberty and extensive commercial activity is direct and immediate. Liberty encourages commerce and industry, thus assuring economic well-being. Free nations, by virtue of the fact that property is secure, are productive, and the industry of the citizens of such countries in turn acts as a further incentive to greater trade. In a surprisingly modern analysis of the flow of capital and labor, Cato observes that when there is Liberty, there are Encouragements to Labour, because People labour for themselves; and no one can take from them the Acquisitions which they make by their Labour: There will be the greatest Numbers of People, because they find Employment and Protection; there will be the greatest Stocks, because most is to be got, and easiest to be got, and safest when it is got; and those Stocks will be always encreasing by a new Accession of Money acquired elsewhere, where there is no Security of enjoying it; there people will be able to work cheapest, because less Taxes will be put upon their Work, and upon the Necessities which must support them whilst they are about it.

Trade cannot be carried on so cheap as in free Countries; and whoever supplies the Commodity cheapest, will command the Market. In free countries, Men bring out their Money for their Use, Pleasure, and Profit, and think of all Ways to employ it for their Interest and Advantage. New Projects are every Day invented, new Trades searched after, new Manufactures set up; and when Tradesmen have nothing to fear but from those whom they trust, Credit will run high, and they will venture in Trade for many times as much as they are worth. (Letter 67, 2:308–9)

Cato's comments are a far cry from the civic-humanist conception of the rentier and the entrepreneur as essentially corrupt (Pocock 1975b:461). Nor is there anything here that suggests that those whose wealth consists in mobile property are less likely to be good citizens or are at greater risk of preserving their independence than are the possessors of land. The independence of which Cato writes is a function of property *in any form*, which frees men from being servants, dependent on the will of others.

Nor did ever any Man that could live satisfactorily without a Master, desire to live under one; and real or fancied Necessity alone makes Men the Servants, Followers, and Creatures of one another. And therefore all Men are animated by the Passion of acquiring and defending Property, because Property is the best Support of that Independency, so passionately desired by all Men. Even Men the most dependent have it constantly in their Heads and their Wishes, to become independent one time or other; and the Property which they are acquiring, or mean to acquire by that Dependency, is intended to bring them out of it, and to procure them an agreeable Independency. (Letter 68, 2:319)

It is true, as Pocock points out, that at one point Cato warns freeholders not to select "men whose estates are embarked in Companies" as their representatives in Parliament, but this admonition must be taken in the context in which it is made. The letter in which this caution appears is addressed both to the freeholders and burghers "of the Counties, Cities and Towns of Great Britain," regarding their choice of representatives. By "Companies," Cato is here referring to the large-scale joint-stock enterprises whose origins and continuing survival require a constant and intimate involvement in Court politics. Cato writes of the men whose own fortunes are linked to those of these companies, whose hands "have dipt in the publick Spoils" (Letter 69, 3:7), that "they will always be against the Interest of general Trade; and they will be but too apt to fall into the Juggling and Artifices of Courts, to raise their Stock to imaginary Values" (Letter 70, 3:24). This warning no more suggests that all men engaged in commerce are in some sense corrupt than does Cato's allusion that some landholders are suspect implicate all those whose wealth is in land. The men whom Cato would raise to public office are those who are truly zealous against "exorbitant Pensions, outrageous Taxes, wild and expensive Expeditions; against encreasing the publick Debts; against standing Troops quartered up and down your Countries; against oppressive Companies, to the Destruction of your Trade and Industry; against private Mens raising immense Estates upon your Ruin" (Letter 69, 3:6). Such men, possessed of a capacity for political judgment and disposed towards liberty, may be found no less easily among manufacturers and tradesmen as among the nation's freeholders.

Indeed, *Cato's Letters* displays a keen awareness of the benefits of the division of labor and of the advantages to be gained from trade. In a passage startling for the fact that Gordon appears to adumbrate a subjective theory of value, Cato grounds the trade that takes place in an advanced monied economy in man's fundamental desire to better his condition in a manner consistent with natural justice.

Men will not spontaneously toil and labour but for their own Advantage, for their Pleasure or their Profit, and to obtain something which they want or desire, and which, for the most part, is not to be obtained

but by Force or Consent. Force is often dangerous; and when employed to acquire what is not ours, it is always unjust; and therefore
Men, to procure from others what they had not before, must gain
their Consent; which is not to be gained, but by giving them in lieu of
the Thing desired, something which they want and value more than
what they part with. This is what we call Trade; which is the Exchange of one Commodity for another, or of that which purchases all
Commodities, Silver and Gold. (Letter 67, 2:304)

This hard-headed definition of trade is hardly consonant with a
semimagical notion of commerce whereby men are led into an illusory
and fantastic world of passion (Pocock 1975b:471). The world of trade is
not Circe's Island but Britain at the outset of the Industrial Revolution.
Nor does Cato have any illusions about the idyllic nature of societies
based exclusively on husbandry: "In Countries where no other Arts are in
Use, but only Husbandry and the Professions necessary to it, all the other
Inhabitants have no Means of purchasing Food and Raiment, but by selling their Persons, and becoming vile Slaves and Vassals to their Princes,
Lords, or other Proprietors of the Land" (Letter 67, 2:305). And again,

Labour in Husbandry is the least profitable Employment in the
World, . . . and the meanest Mechanicks and Artificers earn more
than Husbandmen, and consequently have a Surplus from their own
Labour after they have bought the Production of the other's Industry.
This is the Circumstance of Cities and trading Towns, who have no
Growth of their own, and yet grow rich by retailing and manufactur-
ing the Growth of the neighbouring Countries, over and above what
they consume for their own Subsistence and Use. (Letter 87, 3:183)

The most common conclusion respecting *Cato's Letters* drawn by historians who have accepted a civic-humanist interpretation of the
eighteenth century is that its authors viewed the emergence of credit and
the new, monied interest with abhorrence.[21] Pocock (1975b:469) has written that Cato believed that the crucial evil of the growth of a monied
interest was that it perverted the traditional relationships of executive,
Parliament, and propertied people and thus unbalanced the constitution.
W. A. Speck (1979:224) concludes that Trenchard and Gordon regarded the
financial revolution as having "created an engine for corruption on an
unprecedented scale."[22] And Isaac Kramnick (1968:246) imputes to Cato

the view that credit "transformed all subjects into pickpockets and gamesters."

All these explications of Cato suffer from misinterpreting Cato's strictures respecting the illegal manipulation of the financial markets. Cato's animus is directed at such frauds, especially when they are perpetrated upon the public with the connivance of a corrupt government, and not against credit in general. Not only does Cato not condemn the instruments of public credit, but he in fact embraces them as essential to an advanced economy and to national well-being. Credit, properly understood, Cato writes, may be said to run high

> when Lands and Houses find ready Purchasers, and when Money is to be borrowed at low interest, in order to carry on Trade and Manufacture, at such Rates, as may enable us to undersell our Neighbours.
> . . . When People think it safe and advantageous to venture large Stocks in Trade and Dealing, and do not lock their Money in Chests, or hide it under-ground, And
> . . . When Notes, Mortgages, and Publick and Private Security will pass for Money, or easily procure Money, by selling for as much Silver or Gold as they are Security for: which can never happen, but upon a Presumption that the same Money may be had for them again.
> . . . In all these Cases, 'tis abundantly the Interest of a Nation, to promote Credit. (Letter 4, 1:16)

A reading of the whole of *Cato's Letters* leaves little doubt that Cato is aware of the benefits that follow from increased investment and the mechanisms of large-scale finance that permit such investment. The South Sea swindle is not an instance of property based on credit. Rather, it destroys all property because it provides to private corruption the power and authority of the state. The economy can never be benefited "by raising Stocks and Commodities by Artifice and Fraud, to unnatural and imaginary Values; And consequently, delivering up . . . the ignorant and unwary, but industrious Subject, to be devoured by . . . a sort of Vermin that are bred and nourished in the Corruption of the State" (Letter 4, 1:17).

Kramnick and the other commentators who see in Cato's attack on stock-jobbing a broad assault on all credit markets are making the unwarranted assumption that Cato does not distinguish between dealing in totally unsecured promissory notes and in secured paper. In fact it is only the first, the worthless shares of the South Sea Company and other chimerical enterprises, purchased by an unwary and credulous public gulled into believing that there was no limit to the capital appreciation possible, that Cato inveighs against. Such stocks were equivalent to counterfeit coin upon which the stamp of public authority had been placed. Indeed, what Cato finds most offensive about the South Sea scheme is the collusion of government officials at the very highest levels to defraud the public, thus "inverting the policy of nations." It is dishonesty and greed—and not credit—that "has entered into the Cabinets and Courts; has guided the Counsels of Senates, and employed their whole Wisdom; nay, most of their Time has been employed in keeping up this wild and airy Traffick, as if the Business of Government was not to protect People in their Property, but to cheat them out of it" (Letter 107, 4:17−18).

One further point needs to be made respecting Cato's attitude toward credit and the kind of society in which a thriving credit market exists. The use Cato makes of quotations from Algernon Sidney has been offered as evidence that Cato held that large-scale corruption was inescapable in a society in which men devoted themselves to the pursuit of private wealth. Sidney is quoted at numerous points in the *Letters*, and in fact two of the letters constitute nothing more than extended quotations from Sidney's *Discourses Concerning Government*. Now it is true that one of these two letters has for its subject the decline into corruption and tyranny of what earlier had been vibrant societies as a consequence of men placing their wealth above their honor and their freedom. But the essential point of Sidney's commentary is not so much that men, when acting in their capacity as private men, should not seek riches, but that tyranny is inevitable when wealth becomes the goal of those into whose hands the government is placed. "When the Power is in the Hands of base mercenary Persons," Sidney observes, "they will always . . . make as much Profit of their Places as they can. Not only Matters of Favour, but of Justice too, will be exposed to Sale; and no Way will be open to Honours or Magistracies, but by paying largely for them" (Letter 26, 1:201).[23]

This essay is not the place to debate which aspect of Sidney's thought dominates his writings—his appeals to history or his theoretical claims. That the rights of Englishmen rested on the ancient constitution and that these self-same rights had their origin in the laws of nature from which our rights are directly derived prior to the establishment of civil society are both notions that appear throughout the *Discourses*.[24] But it is, I think, incorrect to assume that Sidney's claims lent themselves far more easily to Augustan civic humanism than to radical Whig ideology.

This link between appeals to history and to classical republican doctrine has been made by Pocock (1975b:420), who notes, "The motive of the neo-Harringtonians was to denounce corruption; they paid the price of obliging themselves to regard all change as corruption. . . . Furthermore, that which was exposed to corruption and degeneration was now the Ancient Constitution, and this must accordingly be envisaged in the form of a balance." Although it is true that Sidney's arguments are often couched in terms of the historical development of the English constitution, it can hardly be argued that he—like Harrington, with whom he is often coupled—viewed good government as the product of a delicate balance of forces that required that men constantly subordinate their private interests to the public weal. Although there are elements in Sidney's writings that reflect his fears concerning luxury and prodigality, it would be wrong to read him as endorsing the view that a society that countenanced the private pursuit of wealth would inevitably decline into corruption and tyranny. Nor does Cato ratify this conclusion. Indeed, for Cato corruption can originate only among those who possess political power: "There is scarce such a Thing under the Sun as a corrupt People, where the Government is uncorrupt: it is that, and that alone, which makes them so; and to calumniate them for what they do not seek, but suffer by, is as great Impudence, as it would be to knock a Man down, and then rail at him for hurting himself" (Letter 94, 3:239). Cato embraces Sidney as a hero not because of his warnings respecting the decline of public spirit but because of his attack on the fatuous claims of Sir Robert Filmer and because of his robust justification of natural rights. Cato writes of Sidney,

> he fell a Sacrifice to the vile and corrupt Court of our pious Charles the Second. He had asserted the Rights of Mankind, and shewed the Odiousness of Tyranny; he had exposed the Absurdity and Vileness of the sacred and fashionable Doctrines of those Days, Passive Obedience and Hereditary Right; Doctrines, which give the Lie to common Sense, and which would destroy all common Happiness and Security amongst Men! (Letter 26, 1:195)

Cato's radical Whig credentials are vouchsafed by what must be regarded as one of the most vigorous defenses of freedom of conscience and speech in Augustan literature. For Cato, our consciences are the most integral part of our being and as such are exempt from all regulation by the civil magistrate. Our innermost religious convictions are contingent upon our will alone and subject only to the authority of God himself. Freedom of conscience is the first of our natural rights and the immunity of our convictions from the jurisdiction of government the clearest implication of the Law of Nature. "Every Man's Religion is his own," Cato observes,

> nor can the Religion of any Man, of what Nature or Figure soever, be the Religion of another Man, unless he also chuses it; which Action utterly excludes all Force, Power, or Government. Religion can never come without Conviction, nor can Conviction come from Civil Authority; Religion, which is the fear of God, cannot be subject to Power, which is the fear of Man. It is a Relation between God and our own Souls only, and consists in a Disposition of Mind to obey the Will of our great Creator, in the Manner which we think most acceptable to him. It is independent upon all human Directions, and superior to them; and consequently uncontroulable by external Force, which cannot reach the free Faculties of the Mind, or inform the Understanding, much less convince it. Religion therefore, which can never be subject to the Jurisdiction of another, can never be alienated to another, or put in his Power. (Letter 60, 2:227)

Natural law, which dictates the limits of state action, precludes any attempt to constrain men in questions of religious belief. We may appeal and entreat, we may reason and debate, but we may go no further. "The utmost Length that the Power of the Magistrate can in this Matter extend beyond that of Exhortation, which is in every Man's Power, can be only to make Hypocrites, Slaves, Fools, or Atheists" (Letter 66, 2:298).

Although there is good reason to conclude that Trenchard and Gordon would in practice have limited the extension of the principles of religious freedom here expressed to Protestant Dissenters,[25] this does not weaken the strength of the theoretical argument put forward in the *Letters*. An abhorrence of popery, which the English mind associated with the most barbarous and depraved forms of superstition and oppression, was too intrinsic a part of the prevailing political orthodoxy to have been overcome by Cato's commitment to religious toleration. Yet even within the limits of this bizarre legacy of antipopery, which apparently contaminated even the most wholesome writers of the age, the *Letters* set forth a broad and vigorous defense of freedom of conscience that is unmatched in the literature of the period.

Cato embraces a broadly extended sphere of free speech with no less fervor. Freedom of speech is as much a natural right as is the right we each have to the fruits of our labor. Without it property is insecure and good government impossible. In a letter from which the American colonists were never to tire of quoting,[26] Cato discusses the intimate connection between free speech and public liberty:

> Without Freedom of Thought, there can be no such Thing as Wisdom; and no such Thing as publick Liberty, without Freedom of Speech; Which is the Right of every Man, as far as by it he does not hurt or controul the Right of another; and this is the only Check which it ought to suffer, the only Bounds which it ought to know. This sacred Privilege is so essential to free Governments, that the Security of Property, and the Freedom of Speech, always go together; and in those wretched Countries where a Man cannot call his Tongue his own, he can scarce call any Thing else his own. Whoever would overthrow the Liberty of a Nation, must begin by subduing the Freedom of Speech; a Thing terrible to publick Traytors. (Letter 15, 1:96)

So vital is the airing of public issues to the preservation of liberty that Cato favors the virtual elimination of seditious libel. This crime, as ultimately fixed by parliamentary statute and the Court of Star Chamber, prohibited any comment that tended to bring the government into disrepute; neither the intent of the utterer nor the truth or falsity of the charge was relevant in determining guilt. Following upon the expiry of the licensing system in 1694, the threat of prosecution for seditious libel became the chief weapon employed by the British government for controlling the press (Levy 1960:11).[27] Trenchard and Gordon were, of course, keenly aware of this threat and held strong views on the political uses of defamation laws. Cato falls short of advocating the repeal of libel laws when the objects of such utterances are "the private Vices or Weaknesses of Governors" and when these vices do not touch upon issues of public administration. However, the *Letters* offers an impassioned assault on the use of the courts to curtail criticism of governmental policy. He who calls the attention of men to corruption in high places is a public benefactor and is to be applauded, not condemned. "The exposing of publick Wickedness," Cato writes (Letter 32, 1:247), "as it is a Duty which every Man owes to Truth and his Country, can never be a Libel in the Nature of Things." In a further passage, Cato argues that a nation is far better off enduring the occasional libel than constraining a free and vigorous press:

As long as there are such Things as Printing and Writing, there will be Libels. It is an Evil arising out of a much greater Good. And as to those who are for locking up the Press, because it produces Monsters, they ought to consider that so do the Sun and the Nile; and that it is something better for the World to bear some particular inconveniencies arising from general Blessings, than to be wholly deprived of Fire and Water.[28] (Letter 32, 1:252)

Cato's treatment of defamation laws are, of course, well known to anyone familiar with the history of the press in Great Britain and America. I offer these comments not because they are meant to cast new light on the history of freedom of thought in the eighteenth century but because I want to suggest that Cato's concern with such issues as freedom of speech is directly relevant to the more basic question of whether the language of the *Letters* is more Lockean than not. Cato's arguments concerning freedom of conscience and seditious libel are, after all, almost purely theoretical. They contain no appeals to the ancient constitution nor to the traditional arrangements of English law; they do not speak to questions of civic virtue or to the dangers of social change. Cato's conclusions are, in fact, inferences that follow from an elaborate chain of reasoning based on a theory of natural law, inalienable rights, and the natural limits of government. Consider the structure of the following argument:

The Administration of Government is nothing else, but the Attendance of the Trustees of the People upon the Interest and Affairs of the People. And as it is the Part and Business of the People, for whose Sake alone all publick Matters are, or ought to be, transacted, to see whether they be well or ill transacted, so it is the Interest, and ought to be the Ambition, of all honest Magistrates, to have their Deeds openly examined, and publickly scanned: Only the wicked Governors of Men dread what is said of them. (Letter 15, 1:97).

This kind of speculative reasoning surely has far more in common with the approach of Locke and the other radical Whigs than with that of the classical republican writers, whose arguments are framed in historical terms.

Pocock (1957:229–51; 1980b) has argued that Locke's *Treatises*, though they well might have been invoked over the course of the eighteenth century as the definitive answer to Filmer, fall outside the mainstream language in which political issues were examined. Rather, political debate, including the character of the revolutionary settlement of 1688, was couched in the language of the ancient constitution and of English feudal law, to which Locke contributed nothing. The *Treatises*, in contrast, offers a purely theoretical argument concerning the nature of political obligation and the proper functions of government that appeal neither to history nor to legal precedent. Nor does Locke address such classical republican concerns as the relation between political participation and public virtue or the threat posed by luxury to good government, subjects, Pocock argues, of recurring interest to Whig writers in the seventeenth and eighteenth centuries.

We are not primarily concerned here with the question of whether Pocock is correct in characterizing the language of political debate following the Revolution of 1688 as heavily historical and legalistic. Harry Dickinson's (1977:73) researches have led him to conclude of Whig literature during this period that, though an appeal to history might well have been emphasized, a "conflation of the theory of an original contract with the notion of an ancient constitution . . . appears again and again." And Richard Ashcraft (1986:190n) has shown that, at least with respect to the Whig writers of the 1680s, it would be incorrect to regard a historical framework as any more important than one based on natural law.[29] But whether or not Ashcraft's conclusions are also applicable to most political discussion in the first half of the eighteenth century, we may safely conclude that *Cato's Letters* adopts a natural-law approach very much like Locke's. Indeed, it would be hard to read the *Letters* and not be struck by how similar Cato's analysis of the origin and proper functions of government is to that which earlier appeared in the *Two Treatises*. This conclusion seems to me to be not inconsistent with John Dunn's finding (1969b) that, in the first half of the eighteenth century, the fundamental theorems of Locke's politics, even though they might not have been subject to detailed critical assessment, were an integral part of orthodox political language.[30] Although it would be hard to believe that Trenchard and Gordon had not read Locke's *Treatises* closely, especially given their deep interest in Whig politics and their familiarity with the political literature,[31] the matter is moot, inasmuch as the *Letters* itself is unquestionably Lockean.

The Lockean character of *Cato's Letters* is perfectly consistent with the popularity accorded the letters in the colonies, a popularity that was to increase as the agitation for a radical solution to the colonists' difficulties with Great Britain swelled. The struggle over independence became the forum for contending ideologies, and the one that proved victorious in 1776 was the contractarian, natural-rights conception of civil society inherited from the radical Whigs and most especially from Locke's *Treatises*. It is within this context that *Cato's Letters* was frequently cited as an authority on political questions (Bailyn 1967:36). Nor is this incompatible with the general thrust of the *Letters*, which perceives government not as an institution natural to men, whose purpose is the moral elevation of the people, but as the product of a contract and designed solely to protect and enforce men's natural rights. It is foolish to claim

> that Government is concerned to meddle with the private Thoughts and Actions of Men, while they injure neither the Society, nor any of its Members. Every Man is, in Nature and Reason, the Judge and Disposer of his own domestick Affairs; and, according to the Rules of Religion and Equity, every Man must carry his own Conscience. So that neither has the Magistrate a Right to direct the private Behaviour of Men; nor has the Magistrate, or any body else, any manner of Power to model People's Speculations, no more than their Dreams. Government being intended to protect Men from the Injuries of one another, and not to direct them in their own Affairs, in which no one is interested but themselves; it is plain that their Thoughts and domestick Concerns are exempted intirely from its Jurisdiction.[32] (Letter 62, 2:246)

The proposition that the sovereign is constrained by the laws of nature and the contract by which civil society is established to safeguarding the lives and estates of his subjects is possibly the most important legacy of Lockean theory and informs the whole of *Cato's Letters*. This proposition defines the limits of legitimate state action for both Locke and Cato. When government seeks to impose constraints upon our natural and absolute liberty beyond those necessary to enforce "the laws of agreement and society," it becomes tyrannous and must eventually fall to revolution. "No Society of Men will groan under Oppressions longer than they know how to throw them off," Cato assures us. "Upon this Principle of People's judging for themselves, and resisting lawless Force, stands our late happy Revolution" (Letter 59, 2:225). This notion was embraced no less warmly in 1776 than when Cato voiced it in 1721 or when it was offered as an integral element of radical Whig ideology in the 1680s.

Pocock's contention that Locke contributed nothing to the vocabulary of orthodox Whig thought during most of the eighteenth century must be reevaluated in light of the Lockean nature of *Cato's Letters*. Certainly the centrality of this work in the Whig canon suggests that radical Whig thought played a more substantial role in shaping the political rhetoric of the period than has recently been conceded. The approval with which the letters were received during the quarter century after their original publication strongly corroborates the view that the Lockean paradigm had in fact constituted a major force in eighteenth-century politics.

NOTES

An earlier version of this essay appeared in the Summer 1990 issue of *History of Political Thought*.

1. Pocock writes of Machiavelli that he was "for the late seventeenth and eighteenth centuries a principal transmitter of the ideals and technical theory of what can be termed either civic humanism or classical republicanism. This revived the ancient assertion that man was by nature a citizen, fulfilling his virtue—an extremely pregnant term—in participation in a self-governing republic, hierarchical in the sense that its members possessed differing qualifications and capacities, egalitarian in the sense that each member must rule and be ruled, respecting the special qualities of others as they respected his" (Pocock 1975a:64—65).

2. Robert Shalhope has provided a summary of current scholarship that seeks to read American political thought in the last half of the eighteenth century as at least partially reflective of civic-humanist concerns (see Shalhope 1972:49—80; Shalhope 1982:334—56).

3. McDonald at one point observes of the Jeffersonians that "though they borrowed some of their ideas from James Harrington and other seventeenth-century writers and some from John Locke, their ideology was borrowed *in toto* from such Oppositionists as Charles Devenant, John Trenchard, Thomas Gordon, James Burgh, and most especially Henry St. John, Viscount Bolingbroke. As a well-rounded system, it is all to be found in the pages of the *Craftsman*, an Oppositionist journal that Bolingbroke published from 1726 to 1737" (McDonald 1976:19).

4. Adam Ferguson particularly, in light of his discussions of the dangers that emerge from the increasing specialization of labor, reflects concerns that are clearly Machiavellian (see Pocock 1975b:498—502).

5. All the papers contained in Hont and Ignatieff, which emerged out of a colloquium on "Scottish Political Economy and the Civic-Humanist Tradition" held at Cambridge in 1979, have as their theme the importance of civic humanism in shaping the language of eighteenth-century Scottish thought.

6. See Edward J. Harpham's (1984a:764—74) telling critique of Winch's conclusions. See also Jeffrey C. Isaac (1988:349—77), who contends, with specific reference to Adam Smith, that both Winch and Harpham are incorrect and that the

languages of Locke and of Harrington are perfectly compatible. Isaac argues that the republican notion of virtue and of an active and independent citizenry can act as an ideological underpinning to liberal individualist values and that this is in fact the case with respect to both Harrington and Smith.

7. Pocock has acknowledged the basic antagonism between the languages of Lockean liberalism and civic humanism, particularly with respect to commercial activity. At one point he notes: "There were [during the eighteenth century] innumerable treatments of the tension between virtue and commerce, and innumerable attempts to resolve it, some of which satisfied their authors and may satisfy the modern critics; but I would like to suggest that there is no greater and no commoner mistake in the history of social thought than to suppose that the tension ever disappeared, that the ideals of virtue and unity of personality were driven from the field, or that a commercial, 'liberal' or 'bourgeois' ideology reigned undisturbed until challenged by the harbingers of Marx" (Pocock 1979:163). More recently, Pocock (1983:235–52) seems to have somewhat modified his position by suggesting that the civic-humanist paradigm is best viewed as an "operational guide" or "interpretative matrix," through which some aspects of eighteenth-century thought can best be understood. It thus appears that the classical republican interpretation need not be regarded as canonical description but rather as one of several analytical frameworks that may be usefully applied to eighteenth-century Anglo-American political thought. It need hardly be pointed out that this modification does not speak to the question of *which* paradigm, the Lockean or the civic-humanist, is most appropriate to which writers.

8. Among the more classic studies concluding that Lockean political philosophy was of seminal influence in shaping American thought are Curti (1937) and Hartz (1955).

9. Kramnick (1982:631) observes that the republican paradigm "insists on the irrelevance of class in political discourse, which in conventional progressive or liberal scholarship has been linked to the later decades of the century via the emergence of the Industrial Revolution. Analyses of the late eighteenth century that refer to class consciousness or conflicting class ideologies or that use concepts such as aristocracy, capitalist, feudal, or bourgeois are thus dismissed by republican scholarship as simplistic or proleptic." See also John Patrick Diggins (1985) on the mutual exclusivity of Marxist and republican perspectives.

10. Even students of the period who have questioned the propriety of applying the classical republican paradigm to Anglo-American thought in the later half of the century have been prepared to concede that *Cato's Letters* falls squarely within the republican tradition, despite the extraordinary popularity these letters were accorded in the colonies immediately prior to the Revolution. See for example, John Patrick Diggins (1984:19), where he writes that "the principle of civic virtue received its most persuasive expression in *Cato's Letters*." Jesse R. Goodale (1980:237–59), on the other hand, has raised questions about Pocock's analysis of Harrington's legacy to eighteenth-century oppositionist literature, including the writings of Trenchard and Gordon.

11. Beginning in September 1722 the letters appeared in the *British Journal*. The change was prompted by the fact that the *London Journal* underwent a shift in editorial policy after its owner was bribed into supporting the government.

12. Of this number, seventy-six were written by Gordon, fifty-six by Trenchard, and the remaining six by the two authors jointly.

13. See also the detailed discussion of the South Sea Bubble in Carswell (1960), Erleigh (1933), and Dickson (1967).

14. The whole of the national debt was to be incorporated into the capital of the company, which in turn would issue stock in the company to holders of government annuities. In return, the company would receive 5 percent on the interest charged the government on its capital (4 percent after 1727). For the privilege of effecting this conversion the company was prepared to pay the government a bonus of between £4 million and £7.5 million, depending on the amount of debt converted to South Sea stock. In addition, the government would realize a savings in interest payments of between £400,000 and £550,000 per year if the whole of the debt were converted.

15. Its one trading asset, the *Asiento*, was in fact worthless. The *Asiento*, the privilege granted by the king of Spain to supply forty-eight hundred Negro slaves per year to the Spanish Indies, had been awarded to the British Crown in 1713—who in turn assigned it to the South Sea Company—as part of the settlement of Utrecht, which ended the War of the Spanish Succession. Spanish obstructiveness and the rigors of the Spanish bureaucracy in America, however, made the slave trade unprofitable for the company, and they eventually abandoned it.

16. Among the more fanciful, impractical schemes that were floated were companies that were to devote themselves to trading in hair, to importing brooms from Germany, to fixing quicksilver, to trading in ambergris and ostrich feathers, to furnishing funerals throughout England, to extracting silver from lead, to suppressing smuggling, to maintaining and educating bastard children, to exploiting the lands "to the west of South America," and so on.

17. The Bubble Act, which received royal assent on 11 June 1720, was passed at the instigation of the South Sea directors, who thought its enactment would reduce the amount of speculation in the stock of companies competing with the South Sea Company for funds. The act sought to check the widespread, unregulated creation of joint-stock companies and to prevent their diverting their charters to unauthorized ends.

18. The origins of the Stock Exchange are treated at some length in the final chapter of Dickson (1967:486–520).

19. All references to *Cato's Letters* are to the letter number and volume and page number of Trenchard and Gordon (1969).

20. At another point Cato writes that "true and impartial Liberty is . . . the Right of every Man to . . . spend his own Money himself, and lay out the Produce of his Labour his own Way; and to labour for his own Pleasure and Profit" (Letter 62, 2:248).

21. It should perhaps be underscored that the neo-Machiavellian indictment of public credit is not limited to governmental borrowing and to the instruments associated with the public debt but includes a denunciation of all forms of credit, including commercial credit. This is the only interpretation consistent with the view that mobile property subverts the benefits of real property, thus undermining the conditions that make civic virtue possible. See Pocock's chapter on "The Augustan Debate over Land, Trade and Credit" (1975b:423–61).

22. Both Pocock and Speck equate Cato's hostility to the instruments of public credit with Cato's fears respecting a standing army. Pocock goes so far as to conclude that both were regarded by Cato as, at bottom, the same phenomenon (1975b:468).

23. The selection is taken from Book 2, chapter 25 of Sidney's *Discourses*.

24. Sidney's recourse to both types of argument possibly accounts in part for the popularity of the *Discourses* in the eighteenth century. See James Conniff (1982:397–416).

25. David L. Jacobson has called attention to this in his introduction to the collection of *Cato's Letters* that he edited (see Jacobson 1965:xxxix–xl).

26. On the popularity of this letter among the colonists, see, among others, Rossiter (1953:299) and Levy (1966:xxiii).

27. On the history of seditious libel, see also the relevant sections of Siebert (1952).

28. It is not unlikely that James Madison was indebted to the point made here by Cato when he noted, in the "Virginia Report of 1799–1800, Touching the Alien and Sedition Laws," that "some degree of abuse is inseparable from the proper use of everything, and in no instance is this more true, than in the press . . . it is better to leave a few of its noxious branches to their luxuriant growth, than by pruning them away, to injure the vigour of those yielding the proper fruits" (Levy 1966:216).

29. Ashcraft concludes that "in the development of the political consciousness of seventeenth-century Englishmen, the historical framework was only one, and not necessarily the most important of several perspectives from which to view political problems. A great many political writers adopted the natural law approach to these problems, in terms of which a custom-oriented legalistic argument was either irrelevant or of secondary importance." And with particular reference to the exclusion debate he writes, "Locke was not an exceptional political writer in his rejection of a legalistic approach" (1986:190n).

30. Dunn notes of the *Treatises*: "In England its status as the outstanding exposition of the principles of 1688 derived more from the enormous esteem in which the *Essay* was held than from any close reading of the book itself. . . . It was a work much recommended to the young and seldom read with any care by the adult" (1969b:57–58). These observations are simply not compatible with the view that Locke's politics were only marginally relevant to eighteenth-century Anglo-American political philosophy, despite the fact that some have claimed that they confirm the civic-humanist reading of political debate during the period.

31. On Gordon's familiarity with Locke, see, for example, Laprade (1936:308).

32. Cato continues: "What is it to a Magistrate how I wash my Hands, or cut my Corns, what Fashion or Colours I wear, or what Notions I entertain, or what Gestures I use, or what Words I pronounce, when they please me, and do him and my Neighbour no hurt? As well may he determine the Colour of my Hair, and controul my Shape and Features" (Letter 62, 2:248).

7 / *Locke's* Two Treatises *and Contemporary Thought: Freedom, Community, and the Liberal Tradition*

STEPHEN L. NEWMAN

In spirit, the seventeenth-century English philosopher John Locke ranks among the founders of the American political tradition. His liberal political philosophy haunts American politics like a family ghost. We Americans, as Louis Hartz once observed, are on the whole an unphilosophical people who have turned liberal theory into practical belief. Oblivious to the ideological character of our thought, we have built a way of life around individualism, private property, and voluntarism (Hartz 1955). Received as a way of life, Locke's philosophy appears to be invincible; no ideological challenger has ever achieved a mass audience in the United States. Typically our political arguments play one reading of Locke off against another, although in our naiveté we frequently mistake these family quarrels for a contest between radically opposed systems of ideas. Thus today proponents of the modest American welfare state are accused of socialism and morally conservative religious traditionalists are branded archreactionaries. Genuine alternatives to Locke are rarely encountered in public discourse.

Much the same is true of our intellectual discourse. Confronting liberal hegemony in the realm of ideas, philosophers have two options. They may cast their arguments within the Lockean framework, in which event they must accept all that this strategy entails for the way society is constituted. Theories of this sort tend to focus on the distribution of rights and liberties, often refining Lockean arguments in light of contemporary social and economic relationships. Such theories typically pit one set of political interests against another but pose no real challenge to the fundamental constitution of political life.[1] Philosophers pursuing a more radical agenda ignore Locke at the peril of their own irrelevance. If they hope to enlarge the nation's cramped political imagination, they have no choice but to attempt to disarm liberal ideology. Critics of the American

Way of Life characteristically seek to undermine our complacency through social criticism. A path to the reconstruction of public discourse may then be cleared by establishing a connection between Locke's conceptual vocabulary and society's ills. Theories of this sort have a subversive intent; they envision nothing less than the reconstitution of political life.

The present essay is concerned with two sets of contemporary political theories, libertarianism and communitarianism, which illustrate the dilemmas of theorizing in the American context. Both are presented by their advocates as critical perspectives on the modern state. All similarity ends there, however. Libertarianism and communitarianism represent diametrically opposed points of view. The former is militantly individualistic and recognizes no higher political value than personal freedom; the latter regards the purportedly excessive individualism of our time as a form of social pathology and places a higher value on shared communal ends than on personal rights and liberties. For their part, libertarians fear the enhancement of state power and regard popular acceptance of the regulatory and redistributive policies of the modern welfare state as evidence of a creeping collectivism. In contrast, communitarians perceive too little regard for collective interests embodied in liberal notions of social welfare and would extend rather than restrain society's influence over its members.

Reading libertarian and communitarian theories invites a sense of déjà vu. The former recall the teachings of classical liberalism; the latter echo the rival political traditions of classical republicanism and majoritarian democracy. Their attitudes toward present-day politics are colored by their historical affinities. Libertarianism understands contemporary liberalism as a departure from first principles; in effect, libertarians invite us to restore liberal theory to its Lockean original. Communitarianism, on the other hand, makes no distinction between the new liberalism and the old. Its partisans condemn all varieties of liberalism for contributing to the decline of civic spirit and the loss of common purpose in modern civil society. In their quest for a politics of fellowship, communitarians urge us to abandon Locke and to take up with the likes of Aristotle and Rousseau.

I cannot pretend to offer a complete survey of these theories in the space of a single essay. Instead, I shall focus on main currents in libertarian and communitarian thought through a discussion of representative thinkers. Throughout, Locke's philosophy as found in the *Two Treatises* will be my touchstone. It is an irony of the triumph of Lockeanism in America that the historical Locke all but disappears from view. By returning to the *Two Treatises* we can see that libertarians are not so very close to Locke nor perhaps communitarians so far removed as they make themselves out to be.[2]

Libertarianism builds on a fragment of Locke's political philosophy. Arguments presented in the *First Treatise* disappear altogether. Much of the *Second Treatise*, especially the later chapters in which Locke discusses the historical origins of government, are neglected. Instead, libertarian theory is preoccupied with themes developed in the early chapters set in the state of nature where Locke provides a hypothetical account of original government. In these chapters Locke's arguments concerning rights, liberty, property, and consent effectively frame the modern libertarian enterprise.

Libertarians depart from Locke in important ways, however. Locke conceived of the politics that emerge from his state of nature as an alternative to historical practice. Rational nature served as a critical vantage point, permitting the imaginative reconstruction of human society. Libertarian theory never looks beyond the state of nature and so remains innocent of the depraved political history that haunts the *Two Treatises*. Consequently, much of the political message contained in the *Second Treatise* is muted or lost altogether in the libertarian reprise of Lockean themes.

Consider first the doctrine of rights. Robert Nozick exemplifies the libertarian perspective when he states at the outset of *Anarchy, State and Utopia* that "individuals have rights, and there are things no person or group may do to them (without violating their rights)" (Nozick 1974:ix). Libertarian theorists share Locke's conviction that the individual is entitled to life, liberty, and property. None that I know of, however, accepts Locke's doctrine of rationally accessible natural rights ultimately validated by divine intention (*ST*: no. 106). Not surprisingly, in a secular age Locke's theology simply drops out of the libertarian reconstruction of his politics. A preferred libertarian strategy is to ground support for rights in an essentially Kantian regard for the status of persons. In Nozick's view, rights "reflect the underlying Kantian principle that individuals are ends and not merely means" (Nozick 1974:30–31).

Nozick treats rights as side-constraints regulating goal-directed activity. The effect is to impose as strong a barrier to rights violation as that supplied by Locke's natural laws. Nozick, though, has curiously little to say about how these side-constraints come into effect. In a recent book Loren Lomasky treats respect for rights as being logically entailed in the structure of practical reason (Lomasky 1987). His argument conceives of persons as "project pursuers," who value the ability to define and carry out their various personal enterprises. These projects have considerable moral significance in that they are at least partially constitutive of the individual's sense of self. Because they recognize the importance of personal projects and the opportunity to pursue them, prudent individuals (who seek their own good) have reason enough to respect one another's "moral space" (i.e., the zone of personal initiative in which projects are brought to life). This results in a cooperative social equilibrium reminiscent of the "State of Peace, Good Will, Mutual Assistance, and Preservation" that initially prevails in Locke's state of nature (ST: no. 19).

For Lomasky, "basic" rights thus come into being independent of the social contract, making them the theoretical equivalent of Locke's natural rights. Locke, who believed in the natural equality of persons, believed also in a natural equality of rights. Lomasky, too, favors equal rights, though not on account of men's common estate in nature as Locke argued (ST: no. 4). Rather, his derivation of basic rights is initially conceived as a two-person bargaining process, which gives it a built-in bias toward equality. (Neither project pursuer is likely to accept less than an equal grant of moral space.) Opened to n persons the story changes, however. Lomasky admits that under these conditions multiple bilateral equilibria with relations between two different classes exhibiting unequal status (as, for example, between whites and blacks or men and women) are possible. Nonetheless, he counters that the moral case for equality of basic rights among project pursuers is implicit in the logic of their situation. Since everyone values his or her own projects most highly, no person "is rationally obliged to accept inferiority in protected moral space, and [no person] can make a good claim to superiority" (Lomasky 1987:78).

Lockean natural rights have natural limits. They create no positive duties (with the possible exception of a weak duty to "preserve the rest of Mankind" so long as one's own preservation "comes not in competition" (ST: no. 6). Instead, their function is to establish a protected zone around the individual (prohibiting what Nozick calls boundary-crossing).[3] The Law of Nature, which Locke identifies with reason, "teaches all Mankind, who will but consult it, that being all equal and independent, no one ought to harm another in his Life, Health, Liberty, or Possessions" (*ST*: no. 6). Although Lomasky has no recourse to natural law, reason steps in to limit the scope of his basic rights in much the same way. He argues that because persons are likely to disagree over just how far basic rights extend, a stable regime of equal rights for all will incline toward the most inclusive, least expansive understanding of those rights. Basic rights, then, become "those moral constraints that impose minimal demands on the forbearance of others such that individuals can pursue projects amidst a world of similar beings, each with his own life to lead, and each owing the same measure of respect to others that they owe to him" (Lomasky 1987:83).

This sort of moral argument contrasts sharply with Friedrich Hayek's argument from utility. He arrives at a Lockean conclusion regarding the individual's right to be left alone by weighing the advantages that accrue to society as a whole. In Hayek's view, interference with the self-regarding actions of individuals is wrong not (only) because it shows disrespect for the moral status of persons but because it deprives society of possible benefits implicit in the creative potential of free agents. Repeating J. S. Mill's plea for tolerance in *On Liberty*, Hayek contends that there is simply no way of knowing in advance what might result from unorthodox experiments in living. By punishing the nonconformist, by silencing the heretic, society risks the loss of useful knowledge that might improve everyone's quality of life (Hayek 1960:22–53).

From the perspective of a Lomasky or a Nozick, the problem with Hayek's utilitarian argument is that it provides at best a conditional ground for rights. Were it shown to be the case that a higher social utility may be obtained from selective rights-violations than from a strict observance of rights, the argument folds. Hayek's understanding of societal evolution bars this conclusion in the long run. Simply stated, his claim is that free (rights-respecting) societies are more efficient than their competitors and hence more likely to survive a Darwinian process of natural selection (Hayek 1973). He is willing to concede, however, that individual rights have no place in a society still governed by cultural norms of collective responsibility. Thus a people truly believing that all will be made to suffer the wrath of the gods on account of even one heretic may rightfully enforce religious conformity (Hayek 1960:145).

Hayek refuses to condone external criticism of such illiberal practices. He takes the position that only "immanent criticism" undertaken in a spirit faithful to the norms and laws of a given society is reasonable. To impose a higher or simply a different standard in his view ignores the proven social utility of the existing normative framework that evolved over time to meet the survival needs of that society (Hayek 1960:63; Hayek 1973:24). This is an essentially Burkean argument directed against the radical (Painite) uses of the doctrine of natural rights, and it blunts the critical edge of libertarian theory. Following Hayek, Nozick's ringing declaration that "individuals have rights" must now be amended to read "individuals (sometimes) have rights, but only in certain societies and to a greater or lesser extent depending on local circumstances."

Lomasky, whose argument is closer to Nozick's (and Locke's) than to Hayek's, nonetheless agrees with the latter that cultural differences will significantly affect the boundaries drawn by basic rights. Though insisting that there is a basic right to noninterference even in a culture that believes in collective responsibility to the gods, he concludes that the right does not prohibit punishing blasphemy as conduct injurious toward others (Lomasky 1987:102). This is the case because basic rights "are enjoyed only insofar as they are instantiated in the concrete form of moral and legal rights" validated by the community (Lomasky 1987:107). Although Lomasky follows Locke in arguing that rights emerge prior to the social contract, he departs from Locke's apparent atomism in assigning a key role in the articulation of basic rights to the preexisting moral community. If this exposes his argument to some of the same difficulties suggested by Hayek's cultural relativism, it also allows him to avoid the charges of utopianism that might be laid against Nozick for presuming the transcultural uniformity of rights.

Hayek's utilitarian argument ironically allows him to portray the ahistorical Lockean concept of individual rights as the outcome of a historical process. The state of nature ceases to function as a starting point for political theory and becomes instead an actual moment in historical time. In effect, Locke's nature, shorn of its moral significance, is reproduced in modern (Western) societies that have evolved liberal political institutions and free-market economies. Lomasky also brings the state of nature to life but without assigning it a particular historical location. Rather, Lockean nature makes its appearance as a set of culturally mediated behavioral norms conducive to the pursuit of personal projects. In contrast, Nozick borrows Locke's own concept of the state of nature, which lacks both historicity and cultural depth. Yet, unlike Locke, he fails to distinguish between a political process that unfolds in timeless nature and the political events recorded in historical time. In consequence, it is impossible to know from Nozick's discussion when, if ever, the two intersect.

Locke is able to avoid the indeterminacy of Nozick's position because his account of original government set in the state of nature is balanced by a subsequent political history of the family. The latter describes how in the remote past political rule emerged spontaneously from the customary deference shown by children to their father. Locke makes it clear that historical subjects submitted to the rule of father-kings without ever drawing up a social compact or elaborating their rights. In essence, there was no need. "The Father's Government of the Childhood of those sprung from him, having accustomed them to the *Rule of one Man*, and taught them that where it was exercised with Care and Skill, with Affection and Love to those under it, it was sufficient to procure and preserve to Men all the Political Happiness they sought for, in Society" (*ST*: no. 107). But Locke asserts that the benign rule of father-kings came to an end with the passing of mankind's Golden Age. In subsequent eras "vain Ambition" and "evil Concupiscence" taught princes to have "distinct and separate interests from their People," and "Men found it necessary to examine more carefully *the Original* and Rights of *Government*" (*ST*: no. 111). Thus the depravity of historical politics creates the historical opening Locke needs to introduce political arguments first conceived in the (ahistorical) state of nature.

Locke's use of history is significant for his doctrine of rights, which is now seen to be grounded in an express political intention. The object of "natural" rights originating outside of history (in reason and revelation) is to legitimize popular resistance to the tyranny of traditional rulers. This strategy of argumentation is consistent with the polemical nature of the *Second Treatise*, an overtly political document whose author may have been deeply involved in revolutionary intrigue (Ashcraft 1986). Also, it further distinguishes Locke from modern libertarians whose formal theories of rights are not nearly so political in character. Reconceived in terms of aggregate social welfare or of the morality of individual conduct, rights supply the foundation for libertarian social theory. To be sure, libertarian rights may still serve as a bulwark against misrule; however, their primary function is to assure that mutually independent individuals can each pursue their separate projects without bumping into one another. If good fences make good neighbors, libertarian rights are well designed to promote social peace.

The preeminent libertarian right is the right to liberty. Following Locke, libertarian theorists define freedom as the capacity for self-determination. Locke introduces his concept of personal liberty in the state of nature, where he describes men as being "perfectly free." Their freedom lies in their ability to "order their Actions, and dispose of their Possessions, and Persons as they think fit, within the bounds of the Law of Nature, without asking leave, or depending upon the Will of any other Man" (*ST*: no. 4). It is clear from this that what makes men free is their independence from another's will. Adherence to the Law of Nature (that is, to reason) is no burden on freedom but rather serves to distinguish liberty from license (*ST*: no. 6). Otherwise men would be free to prey upon one another, and the state of nature would degenerate into a state of war.

Locke's is a classic statement of what Isaiah Berlin called "negative freedom," which deems the absence of coercion more important than the presence of meaningful choices in assessing the status of liberty (Berlin 1969:118–72). Being free in this sense of the term is compatible with having no capacity for action whatsoever, so long as blind circumstance and not deliberate human intervention is to blame. Hayek explains that any circumstantial loss of an individual's capacity for action may be unfortunate, but it is morally unexceptional. A tree felled by a storm may block the path I had wanted to take and compel me to choose another, but I am in no way coerced and hence suffer no loss of freedom. On the other hand, had the tree been cut down by someone who contrived to have me go another way the situation would be quite different. This attempt at manipulation, whether the intended victim knows of it or not, is for Hayek an instance of coercion and an assault on liberty (cf. Hayek 1960:133).

Negative freedom serves Locke as a political doctrine establishing the right to resist a tyrant and is made explicit in the last chapter of the *Second Treatise*. Libertarianism picks up on Locke's portrayal of the state as a potential aggressor. In the words of economist Murray Rothbard, a popularizer of libertarian ideas, "While opposing any and all private aggression against the rights of person and property, the libertarian sees that throughout history and into the present day, there has been one central, dominant, and overriding aggressor upon all these rights: the State" (Rothbard 1978:23–24). Despite this rhetorical parallel, the ideological thrust of the libertarian position is quite different from Locke's. Libertarians discover the specter of Locke's tyrannical sovereign in the Lockean doctrine of popular sovereignty. In their view, there is more to fear (today) from the will of the people than from the arbitrary will of kings.

The problem with democracy is that it inclines toward egalitarianism. Fending off political demands for redistributive social-welfare policies, libertarians employ the concept of negative freedom to defend a policy of social and economic laissez-faire. Hayek argues that the inequalities associated with market outcomes are morally neutral. Although the result of conscious human agency they are not deliberate; so long as markets are not rigged, they do not obey the will of any single agent or group of agents. Hence the relative disadvantages suffered by any given person or class of persons are simply irrelevant from the standpoint of freedom. The inability of some person to achieve her goals may be tragic but creates no valid claim against resources held by others. Our freedom, Hayek observes, "does not ensure us any particular opportunities, but leaves it to us to decide what use we shall make of the circumstances in which we find ourselves." In Lomasky's terms, freedom is the *necessary* but *insufficient* condition for the realization of our projects. Acknowledging the political temptation to "correct" market outcomes in favor of the relatively disadvantaged, Hayek cautions that "above all we must recognize that we may be free and yet miserable" (Hayek 1960:18; Lomasky 1987:92).

That libertarian theorists give relatively little weight to freedom in Locke's political sense of the term is evident in their treatment of civil liberties. The paramount right of free speech, for example, becomes the individual's right to speak his mind on his own property or on property rented for the occasion (Hospers 1971:61–62; Rothbard 1978:94–105). It is therefore possible that some persons may be denied an opportunity to speak either because they cannot afford to publicize their views or because they cannot find a proprietor willing to sell them access to a public forum. The political implications of this, especially in light of the inegalitarian implications of the libertarian defense of market outcomes, is tremendous. Yet libertarian theorists seem not to appreciate the revolutionary turn in their argument. Instead, they reason as though by collapsing traditional civil liberties into the concept of property they have merely clarified the real issue at stake.

Murray Rothbard's discussion of free speech is a case in point. He asks his readers to envision a "purely" libertarian world in which even the streets are privately owned and would-be political demonstrators must apply to the owners for permission to march. "It would then be clear," he contends, "that what is involved is not a 'free speech' or 'free assembly' question at all, but a question of property rights: of the right of the group to offer to rent the street, and of the right of the street owner either to accept or reject the offer" (Rothbard 1978:97). What Rothbard really accomplishes by this example, however, is the depoliticization of speech. In fact, his argument amounts to nothing less than an all-out assault against politics. Rothbard's war on politics, joined by most other libertarian theorists (with greater or lesser degrees of enthusiasm), is motivated by a desire to neutralize the state as a threat to (negative) freedom. The only sure route to victory lies in privatizing the totality of political relationships. The social universe may then be reconstructed on a liberty-respecting foundation buttressed by private property.

Libertarian emphasis on property rights seems appropriately Lockean on its face. Property occupies a central place in Locke's *Second Treatise*, such that life and liberty are subsumed under that category. But Locke is not so easily identified with free-market ideology, and his argument concerning property does not necessarily lead to a libertarian conclusion. Although he is sometimes portrayed as an early theorist of liberal capitalism, recent scholarship suggests that Locke harbored precapitalist and even anticapitalist sentiments (cf. Macpherson 1962; Tully 1980; Vaughn 1980; and Wood 1984).

For Locke, individuals come to have a right to property in things because they first have a right to property in themselves (in their persons) and in their labor. By acting on as yet unappropriated objects in the state of nature, human labor assimilates nature to the personality of the laborer (*ST*: no. 27). Private appropriation enjoys a divine sanction insofar as "God, who hath given the World to Men in common, hath also given them reason to make use of it to the best advantage of Life, and convenience" (*ST*: no. 26). Locke inserts a caveat, however, by claiming that there are divinely ordained limits to accumulation. Persons who remove objects from the common store supplied by a beneficent deity must leave behind "enough, and as good" for others to enjoy (*ST*: no. 27). Further, no one may rightfully appropriate more than he can use before it spoils. "Nothing was made by God for Man to spoil or destroy," to which the voice of reason adds that waste is senseless (*ST*: no. 31).

Locke argues that the constraint of spoilage would effectively ensure a rough equality of condition were it not for "the *Invention of Money*, and the tacit Agreement of Men to put a value on it," which allows industrious persons to amass great wealth without committing injustice (*ST*: nos. 36, 48). Perishable goods may now be exchanged for incorruptible gold or

silver, legitimating vast agricultural holdings and foretelling the (en)clos-
ing of nature's commons. Still, the proviso that individual acts of appropriation must leave behind "enough and as good" for others would seem
to rule this out. James Tully has suggested that the proviso lapses once the
exhaustion of the commons makes its application impossible, forcing
adoption of a new conventional rationale for individualized holdings
(Tully 1980:129). It might be argued to the contrary that the increased
productivity Locke attributes to private holdings so expands the stock of
goods in the world as to meet the requirements of the proviso (*ST*: nos.
40–43). Of course, this will be true only if goods available for trade are
deemed equivalent to the opportunities for appropriation presented by
uncultivated nature (Newman 1984:52–62; cf. Nozick 1974:182).

Admittedly, this reading of Locke makes him more of a capitalist than
Tully is likely to accept. It does not require that he be seen as a modern
possessive individualist, however. Locke never expressly abandons the
moral constraints that reason and revelation jointly impose on appropriation. Moreover, in the *First Treatise* he makes it clear that property rights
are enjoyed in balance with an obligation to be charitable. "As *Justice*
gives every Man a Title to the product of his honest Industry, and the fair
Acquisitions of his Ancestors descended to him; so *Charity* gives every
Man a Title to so much out of another's Plenty, as will keep him from
extream want, where he has no means to subsist otherwise" (*FT*: no. 42).
Undoubtedly, the title conferred by charity becomes all the more important after the invention of money (described in the *Second Treatise*) up-
sets the "natural" equality previously enforced by the limitation of spoilage.

Locke's theory of just acquisition is more or less accepted without
emendation by Rothbard, who quotes the relevant passages of the *Second
Treatise* at length (Rothbard 1978:32–33). Nozick, on the other hand,
thinks it ludicrous to suppose for example that anyone might claim title
to the ocean simply by pouring into it a bottle of tomato juice, thereby
"mixing" his labor with the waters (Nozick 1974:175). Lomasky shares
Nozick's judgment, objecting that far from creating a right in some object,
mere use is morally arbitrary. He cannot see why labor should be thought
to create an exclusive right of ownership in perpetuity (Lomasky
1987:114). Yet Lomasky is also critical of Nozick's entitlement theory of
just holdings, which assumes that "things come into the world already
attached to people having entitlements over them" (Nozick 1974:160;
Lomasky 1987:115). Given the evident injustice that pervades historical

property relations and the impossibility of rectification, he dismisses Nozick's argument as irrelevant to both theory and practice.

If Nozick and Lomasky depart from Locke (and disagree with one another), both stay close to the spirit of Locke's argument. Although he rejects Locke's theory of acquisition, Nozick nonetheless concludes that "whoever makes something, having bought or contracted for all other held resources used in the process (transferring some of his holdings for these cooperating factors), is entitled to it" (Nozick 1974:160). Lomasky differs in not making title depend on entitlement. He argues that a basic right to property follows from the concept of persons as project pursuers insofar as having (though not owning) goods is necessary to a person's plans. Mutual recognition of the value in having one's supply of goods secure from predation provides a reason for each to defer to the others with respect to their personal holdings. At length, the creation of social institutions that recognize and formally define principles of noninterference with respect to personal holdings transforms mere possession (having) into rightful ownership (Lomasky 1987:120–21).

As previously noted, libertarians are antiegalitarians. In Lomasky's version of their position, "Not equality in holdings but equal liberty to acquire holdings is entailed by the normative theory of basic rights" (Lomasky 1987:123). This yields a prima facie case against all redistributive claims. There is no Lockean obligation to be charitable in libertarian theory, even though some libertarians expressly rely on private charity to relieve the distress of the poor in place of the welfare state (e.g., Rothbard 1978:150–51). Lomasky confidently asserts that under a libertarian regime most persons will usually be able to meet their own needs and that voluntary aid from family and friends will be sufficient in those rare cases where self-help fails. But atypically he goes one step further and offers an argument strikingly similar to Locke's use of charity: "If a person is otherwise unable to secure that which is necessary for his ability to live as a project pursuer, then he has a rightful claim to provision by others who have a surplus beyond what they require to live as project pursuers." He justifies this deviation from a strict libertarian regard for property rights prudentially by claiming that it would be irrational for any person to pledge support for a regime under which one's prospects for project pursuit may be extinguished (Lomasky 1987:126–27).

Whether or not this opens the door to more extensive welfare rights than Lomasky allows need not detain us. His argument is more interesting for the way it contrasts with Locke's. The rights-claim Lomasky allows to the (desperately) poor differs from the title conferred by charity in Locke's account largely in regard to its purpose. Lomasky is concerned with protecting the moral status of the person as a pursuer of projects. Locke, on the other hand, clearly indicates that his chief concern is with the *political* status of the impoverished individual, as is seen in the continuation of the passage on charity: "A Man can no more justly make use of another's necessity, to force him to become his Vassal, by with-holding that Relief, God requires him to afford the wants of his Brother, than he that has more strength can seize upon a weaker, master him to his Obedience, and with a Dagger at his Throat offer him Death or Slavery" (*FT*: no. 42). Lomasky's restatement of Locke's argument mutes its political significance, preferring once again to focus instead on the moral parameters bounding human relationships abstractly considered. Absent the context supplied by the *Two Treatises*, Locke's philosophy hangs in a void, allowing Lomasky and other libertarian theorists to drain its political content and substitute their own brand of antipolitics.

The libertarian antipathy for politics is most clearly expressed by antistatism. This hostility toward government recalls Locke's own seeming ambivalence about the state in the *Second Treatise*. Contemplating the ends of government Locke asks, "If Man in the State of Nature be so free, as has been said; if he be absolute Lord of his own Person and Possessions, equal to the greatest, and subject to no Body, why will he part with his Freedom?" (*ST*: no. 123). Libertarian theorists take Locke's question very seriously. Some answer it by claiming that no rational person would or should willingly compromise his freedom by accepting the yoke of government, however benign its ostensible purpose. In place of the state they propose a form of anarchism, sometimes described as "anarcho-capitalism," in which police and judicial services are supplied by private entrepreneurs competing for clients in a free market (e.g., Friedman 1973; Rothbard 1978). To another group of libertarian theorists this seems a recipe for chaos. They counter with some version of the minimal or "night-watchman" state equipped with constitutional checks and balances (e.g., Hospers 1971; Machan 1975; Nozick 1974).

Of course, Locke was no anarchist. Still, his account of the state of nature suggests parallels with both versions of libertarianism. Initially, Lockean nature is a state of peace and plenty for all, thanks to a fortuitous coincidence: Right (the Law of Nature, which every individual is empowered to enforce) and convenience (human self-interest) go together.

For as a Man had a Right to all he could imploy his Labour upon, so he had no temptation to labour for more than he could make use of. This left no room for Controversie about Title, nor for Incroachment on the Right of others; what Portion a Man carved to himself, was easily seen; and it was useless as well as dishonest to carve himself too much, or take more than he needed. (*ST*: no. 51)

Although he early on expresses concern that nature will prove "inconvenient" because men are allowed to be judges in their own cases (*ST*: no. 13), in fact government is hardly missed at this stage in Locke's argument. Had the *Second Treatise* ended here it might be known today as an anarchist manifesto.

Locke's state of nature changes dramatically, however, after the invention of money. It may be supposed that the closing of the commons gives some persons reason enough to steal, for Locke now describes the greater part of mankind as being "no strict Observers of Equity and Justice," making property "very unsafe, very insecure" (*ST*: no. 123). At this point rational persons anxious about their property have every reason to sign the social compact. "The great and *chief end* therefore, of Mens uniting into Commonwealths, and putting themselves under Government, *is the preservation of their Property*" (*ST*: no. 124). Government comes into being as the common judge with authority, whose absence renders the (postmonetary) state of nature unacceptably "inconvenient."

No libertarian theorist disputes the need for Locke's common judge. (If libertarians virtually identify modern society with the state of nature, it is nature as Locke described it subsequent to the invention of money. The rough equality of condition that initially prevails in nature is not on their agenda.) Libertarian anarchists differ from supporters of the minimal state in supposing that the common judge need not be identical with government. Rothbard, for example, envisions a competitive market in police and judicial services performing as the functional equivalent of the Lockean state while avoiding the dangers inherent in granting any "judge" a monopoly.

In a state of libertarian anarchy, persons would be allowed to retain what Locke called the executive power of the law of nature (that is, the right to self-help enforcement in defense of life, liberty, and property). They may choose to exercise this right themselves, or they might decide to purchase additional protection from entrepreneurs specializing in police services. It is assumed by libertarian theorists that the market will offer a range of such services catering to the disparate needs (and differing incomes) of a diverse clientele. It is further assumed that economic rationality will prevent these entrepreneurs from going to war in defense of their clients. "To put it bluntly," Rothbard explains, "such wars would be bad—very bad—for business. Therefore, on the free market, the police agencies would all see to it that there would be no clashes between them, and that all conflicts of opinion would be ironed out in private courts, decided by private judges or arbitrators" (Rothbard 1978:221).

The market mentality taken for granted by theorists of anarcho-capitalism has its parallel in Locke's appreciation of the human desire for "conveniency"; however, Locke was too well-schooled in political history and too deeply imbued with the consequences of Adam's Fall to believe in the saving power of economic rationality. Libertarian supporters of the minimal state may be thought to share his more profound sense of the depth of human depravity. Contemplating anarchist proposals, they are haunted by the grim specter of incessant warfare among competing police forces (cf. Hospers 1971:448–49; Nozick 1974:15–17; and Rand 1964:108–9). Still, libertarian theories of minimal government do not achieve the degree of psychological complexity implicit in the theological and historical dimensions of Locke's argument. Rather, they choose to emphasize the role of instrumental rationality in an agent's decision to adopt the Lockean social compact. They simply believe that consent to the minimal state is more rational than retaining the right to self-help enforcement.

Unexpectedly, the libertarian case for the minimal state stumbles over the consent of the governed. If consent must be unanimous, what becomes of political legitimacy in the event that some person or persons withhold their consent? If consent must be ongoing, what happens when some person or persons dissent from a particular measure? Locke overcomes the latter difficulty by arguing that the social compact establishes "one *Body Politick*, wherein the *Majority* have a Right to act and conclude the rest" (*ST*: no. 95). The former difficulty is met by the doctrine of tacit consent, which holds that anyone enjoying the protection of the laws is obliged to respect them (*ST*: no. 119). Libertarians, however, are wary of majority rule precisely because it subordinates the individual to the will of the group. And Locke's doctrine of tacit consent is suspect because of the burden it imposes on would-be dissenters. In order expressly to reject the state's unwanted "protection," they must remove themselves beyond its territorial jurisdiction. This comes perilously close to recognizing the brute fact of state power as a grant of legitimate authority.

These sorts of considerations lead Nozick to hypothesize an invisible-hand explanation of how minimal government might arise from a condition of anarchy. Starting from the scenario sketched by the anarcho-capitalists, Nozick argues that the very nature of the service they provide brings competing private police forces into violent conflict, leading to the elimination of all but one within a given territory. This "dominant" police force becomes to all intents and purposes an "ultraminimal state." It differs from the minimal state insofar as its monopoly does not preclude self-help enforcement by nonsubscribers. True government comes into being when the nonsubscribers are prohibited from enforcing their claims against paying clients of the ultraminimal state (because it deems their procedures unreliable) and, in compensation, are offered the same services (free or at a reduced fee) in settling their disputes with others (Nozick 1974:pt. 1).

Nozick does not require nonsubscribers to accept this offer, though it is clearly in their interests to do so. Nor does he give the newly established minimal state authority to interfere in disputes between nonsubscribers. For these reasons he cannot be said to have imposed government against the will of the governed. In essence, he has created circumstances under which consent to the authority of government is the prudent course for rational individuals. Yet the fact remains that he allows the state to limit self-enforcement by nonsubscribers. On its face this prohibition seems difficult to square with his commitment to inviolable individual rights. Why does he not have the state evaluate each enforcement action by a nonsubscriber case by case, sustaining those it finds worthy and condemning those it determines to be unjust? How does faulty self-enforcement differ from any other private wrong?

Nozick insists that unlike most wrongful acts faulty self-help enforcement belongs to a class of wrongs having a public component. Such wrongs, he explains, create fear among the general public even though people know they will be compensated fully if and when the wrongs occur. "Even under the strongest compensation proposal which compensates victims for their fear [as well as for any injury], some people (the nonvictims) will not be compensated for *their* fear" (Nozick 1974:67). Public wrongs, then, induce a state of general anxiety for which there is no adequate compensation. On the other hand, Nozick argues that the protection extended to nonsubscribers by the state leaves them no worse off than before. Paying clients of the state, who now must share the cost of protecting nonsubscribers, are morally obliged to shoulder this added burden because prohibited self-help enforcement is *merely risky* and not always wrongful (Nozick 1974:114).

The oddity of Nozick's theory of the state is that it entirely ignores political motives. Whatever else Nozick's minimal state might be, it is not a political community in Locke's sense of "the Body Politick." Locke emphatically states that the social compact creates a new entity, a collective representation of the whole people pledged to the welfare of all. Although personal interests are not made subordinate to the general will, the personal right of judgment in matters pertaining to life, liberty, and property is surrendered to the majoritarian political process. Government in Locke's view is nothing other than a trust exercised by rulers on behalf of the governed. Failure to discharge that trust in good faith gives the people a right to revoke it and to change their government. Nozick's state, on the other hand, is merely the dominant police force dressed up as a government. Persons do not contract with one another to form a civil community as they do in Locke's account. Rather, they become clients of the state, paying the "government" to enforce their rights against others. Public officials are transformed into private entrepreneurs, bound not by a public trust but by a contractual obligation to their clients. Robert Paul Wolff is surely right when he observes that "as a device for guaranteeing individual liberties and enforcing absolute side constraints, this is, to put it gently, a trifle feckless" (Wolff 1977:93).

Politics is swallowed up by the market and disappears in Nozick's theory. This same result is reached by libertarian anarchism and reflects a tendency in libertarian theory to exaggerate one side of Locke's philosophy at the expense of another. Locke's concern with individual rights is detached from his ambition to secure responsible government. By treating the state solely as a guarantor of rights, libertarians can afford to neglect Locke's insistence on popular sovereignty by theorizing about private "government." The loss of political accountability is thought to be made good in the case of libertarian anarchy by the freedom of consumers to abandon an unpopular provider of governmental services in favor of a rival operation. The monopoly enjoyed by the minimal state deprives consumers of this alternative; however, they may still express their displeasure with the state by refusing to pay for its services.

The move from popular sovereignty to consumer sovereignty completes the depoliticization of Locke's philosophy begun with the libertarian doctrine of rights. Libertarianism retains the distinction that Locke draws between state and society and also his pronounced individualism and the conception of personal freedom that goes with it, but the political aims of the *Second Treatise* are abandoned. Locke's libertarian successors casually discard the democratic part of his liberal-democratic theory of government.

FILMER'S REVENGE: THE COMMUNITARIAN CRITIQUE OF LIBERALISM

Locke's *Two Treatises* did more than refute an already tired scriptural defense of the divine right of kings. They introduced a new, decidedly modern political paradigm that would dramatically affect the status of the individual in society and redefine the legitimate ends of government. Locke's version of the social contract prepared the way for subsequent moves against aristocratic privilege by sweeping aside all consideration of rank and title and by liberating traditional subjects from their historical allegiance to inherited social and political institutions. At the same time, Locke deposed the privileged conceptions of the good associated with classical and medieval political theory by having individuals in the state of nature reinvent civil society for their own limited purposes and by making the sum of their private needs and wants supply the complete contents of the public good.

Communitarians object that however much was gained through the Lockean revolution in political thought, as much (or more) was lost. They acknowledge that liberal civil society is highly successful in bringing together autonomous men and women for their mutual advantage without requiring them to give up any significant portion of their autonomy; however, they regard this as a dubious achievement. Concerned about the quality of political relationships, they question the depth of civic attachments born out of respect for the individual's right to be left alone. Rational self-interest, the conventional motive assigned to political actors in liberal theory, seems to them a weak foundation for political loyalties. From the communitarian perspective it appears that fraternity has been sacrificed on the altar of liberty. Believing that Lockean politics can never be more than a rough-and-tumble competition for personal and partisan advantage, communitarian theorists urge us to look beyond liberalism toward a public philosophy rooted in a broader conception of the common good.

The communitarian critique of Lockean individualism is founded on the Aristotelian observation that humans are social creatures who require the polis to achieve their full humanity. Only subhuman or superhuman beings can thrive on their own. Men and women stand in need of a life in common with others. From this perspective the problem with Locke's philosophy is that it conceives of politics too narrowly (cf. Budziszewski 1986:109–10). Rather than facilitating the reconciliation of conflicting individual interests through the discovery of a common good, Locke's politics preserve these interests intact. Civil society differs from the prepolitical state of nature only in having a "common judge with authority" to adjudicate and enforce claims of right.

To be sure, Locke never denied the importance of men's social instincts: "God having made Man such a Creature, that, in his own Judgment, it was not good for him to be alone, put him under strong Obligations of Necessity, Convenience, and Inclination to drive him into *Society*, as well as fitted him with Understanding and Language to continue and enjoy it" (*ST*: no. 77). Locke's understanding of human nature differs from that of Aristotle, however, insofar as Locke never doubted the moral sufficiency of human autonomy. Lockean individuals, endowed with natural rights, do not require membership in the polis to become aware of who and what they are. Personal identity is prior to membership in civil society, and private interests have priority over public (collective) initiatives. Political activity contributes nothing to the development of the liberal self.

Communitarian critics of liberalism return to Aristotle's view, arguing that it is simply wrong to treat individuals as fully formed human subjects prior to and apart from the influence of society. On the contrary, they insist that the individual's sense of self is at least partially constituted by social experience. Thus, according to Charles Taylor, even the archindividualist is who and what he is only "by virtue of the whole society and civilization which brought him to be and which nourishes him" (Taylor 1985:206). Taylor's "social thesis" maintains that the social atomism underlying Locke's political individualism is a faulty premise that fatally weakens the entire liberal edifice. Locke and the liberal theorists who follow in his trail err in neglecting the social significance of political activity since the nature of the choices available to "private" men and women depends on the public character of the community in which they live. To succeed, liberalism itself requires from persons a political commitment to liberal values and a willingness to amend social outcomes in a manner consistent with their commitment (Taylor 1985: 207).

Lockean liberalism goes wrong, Taylor insists, in asserting the primacy of rights outside a context of affirming certain human capacities. Because they view individuals atomistically as entitled to choose (and capable of choosing) their own modes of life, liberals are wary of pronouncing judgment on any person's choice. Yet in emphasizing the capacity for choice they involve themselves in a contradiction.

> To affirm the worth of the human capacity to form moral and religious convictions goes far beyond the assertion of the right to one's convictions. It also says that I ought to become the kind of agent who is capable of authentic conviction, that I ought to be true to my own convictions and not live a lie or a self-delusion out of fear or for favor, that I ought in certain circumstances to help foster this capacity in others, that I ought to bring up my own children to have it, that I ought not inhibit it in others by influencing them toward a facile and shallow complaisance, and so on. (Taylor 1985:194)

Taylor concludes that an assertion of the primacy of rights is impossible, "for to assert the rights in question is to affirm the capacities," and these can be developed only in a society of a certain kind. This implies a commitment to belong; however, the solipsistic liberal reading of rights denies any such commitment and thereby undermines the capacity that supports those rights (Taylor 1985:197–98).

Taylor thinks that his argument is especially telling against the claims of a libertarian like Nozick.

> The crucial point here is this: since the free individual can only maintain his identity within a society/culture of a certain kind, he has to be concerned about the shape of this society/culture as a whole. He cannot, following the libertarian anarchist model that Nozick sketched, be concerned purely with his individual choices and the associations formed from such choices to the neglect of the matrix in which such choices can be open or closed, rich or meager. (Taylor 1985:207)

Interestingly, libertarian theorist Loren Lomasky lodges much the same sort of complaint against Nozick's atomistic views and alternatively endeavors to ground libertarianism in the cultural matrix of a moral community (Lomasky 1987:108). He does not think it necessary, however, to subordinate individual ends to an overriding principle of belonging.

Rather, he treats membership in the community as a given, a necessary background condition to individual choice in the exercise of personal rights. The obligation to perpetuate community values falls to a private association, the family (Lomasky 1987:168–69).

It is a historical irony that Lomasky is able to take for granted the sort of moral community that Locke set out to establish. The prevailing political morality of Locke's own day was not so hospitable to his purpose. Confronted by a tradition of political absolutism, he turned to the state of nature to derive an account of civil society independent of contemporary norms. Community is of scant importance in nature. Extracted from history and beyond the reach of tradition, the independent inhabitants of the state of nature have no greater concern than their own survival needs. Once the "inconvenience" of nature convinces them to establish civil government, their first thought is to limit the ends of political society to the preservation of life, liberty, and property. If they entertain some higher conception of the good (and Locke does not suggest that they do), it can find expression only within the private moral space surrounding each individual.[4]

Both Locke and Lomasky insist on a distinction between public and private (or between the political and the social) that communitarians, arguing along the lines of Taylor's social thesis, deem invalid. In their view political individualism, premised on the atomistic view of society encountered in Locke's state of nature, tends to corrupt all social relations and threatens the very integrity of the community. Christian Bay, for example, laments that liberals "have placed on their humanistic pedestal a cripple of a man, a man without a moral or political nature; a man with plenty of contractual rights and obligations, perhaps; but a man without moorings in any real community; a drifter rather than a being with roots in species solidarity" (Bay 1978:30). In a similar vein Benjamin Barber complains that liberal individualism has spawned "a self that exists only for itself, without regard to species, to justice, to equality, or to obligation" (Barber 1984:71). The deracinated state of nature might be no more than a convenient fiction serving Locke's polemical ends; nonetheless, to the communitarian critics of liberalism, it today appears all too real as a state of mind.

Their concern over the ill effects of liberal individualism recalls the view expressed more than a century ago by Alexis de Tocqueville. Writing of the United States, Tocqueville observed that individualism "disposes each citizen to isolate himself from the mass of his fellows and withdraw into the circle of family and friends . . . [leaving] the greater society to look after itself." Still worse, he believed that individualism tended to merge with "egoism," a "passionate and exaggerated love of self which leads a man to think of all things in terms of himself and to prefer himself to all" (Tocqueville 1969:506, 507). The authors of *Habits of the Heart*, which borrows its title from a line in Tocqueville's classic study of American democracy, believe that his fears are borne out by modern experience (Bellah et al. 1985). Their judgment is seconded by historian and social critic Christopher Lasch, who describes modern American culture as having carried the logic of individualism "to the extreme of a war of all against all" (Lasch 1978:xv).

So unhappy a perspective on the present invites comparison with the past. Alasdair MacIntyre contrasts modern civil society with the premodern "traditional" community where no man is simply an individual; rather, he is identified through his relationships to others as "brother, cousin, grandson, member of this household, that village, this tribe." In the traditional community, MacIntyre explains, these sorts of relationships are essential, not accidental, features of the person they describe. To lack a particular place in the pregiven social matrix is to lack a concrete sense of who one is. Members of such a community "inherit a particular space within an interlocking set of social relationships; lacking that space, they are nobody, or at best a stranger or an outcast." To recognize oneself as a member of the community is to accept life as "a journey with set goals; to move through life is to make progress—or to fail to make progress—toward a given end." In contrast, the modern liberal self "in acquiring sovereignty in its own realm" loses all sense of direction (MacIntyre 1984:33 –34). Freedom risks alienation and anomie.

Modern conservatives have long shared MacIntyre's assessment of the assault on tradition. Edmund Burke argued in the *Reflections* that "antient opinions and rules of life" embodied in custom and unexamined "prejudice" are necessary to civilized existence. Take these things away, he warned, and "from that moment we have no compass to govern us; nor can we know distinctly to what port we steer" (Burke 1973:91). Stripped of the "decent drapery of life" and all the "pleasing illusions" that make it worthy of men's affection, government has no other foundation than base self-interest and fear of the hangman. Beyond traditional politics Burke saw only a Hobbesian world of brute force where "the whole chain and continuity of the commonwealth would be broken," and men "would become little better than the flies of summer" (Burke 1973:90, 108).

Force prevails in the world described by Burke and MacIntyre because reason lacks a common ground. Independent selves freed from the constraints imposed by the traditional community become their own moral legislators. It follows from the absence of shared communal standards that moral conflict is now insoluble. Just as the divorce of self from a socially fixed identity dissolves spontaneous allegiance, the loss of a common good embedded in shared practices places moral consensus beyond the reach of modern society. In MacIntyre's view, principles may contest for political supremacy, but ultimately liberal politics cannot be principled. Norms of toleration and pluralism merely serve to disguise the depth of societal conflicts. Modern politics, he concludes, is in reality "civil war carried on by other means" (MacIntyre 1984:253).

MacIntyre is nostalgic for the politics of virtue, which discovers standards of excellence interior to those social practices that define and unite the community. The politics of virtue, which may again be traced to Aristotle, transcends the liberal distinction between public and private by making the individual good identical with the common good; both are realized in and through cultivation of the virtues.

What are the virtues? MacIntyre initially defines virtue as "an acquired human quality the possession and exercise of which tends to enable us to achieve those goods which are internal to practices and the lack of which effectively prevents us from achieving any such goods" (MacIntyre 1984:191). Virtues, then, transcend the particularities of culture. MacIntyre thinks that truthfulness, justice, and courage, for example, are genuine excellences or virtues in any society, although specific moral codes will vary. Different communities at different times present different environments. Thus, "the exercise of the virtues is itself apt to require a highly determinate attitude toward social and political issues; and it is always within some particular community with its own specific institutional forms that we learn or fail to learn to exercise the virtues" (MacIntyre 1984:196–97).

On this view, liberalism defeats the politics of virtue by treating the community simply as an arena in which self-determining individuals may choose their own conceptions of the good life. It becomes illicit for government to encourage any particular moral outlook, even though certain virtues are integral to the social practices on which liberalism itself depends. MacIntyre here joins Taylor in arguing that liberal theory is morally incoherent. But is the politics of virtue any more coherent?

MacIntyre is able to answer in the affirmative because his teleological conception of human existence assigns the virtues a central role in defining the good. Since the complete human good must transcend the limited goods of discrete practices, MacIntyre argues that it can be manifest only in the course of a whole life; thus we must understand the whole human life as a unity. He invites us to see this in terms of the unity of a narrative quest. "It is in looking for a conception of *the* good which will enable us to order other goods, for a conception of *the* good which will enable us to extend our understanding of the purpose and content of the virtues, for a conception of *the* good which will enable us to understand the place of integrity and constancy in life, that we initially define the kind of life which is a quest for the good" (MacIntyre 1984:219). Finally, the virtues come to represent a set of dispositions that will not only enable persons to achieve goods internal to practices but will also further the quest for this larger, all-encompassing good. "The catalogue of the virtues," MacIntyre explains, "will therefore include the virtues required to sustain the kind of households and the kind of political communities in which men and women seek the good together and the virtues necessary for philosophical inquiry about the character of the good" (MacIntyre 1984:219).

At this point his argument collapses into a mystifying circularity. What is the good life for man? According to MacIntyre, it is "the life spent seeking the good life for man, and the virtues necessary for the seeking are those which will enable us to understand what more and what else the good life for man is" (MacIntyre 1984:219; cf. Budziszewski 1986:104–7). Whatever this entails, it is clear that MacIntyre does not find contemporary society well suited to the quest. "What matters at this stage," he counsels, "is the construction of local forms of community within which civility and the intellectual and moral life can be sustained through the new dark ages which are already upon us" (MacIntyre 1984:263).

The obscurity that clouds MacIntyre's account of the virtues plagues the communitarian search for a common good. Like Humpty-Dumpty, the moral consensus of the traditional community appears shattered beyond repair; still, communitarian theorists dream of somehow piecing it together again. Some, like the authors of *Habits of the Heart*, find inspiration in America's religious history. They approvingly quote John Winthrop's admonition to the first Puritan settlers in Massachusetts: "We must delight in each other, make others condition our own, rejoyce together, mourn together, labor and suffer together, always having before our eyes our community as members of the same body" (Bellah et al.

1985:28). Winthrop's teaching and the personal example that he set as governor of the colony are taken to represent a viable alternative to the liberal tradition still available today to Winthrop's more secular descendants. What this recommendation fails to take into account, however, is that Winthrop and his peers saw their mutual obligations arising from the covenant of shared grace, which made them a peculiar people set apart from the other nations of the earth. Their spiritual covenant with each other and with God bound them specially to observe the gospel law and to love one another. No such obligation binds the unregenerate.

If there can be no true fellowship absent the recognition of shared grace, there would seem to be little hope for this version of the communitarian project. Even in Winthrop's time many in the second and third generation of colonists could not honestly "own the covenant" and take their place as full citizens. Perhaps because they recognize the difficulty of religious commitment, modern prophets of the biblical path to community are content to ask less of people. In their watered-down version of the covenant, a vague moral consensus rather than a strict observance of gospel law outlines the contours of the good. Their brief against liberalism is that by consigning moral questions to the sphere of private opinion it promotes an unhealthy moral relativism and weakens the historical consensus sustained by religious belief.

Richard Neuhaus, for example, argues that America is and always has been a Christian nation. He worries that by attempting to repudiate the nation's religious heritage, modern liberals risk depriving American politics of its moral center of gravity. Neuhaus is no rabid sectarian. He places tolerance at the heart of the nation's religious tradition, but he thinks it foolhardy to maintain a strict separation of church and state. Like MacIntyre, he sees liberal politics as a disguised form of civil war or at best an uneasy truce, and he, too, insists on the need of a common standard: "Without a transcendent or religious point of reference, conflicts of values cannot be resolved; there can only be procedures for their temporary accommodation." He recommends to his secular contemporaries that they furnish "the naked public square" with moral concepts borrowed from the biblical tradition, the only tradition of moral legitimation that is in his view "democratically supportable in [American] society" (Neuhaus 1986:110, 176).

As a sociological observer Neuhaus stands in a line of descent from Tocqueville, who saw in Jacksonian America's broadly diffused Christianity a positive influence that served to check partisanship and self-interest by imposing universal "habits of restraint." It was Tocqueville's judgment that "while the law allows the American people to do everything, there are things which religion prevents them from imagining and forbids them to dare" (Tocqueville 1969:292). Unhappily for Neuhaus, the Christian nation that received Tocqueville in the 1830s no longer exists (if, indeed, America ever was quite as Tocqueville saw it). To the degree that religion might be said to have supplied a national conscience, or universal "habits of restraint," it reflected a pervasive Protestant influence rooted in the common cultural origins of the early settlers and the homogenizing effect of colonial and frontier life. Even in Tocqueville's day, however, America's Protestant identity was being undermined by the first of several massive waves of Catholic immigration, and the nation was already experiencing the secularizing trends associated with modernization (Kelley 1979:171–72).

Moreover, it is not at all clear that "the biblical tradition" is "democratically supportable" in American society. Neuhaus conveniently overlooks the long history of religious controversy in the United States. If nineteenth-century Christians generally agreed that the Bible belonged in the classroom, that did not prevent Protestants and Catholics from waging political warfare to determine which version of the Bible would be taught (e.g., Montgomery 1972). Similar controversies rage today whenever religion and politics are brought into contact, as for example on the question of abortion. The sorts of political dangers inherent in religious conflict led Locke to propose the privatization of conscience in his writings on toleration, and Locke was no enemy of biblical religion. By restricting the public business to men's "civil interests" he hoped not only to save the state from sectarian discord but to save religion from the state (Eisenach 1981:76–83).

The authors of *Habits of the Heart* write of a second alternative to the liberal tradition that in their view complements the religious perspective. This is the legacy of republicanism that recent historiography associates with the Revolution and the Founding (Bellah et al. 1985:27–31; Bailyn 1967; Pocock 1975b; Wood 1969; cf. Diggins 1984). William Sullivan, a contributor to *Habits of the Heart*, has developed this theme extensively elsewhere. On his reading the American past is a story of political corruption, detailing the loss of republican "civic virtue." The villain of the piece is liberal individualism, which Sullivan accuses of having undermined the "public philosophy" of the Revolutionary era. With the loss of the Founders' common vision there grew up the familiar politics of conflicting private interests. The end result, according to Sullivan, is that modern politics, lacking a moral basis, serves only "the unfettered pursuit of desire" (Sullivan 1982:71). In order to redirect human energies toward mutually beneficial, commonly held goals, he believes it necessary to develop a new public philosophy rooted in the republican past.

"A public philosophy," Sullivan explains, "is an expression and vehicle of practical reason in its classical sense, embodied in the life of a people and bound up with that people's reflection upon itself and its project." Republicanism, unlike atomistic liberalism, is a truly "public" philosophy because it "addresses directly the craving of the human self for a life of inclusion in a community of mutual concern." This claim is troubling if we harbor any doubt that most persons do in fact crave community. Sullivan has no doubts. He takes it for granted that "human nature is naturally disposed to find its fulfillment in what is called a life of virtue" (Sullivan 1982:90, 159, 162–63).

The argument is back on MacIntyre's turf, but the conceptual fog surrounding the virtues still lingers. Civic virtue, we are told, "is the excellence of character proper to a citizen." It is "substantive" freedom understood as "the capacity to attain one's good, where *goodness* describes the full enjoyment of those capacities which characterize a flourishing human life." We are in need of virtue because we are by nature social beings for whom living well requires a shared life.

> And a shared life is possible only when members of a community trust and respect one another. To participate in a shared life is to show concern for and reciprocity to one's fellows, and to do so is simultaneously fulfilling for the individual. Thus the individual's true good must consist not in attaining a sum of satisfactions, but in showing in himself, and sharing as a participant, an admirable and worthwhile form of life. (Sullivan 1982:163)

Unhappily, Sullivan's lyric celebration of virtue leaves hanging the concepts of human flourishing and the good. What do trust, respect, and reciprocity require of political actors? What are the institutional requirements of an admirable and worthwhile form of life? We are told that the renewal of civic virtue will end "the domination of social relationships by bureaucratic management and capitalist economics," but we are not told how or why (Sullivan 1982:183).

Sullivan begins to fill in the details of his republican vision when he explains that justice "finds its *telos* and so its orientation beyond itself in *philia*, or fellowship," and that "distribution of the possibilities for sharing the good life must treat all citizens with equal concern but must recognize their different needs and contributions to the overall community." Still, what fellowship demands of justice is not self-evident and yields no clear-cut principles to guide the distribution of possibilities for sharing the good life, whatever that turns out to be. Like MacIntyre, Sullivan cryptically asserts that the key to the treasure *is* the treasure; the enigmatic common good "always depends on shared understandings derived from a tradition of cultivated experience" and thus requires that the civic community "continually struggle to articulate anew the concrete meaning of justice for the situation" (Sullivan 1982:175–76; cf. Hirsch 1986).

Despite the general tenor of communitarian theory, not all communitarians are implacably hostile toward Locke's legacy. Michael Walzer, for instance, might best be described as a friendly adversary. He congratulates Locke and the early architects of liberal theory for drawing the public/private distinction separating politics from other dimensions of society. Contradicting critics who maintain that this distinction is founded on an illusion, he claims that it is "a morally and politically necessary adaptation to the complexities of modern life" (Walzer 1984:319).

The "art of separation," as Walzer calls it, creates a plurality of social spheres protecting conscience, religious observance, economic behavior, and domestic arrangements from unwanted political intervention. Liberal theory goes wrong in Walzer's view when it conceives of rights as placing each individual within his or her own protected sphere. The individual who stands "wholly outside institutions and relationships and enters into them only when he or she chooses or as he or she chooses . . . does not exist and cannot exist in any conceivable social world" (Walzer 1984:324). By pursuing this mistaken conception of freedom, liberals encourage a radical individualism incompatible with organized society. (We know we are in trouble, he observes, when discussions of a child's right to divorce her parents are taken seriously.) Walzer argues that contrary to the prevailing view of rights, "we do not separate individuals; we separate institutions, practices, relationships of different sorts. The lines we draw encircle churches and schools and markets and families, not you and me. We aim, or we should aim, not at the freedom of the solitary individual but at what can best be called institutional integrity. Individuals should be free, indeed, in all sorts of ways, but we don't set them free by separating them from their fellows" (Walzer 1984:325).

The integrity of the several distinct social spheres is necessary to protect the various practices that occur within them. To allow boundary crossing at this level is to risk the corruption of those practices. Thus, for example, if money—which has an appropriate role to play in the economic sphere—is used to buy love or religious salvation, their meaning is altered; gifts of affection and of grace become commodities of a sort and wealth comes to dominate where previously it bought no advantage (Walzer 1983:227–29, 243–45).

The integrity of the spheres is vitally important to politics. In Walzer's view, the logic internal to the art of separation leaves no alternative to democracy in the political sphere. Democracy, he writes, is "*the political way* of allocating power." What distinguishes democracy from other ways of allocating power in society is that it prizes speech above all other human talents. "Ideally, the citizen who makes the most persuasive argument—that is, the argument that actually persuades the largest number of citizens—gets his way." Force, bribery, and intimidation are out of place in political life because they violate our shared understanding of what counts as a good argument (Walzer 1983:304). Ideally, reason monopolizes the political sphere.

Historically, strength, knowledge, status, and wealth have all intruded on the domain of reasoned argument. Locke's philosophy effectively neutralizes the claims of the first three, but it leaves politics vulnerable to the fourth. The political claims of ownership are such that Locke's libertarian successors would happily depose politics in favor of the market. Walzer confronts the libertarian case for private "government" in discussing the historical example of Pullman, Illinois, a town built by nineteenth-century industrialist George Pullman for the workers in his factories near Chicago. Pullman owned the town and set strict rules of personal conduct for the people who lived there, who were of course free to live elsewhere if they chose. Thus, the worker's (negative) freedom was undiminished, and Pullman acted entirely within his rights as a property owner. But Pullman's "benevolent, well-wishing feudalism" as one contemporary journalist called it, did not sit well with the residents. Some twenty years after the experiment was begun the Illinois Supreme Court ordered the Pullman Company to divest itself of all property in the town not used for manufacturing purposes. The court ruled, and Walzer agrees, that ownership of a town violates the spirit of American democracy. Pullman went too far when he assumed that a right of ownership entitled him to exercise political rule as well. If he wanted power, Walzer comments, "he should have run for mayor" (Walzer 1983:295–303).

The moral that Walzer draws from the history of Pullman is designed to illustrate what he takes to be our shared understanding of politics. If in our culture we did not distinguish between the sorts of power that flow from the rights of property and from political power, the story would serve no point. Indeed, Walzer is unwilling to judge harshly an undemocratic culture where illiberal social practices receive genuine popular support, as may have once been true of the Indian caste system (Walzer 1983:27). This reticence to judge other cultures, which has drawn accusations of moral relativism (Dworkin 1985), owes to Walzer's insistence that social meaning is internal to social practices. On this view, criticism of a practice is misplaced if it imposes a judgment not shared by (or simply unintelligible to) the participants (cf. Downing and Thigpen 1985 and 1986).

The importance of shared understandings underscores the communitarian bias to Walzer's argument. Social practices cohere within a dense network of shared understandings that constitute the collective identity of a particular people. Yet these understandings need not be entirely consistent; after all, communitarians like Walzer abide with libertarians like Nozick. As adversaries who share membership in a liberal-democratic political community, their quarrel has largely to do with the appropriate interpretation of communal values. And because we consider the political sphere autonomous in our community (or so Walzer claims), all such arguments must be settled democratically.

It may be questioned, however, whether liberal democracy does in fact sufficiently insulate the political sphere from external influence. Benjamin Barber contends that it does not. In Barber's view, liberal democracy is not strongly democratic enough; liberalism, he complains, treats public life solely as a means to private ends. This legitimates the substitution of economic for political power in an unequal competition among social groups. Ironically, it also favors paternalism at the expense of participation; under liberal auspices the modern state has established a passive client-consumer of bureaucratic services in place of the active citizen-participant envisioned by classical democratic theory. Still, Barber follows Walzer in not rejecting liberalism out of hand. Optimistically, he writes that "there is little wrong with liberal institutions that a strong dose of political participation and reactivated citizenship cannot cure" (Barber 1984:xi).

Barber proposes a conception of politics that he calls "strong democracy," a communitarian reading of democratic politics in which partisan conflict gives way to a process of mutual accommodation through the discovery of shared values and the invention of common ends. Like Walzer, he believes that democracy is about reasoned argument. At the heart of his theory of strong democracy lies the concept of "political talk." In contrast with liberal democratic conversation ("animal expletives meant to signify bargaining positions in a world of base competition"), strong democratic talk goes beyond the articulation of interests to the exploration of mutuality and the cultivation of friendship. Barber likens what he has in mind to the conversation of neighbors who listen to one another in a spirit of empathy. "Politics," he explains, "is the art of engaging strangers in talk and of stimulating in them an artificial kinship made in equal parts of empathy, common cause, and enlightened self-interest" (Barber 1984:189).

In strong democracy the common good must be consciously fashioned by the citizens themselves as they confront matters of public importance that demand a collective choice. Unlike theories of community that rely on teleological conceptions of virtue, Barber's strong democracy knows nothing of *the* human good; instead, it entertains the notion of "alternative visions that compete for communal acceptance." The challenge facing participants in Barber's communitarian democracy "is to envision the human future and then to inspire a passion in others for that vision—often by adapting it to their vision" (Barber 1984:169, 170). This approach to the good makes no special claims about human nature. It assumes only that human beings are capable of fellowship and that fellowship may be encouraged through participation in the political process. Barber hopes that active participation will make tangible the full significance of membership in the community and thereby promote a general sense of civic responsibility. In this manner, the excessively self-regarding behavior that Rousseau described in terms of the particular political will might be replaced by a truly democratic (and uncoerced) general will. Barber observes that among strong democrats the political demand "I want X" must be reconceived as "X would be good for the community to which I belong." This, he insists, is "an exercise in social algebra for which not every 'X' will be suitable" (Barber 1984:171).

Yet Barber's conception of the common good is problematic. He wants a strong form of community—true fellowship animated by a sense of shared purpose—that at the same time respects individuality and personal autonomy. As he himself seems ready to admit, this is a tall order; "institutions that can facilitate the search for common ends without sabotaging the individuality of the searchers, and that can acknowledge pluralism and conflict as starting points of the political process without abdicating the quest for a world of common ends, may be much more difficult to come by than a pretty paragraph about the dialectical interplay between participation and community" (Barber 1984:155). How are the demands of community and the desire for autonomy to be kept in balance?

Liberals answer this question by turning to the doctrine of rights; communitarians, however, are wary of this stratagem. Rights-centered theories of politics characteristically set the right (or principles of justice) prior to the good (in this case, the common ends chosen or affirmed by the democratic community). Drawing on the logic of Taylor's social thesis, Michael Sandel argues that this approach to politics treats our political commitments superficially, as though no person's commitment to a way of life could be so deeply felt that it constituted a portion of his or her self-identity. He further argues that because rights apply to persons who are at least partially defined by their commitments, they need to be anchored in shared political understandings; otherwise they have no solid purchase in the world. Thus, Sandel prefers to ground the argument for extending civil rights to previously excluded social groups not as a Kantian might in respect for the dignity of persons abstractly considered but in the community's understanding of what citizenship requires; the socially agreed-upon meaning of the term demands that everyone recognize "the full membership of fellow citizens wrongly excluded from the common life of the nation" (Sandel 1987:91; 1984).

Similarly, Barber avoids entrenching rights in the constitution of strong democracy. Still, he retains a liberal sensibility. He fully expects that citizens imbued with democratic consciousness will value fellowship so highly that no majority would ever abuse its power. How could one citizen harm another when the reciprocal obligations of membership in the community are at least partially constitutive of every citizen's sense of self? Intolerance, discrimination, and the oppression of others become a form of self-betrayal. In Sandel's terms, the political community should be thought of more like a family, where benevolence rather than justice governs personal relationships (Sandel 1982:31–33). Yet what if benevolence fails or the spirit of democratic mutualism wavers? Ultimately, the best defense of freedom Barber can recommend is constant vigilance. "A moment's complacency," he warns, "may mean the death of liberty" (Barber 1984:191).

POLITICS AFTER LOCKE

In the Reagan era American conservatives combined libertarian and communitarian themes in their campaign against Big Government. It made for a successful electoral strategy, but ideologically there was dissonance. While libertarians in the Reagan coalition railed against state intervention in the economy, the communitarians of the religious right complained of a decline in public morals facilitated by liberal jurists, educators, and federal bureaucrats. Libertarian activists had no use for the power of leviathan beyond the requirements of the national defense; the moral majoritarians, on the other hand, sought political power to enforce their notion of decent community standards (Newman 1989).

Libertarian opposition to the welfare state is not very popular on the Left. Community, however, may be catching on. Consider the advice offered to the Democratic party in 1988 by Harvard political theorist Michael Sandel. Writing in *The New Republic* he urged the Democrats to make the recovery of community a prominent theme in their presidential campaign. Lifting a page from the conservatives he blamed the anxieties of the age on "the erosion of those communities intermediate between the individual and the nation, from families and neighborhoods to cities and towns to communities defined by religious or ethnic or cultural traditions." This was unfortunate because American democracy historically relied on communities to generate a socially necessary public spiritedness. "Self-government requires community," he argued, "for people aspire to control their destiny not only as individuals, but as participants in a common life with which they can identify" (Sandel 1988:22).

Sandel believes that the public philosophy of rights and entitlements inaugurated by the New Deal led the Democratic party to ignore the "longing" for community in the electorate, and this gave an opening to Ronald Reagan and the religious right in the 1980s. On a rhetorical level, the Reagan administration successfully played up the moral dimension to common life by condemning the local impact of intrusive federal policies; however, the Reaganites were silent about the equally disruptive effects of private (market) power. It is in this regard that Sandel spies an opening on the Left: "Leaving local communities to the mercy of corporate decisions made in distant places does not empower them; if anything it diminishes their ability to shape their destiny." In a populist vein he advises liberals to put aside their preoccupation with individual rights. By rediscovering the common good, he proposes, they can set communitarian ideals to work for liberal purposes (i.e., Great Society–style social programs).

Community turned out to be a popular buzz word in both the Democratic and Republican campaigns in 1988, suggesting that speech writers are indeed attentive to intellectual trends. Still, communitarian theorists to the contrary, it is not evident that a majority of voters are ready to cast their ballots for one or another version of the communitarian ideal. Indeed, despite the demonstrated electoral appeal of Reaganism, recent polling data show that only 14 percent of the electorate provide a constituency for the moralistic communitarianism of the Right. And there is simply no reason to believe that a Left communitarianism, distinguished by its populist economic platform, would fare any better. Communitarians will be disappointed that in the same survey roughly 16 percent of the voters expressed support for hyperindividualistic libertarianism (*New York Times*, 1988).

The libertarian constituency is young, affluent, well educated, highly secular, and mostly white (Maddox and Lilie 1984). In contrast, the most prominent communitarian constituency, the religious right, draws the bulk of its fundamentalist Christian supporters from the working and lower classes (Simpson 1983). The popularity of libertarian individualism may be thought to reflect the antipaternalist sentiments of a cosmopolitan elite, a sort of Yuppie radicalism asserting the inalienable right of individuals to choose their lifestyle according to their own likes and the size of their bank accounts. Moralistic communitarianism, on the other hand, expresses the cultural anxieties experienced by groups on the periphery of society and occasioned by their normative differences with the dominant center. Libertarianism and communitarianism in this sense stand opposite one another in America's cultural politics.

It is a curious legacy of America's monolithic Lockean heritage that cultural conflict of this sort displaces class conflict and that class differences are expressed in terms of opposing lifestyles. So strong is Locke's hold on the American political imagination, and so closely is his political legacy bound up with modern capitalism, that conservative and socialist ideas must be smuggled in under another name. This, I think, is the real significance of communitarianism. In a splendid irony, it provides the vehicle for both a moral majoritarianism that seems close in spirit to Filmer's political authoritarianism and notions of economic democracy that look like socialism but scrupulously avoid the label.

The popularity of libertarian and communitarian ideas suggests both the enduring strength and the peculiar weakness of the American liberal tradition. It is a telling comment on the persistence of Lockean ideology in American culture that the strained libertarian reading of the *Second Treatise* has as much influence as it does. At the same time, the emotionally powerful quest for community indicates the presence of a gap in contemporary liberal theory that an atomistic reading of Locke's philosophy cannot fill. What is generally missing from both libertarian and communitarian political theory is a Lockean appreciation of the importance of politics. Locke effectively narrowed the classical conception of politics, creating room for a social space inhabited not by citizens but by private individuals (Wolin 1960); nonetheless, in the *Second Treatise* politics still has its own sphere, and Locke is careful not to confuse political matters with the economic or moral concerns of domestic and social life. Libertarians and communitarians (Michael Walzer excepted) depart from Locke insofar as they dissolve politics in one or the other of these until nothing else remains. In effect, we are left with a choice of modeling the political community on either the market or on the family, neither of which is adequate to the ends Locke set for civil society.

Ultimately, libertarian and communitarian theories invite cynical reply. Fanciful proposals to resurrect the night-watchman state or the virtuous republic seem oddly ill-equipped to meet the challenges posed by corporate capitalism at home, superpower confrontations abroad, and the omnipresent threat of nuclear devastation. Can anyone doubt that in the modern world freedom and community are hostage to powers beyond the reach of private individuals acting alone or in small or close-knit groups? Yet the temptation to believe otherwise is strong. Our folklore has mythologized both libertarian and communitarian icons: The heroic figure of the rugged individualist persists alongside cherished images of the extended family, the local church, and the old neighborhood. Disturbed by the complexity, impersonalism, and interdependence characteristic of modern society, we may find ourselves longing wistfully for the romantic independence of life on the frontier two hundred years ago or for the comforting intimacy associated with small towns and rural communities in the last century. In such moments we would do well to recall the words of Louis Hartz, the sagacious chronicler of our liberal tradition, who warned against the politics of nostalgia: "As for a child who is leaving adolescence, there is no going home again for America" (Hartz 1955:32). Hartz was mistaken, though, if he believed that Locke's philosophy was necessarily one of the childish things to be put away. The politically impoverished theories offered by libertarians and communitarians unintentionally suggest how much we still might learn from a careful reading of the *Second Treatise*.

NOTES

1. I have in mind theories of the sort put forward in recent years by Bruce Ackerman, John Rawls, and Robert Nozick. Though these theorists draw on philosophers other than Locke (notably Kant), I maintain that each of their arguments easily accommodates—indeed, seems intended for—the Lockean American polity. Despite their well-known disagreements with one another, all three share a commitment to some form of individualism, claim-rights, and voluntarism.

2. Much of what follows is drawn from my book, *Liberalism at Wit's End: The Libertarian Revolt against the Modern State*. I have updated and extended the discussion through inclusion of recently published material.

3. Since writing this paper I have been persuaded by Richard Ashcraft that Locke intended the duty to preserve the rest of mankind to be stronger than I make out here. Ashcraft points out that the duty to preserve mankind is a divine commandment and must be accorded serious weight if we are to take Locke's religious arguments seriously, and nothing in the text gives us warrant to do otherwise.

4. Discussions with Richard Ashcraft, Ruth Grant, and Nathan Tarcov have convinced me that Locke's thought was less atomistic than I have portrayed it here. Although I insist on continuing to view Locke as an individualist, I am now willing to concede that Lockean nature not only allows for a community of interest but also constitutes a moral community defined by the divine precepts embodied in natural law. The repudiation of this community in the name of individual conscience would remove the foundation of the social compact and doom Locke's project to failure. See Ashcraft (1986), Grant (1988), and Tarcov (1983). In one sense Lockean nature lacks institutional expression prior to the social compact. It is entirely possible for the members of this moral community in the state of nature to be complete strangers to one another!

Bibliography

The bibliography includes leading books and articles written about or related to Locke's *Two Treatises of Government* as well as those cited in the text.

Aaron, Richard I. (1971). *John Locke*. 3d ed. Oxford: Clarendon Press.

Aarsleff, Hans (1969). "The State of Nature and the Nature of Man in Locke." In *John Locke: Problems and Perspectives*. Ed. John W. Yolton, 99–136. Cambridge: Cambridge University Press.

Abrams, M. H. (1971). *Natural Supernaturalism: Tradition and Revolution in Romantic Literature*. New York: W. W. Norton.

Abrams, Philip (1967). "John Locke as a Conservative: An Edition of Locke's Writings on Political Obligation." Ph.D. diss., Cambridge University. Revised for publication in Philip Abrams, ed. *Two Tracts on Government*. Cambridge: Cambridge University Press.

Albritton, Robert R. (1976). "The Politics of Locke's Philosophy." *Political Studies* 24(June): 253–267.

Allen, Jerry Brent (1976). "Hegel's Political Theory as a Critique of Modern Natural Right and Especially Lockean Liberalism." Ph.D. diss., Claremont Graduate School.

Allen, J. W. (1967). *English Political Thought, 1603–1644*. Hamden, Conn.: Archon Books.

Alston, W. P., and J. Bennett (1988). "Locke on People and Substances." *Philosophical Review* 97(January): 25–46.

Andrew, Edward (1988). *Shylock's Rights: A Grammar of Lockean Claims*. Toronto: University of Toronto Press.

Anglim, John Gerald (1975). "Locke and Toleration." Ph.D. diss., Harvard University.

———(1978). "On Locke's State of Nature." *Political Studies* 26(March): 78–90.

Appleby, Joyce D. (1976a). "Ideology and Theory: Tension between Political and Economic Liberalism in Seventeenth Century England." *American Historical Review* 81(June): 499–515.

———(1976b). "Locke, Liberalism and the Natural Law of Money." *Past and Present* 71(May): 43–69.

———(1978). *Economic Thought and Ideology in Seventeenth-Century England*. Princeton, N.J.: Princeton University Press.

———(1982). "What Is Still American in the Political Philosophy of Thomas Jefferson?" *William and Mary Quarterly*, 3d ser., 39(April): 287–309.

———(1984). *Capitalism and a New Social Order: The Republican Vision of the 1790s*. New York: New York University Press.

———(1986). "Republicanism in Old and New Contexts." *William and Mary Quarterly*, 3d ser., 43(January): 20–34.

Arenilla, Lavis (1986). "The Notion of Civil Disobedience According to Locke." *Diogenes* 35(Fall): 109–135.

Arnhart, Larry (1979). "'The God-Like Prince': John Locke, Executive Prerogative and the American Presidency." *Presidential Studies Quarterly* 9(Spring): 121–130.

Ashcraft, Richard E[ldon] (1966). "The Foundations of John Locke's Political Thought." Ph.D. diss., University of California at Berkeley.

———(1968). "Locke's State of Nature: Historical Fact or Moral Fiction?" *American Political Science Review* 62(September): 898–915.

———(1969). "Faith and Knowledge in Locke's Philosophy." In *John Locke: Problems and Perspectives*. Ed. John Yolton, 194–233. Cambridge: Cambridge University Press.

———(1972). "John Locke Belimed: The Case of Political Philosophy." *Political Studies* 20(June): 190–194.

———(1980a). "Political Theory and the Problem of Ideology." *Journal of Politics* 42(August): 687–705.

———(1980b). "Revolutionary Politics and Locke's *Two Treatises of Government*: Radicalism and Lockean Political Theory." *Political Theory* 8(November): 429–486.

———(1980c). "The *Two Treatises* and the Exclusion Crisis: The Problem of Lockean Political Theory as Bourgeois Ideology." In *John Locke: Papers Read at a Clark Library Seminar, 10 December 1977*, 27–114. Los Angeles: William Andrews Clark Memorial Library, University of California.

———(1984). "Marx and Political Theory." *Comparative Studies in Society and History* 26 (October): 637–671.

———(1986). *Revolutionary Politics and Locke's Two Treatises of Government*. Princeton, N.J.: Princeton University Press.

———(1987). *Locke's Two Treatises of Government*. London: Allen & Unwin.

Ashcraft, Richard, and M. M. Goldsmith (1983). "Locke, Revolution Principles, and the Formation of Whig Ideology." *Historical Journal* 26(December): 773–800.

Axtell, James L., ed. (1968). "Some Thoughts Concerning Education." In *The Educational Writings of John Locke*. Cambridge: Cambridge University Press.

Backscheider, P. R. (1988). "The Verse Essay, John Locke and Defoe's Jure Divino." *English Literary History* 55(Spring): 99–123.

Bailyn, Bernard (1967). *The Ideological Origins of the American Revolution*. Cambridge, Mass.: Belknap Press of Harvard University Press.

Banning, Lance (1978). *The Jeffersonian Persuasion: Evolution of a Party Ideology*. Ithaca, N.Y.: Cornell University Press.

Barber, Benjamin (1984). *Strong Democracy*. Berkeley: University of California Press.

Batz, William G. (1974). "The Historical Anthropology of John Locke." *Journal of the History of Ideas* 35(October/December): 663–670.

Bay, Christian (1978). "From Contract to Community." In *From Contract to Community: Political Theory at the Crossroads*. Ed. F. Dallmayer. New York: Marcel Kekkere.

Becker, Lawrence C. (1976). "The Labor Theory of Property Acquisition." *Journal of Philosophy* 73(21 October): 653–664.

Beitz, Charles (1980). "Tacit Consent and Property Rights." *Political Theory* 8(November): 487–502.

Bellah, Robert, Richard Madsen, William Sullivan, Ann Swindler, and Steven Tipton (1985). *Habits of the Heart: Individualism and Commitment in American Life*. Berkeley: University of California Press.

Bennett, John G. (1979). "A Note on Locke's Theory of Tacit Consent." *Philosophical Review* 88(April): 224–234.

Bercovitch, Sacvan (1975). *The Puritan Origins of the American Self*. New Haven, Conn.: Yale University Press.

Berlin, Isaiah (1964). "Hobbes, Locke and Professor Macpherson." *Political Quarterly* 35(October/December): 444–468.

———(1969). *Four Essays on Liberty*. London: Oxford University Press.

Biddle, J. C. (1976). "Locke's Critique of Innate Principles and Toland's Deism." *Journal of the History of Ideas* 37(July): 411–422.

Bourne, Henry Richard Fox (1876). *The Life of John Locke*, 2 vols. London: H. S. King.

Bracken, Harry M. (1961). "Locke, Berkeley, Hume: The End of a Triumvirate." *Indian Journal of Philosophy* 3(August): 1–8.

Brandt, Reinhard, ed. (1981). *John Locke Symposium*. Berlin: de Gruyter.

Brennan, Teresa, and Carole Pateman (1979). "Mere Auxiliaries to the Commonwealth: Women and the Origins of Liberalism." *Political Studies* 27(June): 183–200.

Bronowski, Jacob, and Bruce Mazlisk (1960). "Hobbes and Locke." In *The Western Tradition: From Leonardo to Hegel*, 193–215. New York: Harper.

Budziszewski, J. (1986). *The Resurrection of Nature*. Ithaca, N.Y.: Cornell University Press.

Burke, Edmund (1973). *Reflections on the Revolution in France*. Garden City, N.Y.: Anchor/Doubleday.

Burns, J. H. (1983). "Jus Gladii and Jurisdictio: Jacques Atmain and John Locke." *Historical Journal* 26(June): 369–374.

Byrne, James W. (1964). "The Basis of Natural Law in Locke's Philosophy." *Catholic Lawyer* 10(Winter): 55–68, 87.

———(1968). "The Meaning of Natural Law in Locke's Philosophy." *Personalist* 49(Winter): 142–158.

Caffentzis, Constantina George (1989). *Clipped Coins, Abused Words and Civil Government: John Locke's Philosophy of Money*. Brooklyn: Autonomedia.

Carswell, John (1960). *The South Sea Bubble*. London: Cresset Press.

Clark, L. M. G. (1977). "Woman and John Locke, or Who Owns the Apples in the Garden of Eden?" *Canadian Journal of Philosophy* 7:699–724.

Cohen, Joshua (1986). "Structure, Choice, and Legitimacy: Locke's Theory of the State." *Philosophy and Public Affairs* 15(Fall): 301–324.

Colella, E. P. (1984). "The Commodity Form and Socialization in Locke's State of Nature." *International Studies in Philosophy* 16:1–13.

Coleman, John (1983). *John Locke's Moral Philosophy*. Edinburgh: Edinburgh University Press.

Conniff, James (1982). "Reason and History in Early Whig Thought: The Case of Algernon Sidney." *Journal of the History of Ideas* 93(July–September): 397–416.

Cox, Richard Howard (1960). *Locke on War and Peace*. Oxford: Clarendon Press.

———(1963). "Justice as the Basis of Political Order in Locke." In *Nomas: Yearbook* 6, Justice, 243–261.

Cranston, Maurice (1957). *John Locke: A Biography*. New York: Macmillan.

———(1961a). *Locke*. London: Longmans, Green.

———(1961b). "The Politics of a Philosopher." *Listener* 5 January, 17–19.

———(1966). "John Locke and Government by Consent." In *Political Ideas*. Ed. David Thomson, 64–78. Culture and Discovery Series. New York: Basic Books.

Critelli, Ida Joann (1965). "The Political Good in the Philosophy of John Locke." Ph.D. diss., Marquette University.

Cuervo, Robert T. (1988). "Ruth W. Grant: *John Locke's Liberalism*." *Journal of Politics* 50(August): 800–803.

Curry, Patricia Elaine (1973). "The American Experience through a Glass Darkly: Three Case Studies in the Political Thought of John Locke and the Novels of James Fenimore Cooper." Ph.D. diss., Indiana University.

Curti, Merle (1937). "The Great Mr. Locke: America's Philosopher, 1783–1861." *Huntington Library Bulletin* 11(April): 107–151.

Cvek, P. P. (1984). "Locke's Theory of Property: A Reexamination." *Auslesung* 11.

Dawson, D. J. (1974). "John Locke, the Draft, and the Divine Right of Kings." In *The Libertarian Alternative*. Ed. Tibor R. Machan, 466–477. Chicago: Nelson Hall.

Day, J. Patrick (1966). "Locke on Property." *Philosophical Quarterly* 16(July): 207–220.

DeBeer, E. S., ed. (1976–1985). *The Correspondence of John Locke*. 8 vols. Oxford: Clarendon Press.

DeMarchi, Ernesto R. (1962). "The Origin of John Locke's Theory of Toleration." D. Phil. diss., Oxford University.

Dempsey, Bernard W. (1965). "Just Price in a Functional Economy." In *Economic Thought: A Historical Anthology*. Ed. James Arthur Gherity. New York: Random House.

d'Entreves, A. P. (1951). *Natural Law*. London: Hutchinson.

Derringh, Frank William (1980). "Personal Autonomy and Locke's Theory of Property, with Special Attention to Modern Commentators." Ph.D. diss., Columbia University.

Devine, Donald J. (1978). "John Locke: His Harmony between Liberty and Virtue." *Modern Age* 22(Summer): 246–257.

———(1988). "The Opening of the Socratic Mind." *Modern Age* 32(Winter): 14–20.

Devine, Francis Edward (1975). "Absolute Democracy or Indefeasible Right: Hobbes versus Locke." *Journal of Politics* 37(August): 736–768.

Dickinson, H. T. (1977). *Liberty and Property: Political Ideology in Eighteenth-Century Britain*. New York: Holmes and Meier.

Dickson, P. G. M. (1967). *The Financial Revolution in England: A Study in the Development of Public Credit, 1688–1756*. London: Macmillan.

Diggins, John Patrick (1984). *The Lost Soul of American Politics: Virtue, Self-Interest, and the Foundations of Liberalism*. New York: Basic Books.

———(1985). "Comrades and Citizens: New Mythologies in American Historiography." *American Historical Review* 90 (June 1988): 614–638.

Downing, Lyle, and Robert B. Thigpen (1985). "Communitarian Theory and Domination." Paper presented at the 1985 meeting of the American Political Science Association, New Orleans. Mimeo.

———(1986). "Beyond Shared Understandings." *Political Theory* 14(August): 451–472.

Downing, Paul Mayhen (1960). "A Comparison of the Doctrines of St. Thomas and John Locke on the Right of Political Authority." Ph.D. diss., Columbia University.

Downs, Robert Bingham (1961). "Apologist for Revolution." In *Molders of the Modern Mind*, 91–94. New York: Barnes & Noble.

Driver, Charles (1967). "John Locke." In *The Social and Political Ideas of Some English Thinkers of the Augustan Age 1650–1750*. Ed. F. J. C. Hearnshaw. New York: Barnes and Noble.

Drury, Shadia B. (1982). "Locke and Nozick on Property." *Political Studies* 30(March): 28–41.

Dunn, John (1962). "The Identity of the History of Ideas." In *Philosophy, Politics and Society*. Ser. 4. Ed. Peter Laslett, W. G. Runciman, and Quentin Skinner, 158–173. New York: Harper and Row, 1972.

———(1967). "Consent in the Political Theory of John Locke." *Historical Journal* 10(July): 153–182.

———(1968). "Justice and the Interpretation of Locke's Political Theory." *Political Studies* 16(February): 68–87.

———(1969a). *The Political Thought of John Locke: An Historical Account of the Argument of the "Two Treatises of Government."* Cambridge: Cambridge University Press.

———(1969b). "The Politics of Locke in England and America in the Eighteenth Century." In *John Locke: Problems and Perspectives*. Ed. John Yolton, 45–80. Cambridge: Cambridge University Press.

———(1980). "Consent in the Political Theory of John Locke." In *Political Obligation in Its Historical Context*, 29–52. Cambridge: Cambridge University Press.

——— (1981). "Individuality and Clientage in the Formation of Locke's Social Imagination." In *John Locke Symposium, Wolfenbuttel 1979*, 43–73. Berlin: 1981.

———(1983). "From Applied Theology to Social Analysis: The Break between John Locke and the Scottish Enlightenment." In *Wealth and Virtue: The Shaping of the Political Economy in the Scottish Enlightenment*. Ed. Istvan Hont and Michael Ignatieff, 119–136. Cambridge: Cambridge University Press.

———(1984). *John Locke*. Oxford: Clarendon Press.

———(1985). "'Trust' in the Politics of John Locke." In *Rethinking Modern Political Theory*. Cambridge: Cambridge University Press.

———(1988). "Richard Ashcraft, Revolutionary Politics and Locke's *Two Treatises of Government.*" *Journal of Modern History* 60(June): 366–368.

Duty, Ronald William (1979). "The Theory of Property in British Political Thought: Locke, Hume, Burke and Bentham." Ph.D. diss., University of Minnesota.

Dworetz, Steven Michael (1986). "The Radical Side of American Constitutionalism: Locke and the New England Clergy, Revisited." Paper presented, April, New England Political Science Association Annual Convention, Hartford.

———(1990). The *Unvarnished Doctrine: Locke, Liberalism, and the American Revolution.* Durham, N.C.: Duke University Press.

Dworkin, Robert (1985). "What Justice Isn't." In his *A Matter of Principle.* Cambridge, Mass.: Harvard University Press.

Edwards, Stewart (1969). "Political Philosophy Belimed: The Case of Locke." *Political Studies* 17(September): 273–293.

Eisenach, Eldon J. (1978). "Crime, Death, and Loyalty in English Liberalism." *Political Theory* 6(May): 213–232.

———(1981). "John Locke." In *Two Worlds of Liberalism: Religion and Politics in Hobbes, Locke and Mill.* Chicago: University of Chicago Press.

———(1982). "Hobbes on Church, State and Religion." *History of Political Thought.* 3(Summer): 215–243.

Erleigh, Viscount (Gerald Refus Isaacs, 2d marquis of Reading) (1933). *The South Sea Bubble.* London: Peter Davies.

Evnine, Simon (1987). "Innate Principles and Radical Interpretations." *Locke News* 18:33–44.

Farr, James (1986). "'So Vile and Miserable an Estate': The Problem of Slavery in Locke's Political Thought." *Political Theory* 14(May): 263–289.

Farr, James, and Clayton Roberts (1985). "John Locke on the Glorious Revolution: A Rediscovered Document." *Historical Journal* 28(June): 385–398.

Ferguson, Adam (1980). *An Essay on the History of Civil Society.* New Brunswick, N.J.: Transaction Books.

Fishkin, James S. (1988). "Bargaining, Justice, and Justification: Towards Reconstruction." *Social Philosophy and Policy* 5(Spring): 46–64.

Fournier, J. (1978). "The Rise and Right of Commonwealths: An Exploration of John Locke's Considerations Concerning Political Association." M. Litt. diss., Oxford University.

Franklin, Julian H. (1978). *John Locke and the Theory of Sovereignty: Mixed Monarchy and the Right of Resistance in the Political Thought of the English Revolution.* Cambridge Studies in the History and Theory of Politics. Cambridge: Cambridge University Press.

———(1988). "Bodin and Locke on Consent to Taxation." *History of Political Thought* 7(Spring): 89–92.

Friedman, David (1973). *The Machinery of Freedom.* New York: Harper and Row.

Friedman, Jeffrey (1988). "Locke as Politician." *Critical Review* 2(Spring/Summer): 64–101.

Friedrich, Carl J. (1967). "The Doctrine of Liberalism: Locke and Mill." In *An Introduction to Political Theory: Twelve Lectures at Harvard University,* 14–28. New York: Harper.

Frye, Northrup (1983). *The Great Code: The Bible in Literature*. San Diego, Calif.: Harcourt Brace Jovanovich.

Gale, George (1973). "John Locke, an Unnoticed Aspect of the *Second Treatise*." *Political Theory* 4(November): 472–485.

Gauthier, Davide P. (1966). "The Role of Inheritance in Locke's Political Theory." *Canadian Journal of Economics and Political Science* 32(February): 38–45.

George, Charles H., and Catherine George (1961). *The Protestant Mind of the English Reformation, 1560–1640*. Princeton. N.J.: Princeton University Press.

———(1968). "Puritanism as History and Historiography." *Past and Present* 41(December): 77–104.

Glat, Mark (1978). "The Political Anthropology of John Locke and the Origin of Modern Politics." Ph.D. diss., Rutgers University.

———(1981). "John Locke's Historical Sense." *Review of Politics* 42(January): 3–21.

Glenn, Gary D. (1984). "Inalienable Rights and Locke's Argument for Limited Government: Political Implications for a Right to Suicide." *Journal of Politics* 46(February): 80–105.

Goldie, Mark (1980a). "The Roots of True Whiggism, 1688–94." *History of Political Thought* 1(June): 195–236.

———(1980b). "The Revolution of 1689 and the Structure of Political Argument." *Bulletin of Research in the Humanities* 83(Winter).

———(1983). "John Locke and Anglican Royalism." *Political Studies* 31(March): 61–85.

———(1987). "The Civil Religion of James Harrington." In *Ideas in Context: The Languages of Political Theory in Early Modern Europe*. Ed. Anthony Pagen. Cambridge: Cambridge University Press.

Goldsmith, M. M. (1979). "Entitlement Theory of Justice Considered." *Political Studies* 27(December): 578–593.

Goldwin, Robert Allen (1964). "Locke on Property." Ph.D. diss., University of Chicago.

———(1976). "Locke's State of Nature in Political Society." *Western Political Quarterly* 29(March): 126–135.

———(1981). "Locke and the Law of the Sea." *Commentary*, June, 46–50.

Goodale, Jessie R. (1980). "J. G. A. Pocock's Neo-Harringtonians: A Reconsideration." *History of Political Thought* 1(Summer): 237–259.

Goodwin, Barbara (1986). "The Political Philosophy of Money." *History of Political Thought* 7(Winter): 537–568.

Gough, John Wiedhofft (1956). *Locke's Political Philosophy*. Oxford: Clarendon Press.

———(1961). *Fundamental Law in English Constitutional History*. Oxford: Clarendon Press.

———(1973). *John Locke's Political Philosophy*. 2d ed. Oxford: Clarendon Press.

Gould, James A. (1971). "The Epistemological Grounds of Locke's Political Theory." In *Akten des 14. Internationalism Kongresses für Philosophie in Vienna, 2–9 September* 6:279–284. Vienna: Herder.

Grady, Robert Cowan (1972). "Political Obligation and Individualism: Hobbes and Locke." Ph.D. diss., Vanderbilt University.

————(1976). "Obligation, Consent, and Locke's Right to Revolution: Who Is to Judge?" *Canadian Journal of Political Science* 9(June): 277–292.

————(1977). "Property and 'Natural Political Virtue': The Implications of Locke as a 'Liberal'." *Polity* 10(Fall): 86–103.

Grant, Ruth W. (1984). *John Locke's Liberalism*. Chicago: University of Chicago Press.

————(1988). "Locke's Political Anthropology and Lockean Individualism." *Journal of Politics* 50(February): 42–63.

Gruendling, John E. (1970). "Nature as a Political and Legal Norm: Locke's Contribution." *Enlightenment Essays* 1(Spring): 33–49.

Gunn, J. A. W. (1969). *Politics and the Public Interest in the Seventeenth Century*. London and Toronto: University of Toronto Press.

————(1983). *Beyond Liberty and Property: The Process of Self-Recognition in Eighteenth-Century Political Thought*. Kingston and Montreal: McGill-Queen's University Press.

Habermas, Jurgen (1984). *The Theory of Communicative Action*. Boston: Beacon Press.

Hall, Robert Dennis (1981). "John Locke and Natural Human Rights: An Inconsistency between His Metaphysical and Epistemological Positions and His Moral and Political Theories." Ph.D. diss., St. John's University.

Hall, Ronald, and Roger Woolhouse (1983). *80 Years of Locke Scholarship*. Edinburgh: University Press.

Hampsher-Monk, Iain (1978). "Resistance and Economy in Dr. Anglim's Locke." *Political Studies* 26(March): 91–100.

————(1979). "Tacit Concept of Consent in Locke's *Two Treatises of Government*: A Note on Citizens, Travellers, and Patriarchalism." *Journal of the History of Ideas* 40(January/March): 135–139.

Hancey, James D. (1976). "John Locke and the Law of Nature." *Political Theory* 4(November): 439–454.

Handlin, Oscar, and Lilian Handlin (1989). "Who Read John Locke?" *American Scholar*, Autumn, 545–556.

Harpham, Edward J. (1984a). "Liberalism, Civic Humanism, and the Case of Adam Smith." *American Political Science Review* 78(September): 764–774.

————(1984b). "Natural Law and Early Liberal Economic Thought: A Reconsideration of Locke's Theories of Value." *Social Science Quarterly* 65(December): 966–974.

————(1985). "Class, Commerce and the State: Economic Discourse and Lockean Liberalism in the Seventeenth Century." *Western Political Quarterly* 38(December): 565–582.

Harris, N. G. E. (1988). "Locke's Triangles." *Canadian Journal of Philosophy* 18(March): 31–42.

Hartz, Louis (1955). *The Liberal Tradition in America: An Interpretation of American Political Thought since the Revolution*. New York: Harcourt, Brace and World.

Hayek, Friedrich (1960). *The Constitution of Liberty*. Chicago: University of Chicago Press.

————(1967). "The Result of Human Action, but Not of Human Design." *Studies in Philosophy, Politics and Economics*. Chicago: University of Chicago Press.

———(1973). *Law, Legislation and Liberty.* Vol. 1. Chicago: University of Chicago Press.

Hearn, Robert Wesley (1969). "Revolutionary Action and Political Society: The Lockean Formulation." Ph.D. diss., Yale University.

Herzog, Don (1989). *Happy Slaves: A Critique of Consent Theory.* Chicago: University of Chicago Press.

Hill, Christopher (1958). *Puritanism and Revolution.* London: Secker and Warburg.

———(1971). *Anti-Christ in Seventeenth-Century England.* London: Oxford University Press.

———(1975). *The World Upside Down.* Harmondsworth, U.K.: Penguin Books.

Hinton, R. W. K. (1974). "A Note on the Dating of Locke's *Second Treatise.*" *Political Studies* 22(December): 471–478.

———(1977). "On Recovering the Original of the *Second Treatise.*" *Locke Newsletter* 8.

Hirsch, N. H. (1986). "The Threnody of Liberalism: Constitutional Liberty and the Renewal of Community." *Political Theory* 14(August): 423–449.

Hoffheimer, Michael H. (1986). "Locke, Spinoza, and the Idea of Political Equality." *History of Political Thought* 7(Summer): 341–360.

Hont, Istvan, and Michael Ignatieff (1983a). "Needs and Justice in *The Wealth of Nations*: An Introductory Essay." In their *Wealth and Virtue: The Shaping of Political Economy in the Scottish Enlightenment.* Cambridge: Cambridge University Press.

———(1983b). *Wealth and Virtue: The Shaping of Political Economy in the Scottish Enlightenment.* Cambridge: Cambridge University Press.

Horwitz, Robert (1990). "Introduction." In John Locke's *Questions Concerning the Law of Nature.* Ed. Robert Horwitz, Jenny Strauss Clay, and Diskin Clay. 1–62. Ithaca, N.Y.: Cornell University Press.

Hospers, John (1971). *Libertarianism.* Los Angeles: Nash.

Hudson, Winthrop S. (1964). "John Locke—Preparing the Way for the Revolution." *Journal of Presbyterian History* 42(March): 19–38.

Hughes, Philip Edgcumbe (1965). *Theology of the English Reformers.* London: Hodder and Stoughton.

Hundert, E. J. (1972). "The Making of *Homo Faber*: John Locke between Ideology and History." *Journal of the History of Ideas* 33(January/March): 3–22.

———(1977). "Market Society and Meaning in Locke's Political Philosophy." *Journal of the History of Philosophy* 15(January): 33–44.

Hunt, John (1870–1871). *Religious Thought in England from the Reformation to the End of the Last Century.* 2 vols. London: Strahan.

Isaac, Jeffrey C. (1988). "Republicanism vs. Liberalism? A Reconsideration." *History of Political Thought* 9(Summer): 349–377.

Jacob, M. D. (1976). *The Newtonians and the English Revolution, 1689–1720.* Hassocks, Sussex: Harvester Press.

Jacobson, David L. (1965). "Introduction." In *The English Libertarian Heritage: From the Writings of John Trenchard and Thomas Gordon in "The Independent Whig" and "Cato's Letters".* Ed. David L. Jacobson. American Heritage Series. Indianapolis: Bobbs-Merrill.

Jaffa, Harry V. (1987). "Equality, Liberty, Wisdom, Morality and Consent in the Idea of Political Freedom." *Interpretation* 15(January): 3–28.

James, D. G. (1949). *The Life of Reason: Hobbes, Locke and Bolingbroke*. London: Longmans, Green.

Jenkins, J. J. (1967). "Locke and Natural Rights." *Philosophy* 42(April): 149–154.

Johnson, Merwyn Stratford (1977). *Locke on Freedom: An Incisive Study of the Thought of John Locke*. Austin, Tex.: Best.

Jolley, S. Nicholas (1975). "Leibniz on Hobbes, Locke's *Two Treatises* and Sherlock's *Case of Allegiance*." *Historical Journal* 18(March): 21–35.

Jonghe, E. De (1988). "Locke and Hooker on the Finding of the Law." *Review of Metaphysics* 42(December 1988): 301–325.

Kalberg, Stephen (1980). "Max Weber's Types of Rationality." *American Journal of Sociology* 85(March): 1145–1179.

Kelley, Patrick (1983). "James Tully, *A Discourse on Property: John Locke and His Adversaries*." *Journal of the History of Philosophy* 21(April): 240–242.

———(1988). "'All Things Richly to Enjoy': Economics and Politics in Locke's *Two Treatises of Government*." *Political Studies* 36(June): 273–293.

Kelley, Robert (1979). *The Cultural Pattern in American Politics*. Washington, D.C.: University Press of America.

Kemp, John (1962). "Critical Studies." *Philosophical Quarterly* 12(October): 356–364.

Kendall, Willmoore (1941). *John Locke and the Doctrine of Majority Rule. Illinois Studies in the Social Sciences*. Vol. 26, no. 2. Urbana: University of Illinois Press.

———(1966). "John Locke Revisited." *Intercollegiate Review* 2(January/February): 217–234.

Kenyon, J. P. (1972). *The Popish Plot*. London: Heinemann.

———(1977). *Revolutionary Principles: The Politics of Party, 1689–1720*. Cambridge: Cambridge University Press.

Khan, Galib A. (1987). "Locke's Theory of Significance." *Indian Philosophy Quarterly* 14(April/June): 135–140.

Kidder, Frederick E. (1965). "The Fundamental Constitutions of Carolina in the Light of John Locke's Political Theory." *Atenea* (Mayaquez, P.R.) 2, no. 1:47–60.

Kilcullen, John (1983). "Locke on Political Obligation." *Review of Politics* 45(July): 323–344.

Kim, Ha Poong (1964). "Locke's Political Theory: A Reconsideration of Its Systematic Unity." Ph.D. diss., Boston University.

King, Peter (1830). *The Life of John Locke*. 2 vols. London: H. Colburn and R. Bentley.

Kontos, Alkis Apostolou (1968). "The Idea of Revolution in the Political Philosophy of John Locke." Ph.D. diss., University of Pittsburgh.

Kramnick, Isaac (1967). "An Augustan Reply to Locke: Bolingbroke on Natural Law and the Origin of Government." *Political Science Quarterly* 82(December): 571–594.

———(1968). *Bolingbroke and His Circle: The Politics of Nostalgia in the Age of Walpole*. Cambridge, Mass.: Harvard University Press.

———(1982). "Republican Revisionism Revisited." *American Historical Review* 87(June): 629–664.

———(1990). *Republicanism and Bourgeois Radicalism: Political Ideology in*

Late Eighteenth-Century England and America. Ithaca, N.Y.: Cornell University Press.

Kraynak, Robert P. (1980). "John Locke: From Absolutism to Toleration." *American Political Science Review* 74(March): 53–69.

Kuhn, Thomas S. (1970). *The Structure of Scientific Revolutions*. 2d ed. Chicago: University of Chicago Press.

Lamprecht, Sterling P. (1962). *The Moral and Political Philosophy of John Locke*. New York: Russell and Russell.

Langford, M. J. (1967). "Natural Law in Seventeenth-Century Political Thought." Ph.D. diss., King's College, London.

Laprade, William Thomas (1936). *Public Opinion and Politics in Eighteenth-Century England to the Fall of Walpole*. New York: Macmillan.

Larkin, William Paschal (1930/1969). *Property in the Eighteenth Century with Special Reference to England and Locke*. New York: Kennikat Press.

Lasch, Christopher (1978). *The Culture of Narcissism*. New York: W. W. Norton.

Laski, Harold J. (1920). *Political Thought in England from Locke to Bentham*. New York: Henry Holt.

———(1936/1971). *The Rise of European Liberalism*. London: Unwin.

Laslett, Peter (1952). "Locke and the First Earl of Shaftesbury: Another Early Writing on the Understanding." *Mind* 61 (January): 89–92.

———(1956). "The English Revolution and Locke's *Two Treatises of Government*." *Cambridge Historical Journal* 12:40–55.

———(1957). "John Locke and the Great Recoinage and the Board of Trade, 1695–1698. *William and Mary Quarterly*, 3d ser., 14(July): 370–392.

———(1960, 1967, 1988). "Introduction" to John Locke's *Two Treatises of Government*. Ed. Peter Laslett. Cambridge: Cambridge University Press.

———(1964). "Market Society and Political Theory." *Historical Journal* 7:150–154.

Lebovics, Herman (1986). "The Uses of America in Locke's *Second Treatise of Government*." *Journal of the History of Ideas* 47(October/December): 567–581.

Leigh, Arthur E. (1974). "John Locke and the Quantity Theory of Money." *History of Political Economy* 6(Summer): 200–219.

Leites, Edmund (1979). "Locke's Liberal Theory of Parenthood." In *Having Children: Philosophical and Legal Reflections on Parenthood*. Ed. O. O'Neill and W. Ruddick. New York: Oxford University Press.

Lemas, Ramon M. (1975). "Locke's Theory of Property." *Interpretation* 5(Winter): 226–244.

———(1978). *Hobbes and Locke: Power and Consent*. Athens: University of Georgia Press.

Lence, Ross Marlo (1974). "The American Declaration of Independence: A Study of Its Polemical and Philosophical Antecedents." Ph.D. diss., Indiana University.

Letwin, William (1965). *The Origins of Scientific Economics*. Garden City, N.Y.: Doubleday.

Levin, M. (1971). "Uses of the Social Contract Method: Locke to Paine." Ph.D. diss., Leicester University.

Levy, Leonard W. (1960). *Legacy of Suppression: Freedom of Speech and Press in Early American History*. Cambridge, Mass.: Belknap Press of Harvard University Press.

———(1966). "Introduction." In *Freedom of the Press from Zenger to Jefferson: Early American Libertarian Theories*. Ed. Leonard W. Levy. American Heritage Series. Indianapolis: Bobbs-Merrill.

Lewis, Thomas J. (1975). "Environmental Case against Equality of Right." *Canadian Journal of Political Science* 8(June): 254–273.

Leyden, Wolfgang von (1954). "Introduction." In John Locke, *Essays on the Law of Nature*. Ed. W. von Leyden, 1–92. Oxford: Clarendon Press.

———(1956). "John Locke and Natural Law." *Philosophy* 31(January): 23–35.

———(1981). *Hobbes and Locke: The Politics of Freedom and Obligation*. London: Macmillan and the London School of Economics and Political Science.

Lomasky, Loren (1987). *Persons, Rights, and the Moral Community*. New York: Oxford University Press.

Lowenthal, David (1988). "Locke on Conquest." In *Understanding the Political Spirit*. Ed. Catherine H. Zuckert, 126–135. New Haven, Conn.: Yale University Press.

Lundgren, Gerald George (1976). "Justice and the Social Contract: An Interpretation and Reconstruction of the Concept of Justice in John Locke's Political Philosophy." Ph.D. diss., Pennsylvania State University.

Mabbott, John David (1973). *John Locke*. Philosophers in Perspective. London: Macmillan.

McCoy, Drew R. (1980). *The Elusive Republic: Political Economy in Jeffersonian America*. Chapel Hill: University of North Carolina Press.

McDonald, Forrest (1976). *The Presidency of Thomas Jefferson*. Lawrence: University Press of Kansas.

MacDonald, H. Malcolm (1987). "Ashcraft, Revolutionary Politics and Locke's *Two Treatises of Government*" *Social Science Quarterly* 68(December): 906.

McDonald, Virginia (1973). "A Guide to the Interpretation of Locke as Political Theorist." *Canadian Journal of Political Science* 6(December): 602–623.

———(1975). "A Model of Normative Discourse for Liberal-Democratic Man: Another Look at In/Out Relation." *Canadian Journal of Political Science* 8(September): 381–402.

Mace, George (1979). *Hobbes and the Federalist Papers: An Essay on the Genesis of the American Political Heritage*. Carbondale: Southern Illinois University Press.

Machan, Tibor (1975). *Human Rights and Human Liberties*. Chicago: Nelson Hall.

MacIntyre, Alisdair (1984). *After Virtue*. Notre Dame, Ind.: University of Notre Dame Press.

Mack, Eric (1980). "Locke's Arguments for Natural Rights." *Southwestern Journal of Philosophy* 11(Spring): 51–60.

McKinney, Daphne Georgina (1979). "Locke's Concept of Natural Law." Ph.D. diss., City University of New York.

McNally, D. (1989). "Locke, Levellers and Liberty: Property and Democracy in the First Whigs." *History of Political Thought* 10(Spring): 17–40.

Macpherson, C. Brough (1951). "Locke on Capitalist Appropriation." *Western Political Quarterly* 4 (December): 550–566.

———(1954). "The Social Bearing of Locke's Political Theory." *Western Political Quarterly* 7:1–22.

———(1962). *The Political Theory of Possessive Individualism: Hobbes to Locke*. Oxford: Clarendon Press.

———(1967). "Natural Rights in Hobbes and Locke." In *Political Thought and the Rights of Man*. Ed. D. D. Raphael, 1–15. London: Macmillan.

Maddox, William S., and Stuart A. Lilie (1984). *Beyond Liberal and Conservative*. Washington, D.C.: Cato Institution.

Malekin, Peter (1981). "Liberty and Order, the Wider Spectrum: Filmer, Hobbes, the Putney Debates, Locke." In *Liberty and Love*, 66–76. New York: St. Martin's Press.

Mansfield, Harvey C., Jr. (1979). "On the Political Character of Property in Locke." In *Powers, Possessions and Freedom: Essays in Honor of C. B. Macpherson*. Ed. Alkis Kontos, 23–28. Toronto: University of Toronto Press.

Marini, Frank (1969). "John Locke and the Revision of Classical Democratic Theory." *Western Political Quarterly* 22(March): 5–18.

Marshall, Paul (1979). "John Locke: Between God and Mammon." *Canadian Journal of Political Science* 12(March): 73–96.

Marx, Karl (1906). *Capital*. Vol. 1. Chicago: Charles H. Kerr Co.

———(no date). *The Poverty of Philosophy*. Moscow: Foreign Languages Publishing House.

Marx, Karl, and Friedrich Engels (1978). *Marx Engels Reader*. 2d ed., ed. Robert Tucker. New York: Norton.

Masters, Roger D. (1967). "The Lockean Tradition in American Foreign Policy." *Journal of International Affairs* 21(November): 250–277.

Mautner, Thomas (1982). "Locke on Original Appropriation." *American Philosophical Quarterly* 19(July): 259–270.

Meek, Ronald L. (1976). *Social Science and the Ignoble Savage*. Cambridge: Cambridge University Press.

Menake, George T. (1981). "A Research Note and Query on the Dating of Locke's *Two Treatises*." *Political Theory* 9(November): 547–548.

———(1982). "Research Note and Query on the Dating of Locke's *Two Treatises*. A Sequel." *Political Theory*. 10(November): 609–611.

Menger, Carl (1871/1981). *Principles of Economics*. New York: New York University Press.

Milam, Max (1967). "The Epistemological Basis of Locke's Idea of Property." *Western Political Quarterly* 20(March): 16–30.

Miller, John (1973). *Popery and Politics in England, 1660–1688*. Cambridge: Cambridge University Press.

Montgomery, David (1972). "The Shuttle and the Cross: Weavers and Artisans in the Kensington Riots of 1844." *Journal of Social History* 5:441–446.

Moore-Russell, Martha Elizabeth (1978). "The Philosopher and Society: John Locke and the English Revolution." *Journal of the History of the Behavioral Sciences* 14(January): 65–72.

Moulds, Henry (1961). "John Locke's Four Freedoms Seen in a New Light." *Ethics* 71(January): 121–126.

———(1964). "Private Property in John Locke's State of Nature." *American Journal of Economics and Sociology* 23(April): 179–188.

———(1965). "John Locke and Rugged Individualism." *American Journal of Economics and Sociology* 24(January): 97–109.

Murphy, Jeffrie G. (1969). "A Paradox in Locke's Theory of Natural Rights." *Dialogue* 8(September): 256–271.

Murrin, John M. (1980). "The Great Inversion, or Court versus Country: A Comparison of the Revolutionary Settlements in England (1688–1721) and America (1776–1816)." In *Three British Revolutions: 1641, 1688, 1776.* Ed. J. G. A. Pocock, 368–453. Princeton, N.J.: Princeton University Press.

Nash, A. E. Keir (1971). "Going beyond Locke? Influencing American Population Growth." *Milbank Memorial Fund Quarterly* 49(January): 7–31.

Natanson, Harvey B. (1970). "Locke and Hume: Bearings on the Legal Obligation of the Negro." *Journal of Value Inquiry* 5(Winter): 35–43.

Nelson, J. M. (1978). "Unlocking Locke's Legacy: A Comment." *Political Studies* 26 (June): 241–256.

Neuhaus, Richard John (1986). *The Naked Public Square: Religion and Democracy in America.* 2d ed. Grand Rapids, Mich.: William Erdmans.

Newman, Stephen L. (1984). *Liberalism at Wits' End: The Libertarian Revolt against the Modern State.* Ithaca, N.Y.: Cornell University Press.

———(1989). "Libertarianism and the Divided Mind of the American Right." *Polity* 22(Fall): 75–96.

New York Times (1988). Gallup Poll data. 10 January, E35.

Nozick, Robert (1974). *Anarchy, State and Utopia.* New York: Basic Books.

Oakley, Francis, and Elliot Urdang (1966). "Locke, Natural Law, and God." *Natural Law Forum* 2:92–109.

O'Conner, D. J. (1964). "Locke." In *A Critical History of Western Philosophy,* 204–219. New York: Macmillan, Free Press.

———(1967). *John Locke.* New York: Dover Publications.

O'Hara, John Bryant (1963). "John Locke's Philosophy of Discourse." Ph.D. diss., University of Oklahoma. See *Dissertation Abstracts International* 23 (1964):2625.

Olivecrona, Karl (1974a). "Appropriation in the State of Nature: Locke on the Origin of Property." *Journal of the History of Ideas* 5(April/June): 211–230.

———(1974b). "Locke's Theory of Appropriation." *Philosophical Quarterly* 24(July): 220–234.

———(1975a). "An Insertion in Para. 25 of the *Second Treatise of Government.*" *Locke Newsletter* 6:63–66.

———(1975b). "The Term 'Property' in Locke's *Two Treatises of Government.*" *Archiv für Rechts- und Sozialphilosophie* 61, no. 1:109–115.

Pagden, Anthony, ed. (1987). *The Language of Political Theory in Early-Modern Europe.* Cambridge: Cambridge University Press.

Pangle, Thomas (1988). *The Spirit of Modern Republicanism: The Moral Vision of the American Founders and the Philosophy of Locke.* Chicago: University of Chicago Press.

Parry, Geraint (1964). "Individuality, Politics and the Critique of Paternalism in John Locke." *Political Studies* 12(June): 163–177.

———(1978). *John Locke.* London: Allen & Unwin.

————(1982). "Locke on Representation in Politics." *History of European Ideas* 3, no. 4:403–414.

Parsons, J. E. (1965). "Locke's Doctrine of Natural Law." Ph.D. diss., London University (external).

————(1969). "Locke's Doctrine of Property." *Social Research* 36(Autumn): 389–411.

Pateman, Carole (1975). "Sublimation and Reification: Locke, Wolin and the Liberal Democratic Conception of the Political." *Politics and Society* 5(August): 441–467.

Paul, Ellen Frankel (1978). "On the Theory of the Social Contract within the Natural Rights Tradition." *Personalist* 59(January): 9–21.

Paul, Jeffrey, and Ellen Frankel Paul (1980). "Locke's Usufructuary Theory of Self-Ownership." *Pacific Philosophical Quarterly* 61(October): 384–395.

Peters, Richard S. (1964). "Locke." In *Western Political Philosophers*. Ed. M. Cranston, 53–64. London: Bodley Head.

Pitkin, Hanna (1965). "Obligation and Consent." *American Political Science Review* 59(December): 990–999.

————(1966). "Obligation and Consent." *American Political Science Review* 60(March): 39–52.

Plamenatz, John P. (1963). "Locke." In *Man and Society*, 1:209–256. London: Longmans.

Pocock, J. G. A. (1957). *The Ancient Constitution and the Feudal Law: A Study of English Historical Thought in the Seventeenth Century*. Cambridge: Cambridge University Press.

————(1971a). "Civic Humanism and Its Role in Anglo-American Thought." Rep. in J. G. A. Pocock, *Politics, Language and Time: Essays in Political Thought and History*, 80–103. New York: Atheneum.

————(1971b). "Machiavelli, Harrington and English Political Ideologies in the Eighteenth Century." In J. G. A. Pocock, *Politics, Language and Time: Essays in Political Thought and History*, 104–147. New York: Atheneum.

————(1971c). *Politics, Language and Time: Essays in Political Thought and History*. New York: Atheneum.

————(1972). "Virtue and Commerce in the Eighteenth Century." *Journal of Interdisciplinary History* 3:119–134.

————(1975a). "Early Modern Capitalism—the Augustan Perception." In *Feudalism, Capitalism, and Beyond*. Ed. Eugene Kamenka and R. S. Neale, 62–83. Canberra: Australian National University Press.

————(1975b). *The Machiavellian Moment: Florentine Political Thought and the Atlantic Republican Tradition*. Princeton, N.J.: Princeton University Press.

————(1977). "Historical Introduction." In *The Political Works of James Harrington*. Ed. J. G. A. Pocock. Cambridge: Cambridge University Press.

————(1979). "The Mobility of Property and the Rise of Eighteenth-Century Sociology." In *Theories of Property: Aristotle to the Present*. Ed. Anthony Parel and Thomas Flanagan, 141–166. Ottawa: Wilfrid Laurier University Press.

————, ed. (1980a). *Three British Revolutions: 1644, 1688, 1776*. Princeton, N.J.: Princeton University Press.

————(1980b). "The Myth of John Locke and the Obsession with Liberalism." In *John Locke: Papers Read at a Clark Library Seminar, 10 December 1977.* By J. G. A. Pocock and R. Ashcraft. Los Angeles: William Andrews Clark Memorial Library, University of California.

————(1983). "Cambridge Paradigms and Scotch Philosophers: A Study of the Relations between the Civil Humanist and the Civil Jurisprudential Interpretation of Eighteenth-Century Social Thought." In *Wealth and Virtue: The Shaping of Political Economy in the Scottish Enlightenment.* Ed. Istvan Hont and Michael Ignatieff, 235–252. Cambridge: Cambridge University Press.

————(1985). *Virtue, Commerce and History.* Cambridge: Cambridge University Press.

————(1987). *The Ancient Constitution and the Feudal Law: A Study of English Historical Thought in the Seventeenth Century. A Reissue with a Retrospective.* Cambridge: Cambridge University Press.

Polin, Raymond (1960). "Justice in Locke's Philosophy." *Nomos: Yearbook 6, Justice,* 262–283.

————(1967). "The Rights of Man in Hobbes and Locke." In *Political Theory and the Rights of Man.* Ed. D. D. Raphael, 16–26. London: Macmillan.

Pona, Gardner Dwinell (1971). "John Locke and Democratic Theory." Ph.D. diss., Johns Hopkins University.

Poole, Ross (1980). "Locke and the Bourgeois State." *Political Studies* 28(June): 222–237.

Post, David M. (1986). "Jeffersonian Revision of Locke: Education, Property Rights, and Liberty." *Journal of the History of Ideas* 47(January/March): 147–157.

Power, Susan (1981). "John Locke: Revolution, Resistance, or Opposition?" *Interpretation* 9(September): 229–244.

Preece, Rod (1980). "The Anglo-Saxon Conservative Tradition." *Canadian Journal of Political Science* 13(March): 3–32.

Prosch, Harry (1967). "Towards an Ethics of Civil Disobedience." *Ethics* 77(April): 176–192.

Pynn, Ronald Earl (1970). "The Influence of John Locke's Political Philosophy in American Political Tradition." Ph.D. diss., University of Michigan.

Rand, Ayn (1964). *The Virtue of Selfishness.* New York: New American Library.

Rapaczynski, Andrzej (1981). "Locke's Conception of Property and the Principle of Sufficient Reason." *Journal of the History of Ideas* 42(April/June): 305–315.

————(1987). *Nature and Politics: Liberalism in the Philosophies of Hobbes, Locke, and Rousseau.* Ithaca, N.Y.: Cornell University Press.

Rauch, Leo (1981). "Locke: The Individual as Atom." In *The Political Animal: Studies in Political Philosophy from Machiavelli to Marx,* 55–82. Amherst: University of Massachusetts Press.

Rea, Bruno (1987). "John Locke: Between Charity and Welfare Rights." *Journal of Social Philosophy* 18(Fall): 13–26.

Realey, Charles Rechdolt (1935). "*The London Journal* and Its Authors, 1720–1723." *Bulletin of the University of Kansas,* vol. 36, no. 23. *Humanistic Studies,* vol. 5, no. 3 (December).

Redpath, Theodore (1964). "John Locke and the Rhetoric of the Second Treatise." In *The English Mind: Studies in the English Moralists, Presented to Basil*

Willey. Ed. Hugh Davies and George Watson, 55–78. Cambridge: Cambridge University Press.

Redwood, John (1976). *Reason, Ridicule and Religion: The Age of Enlightenment in England, 1660—1750.* Cambridge, Mass.: Harvard University Press.

Resnick, David (1984). "Locke and the Rejection of the Ancient Constitution." *Political Theory* 12(February): 97–114.

——(1987). "John Locke and the Problem of Naturalization." *Review of Politics* 49(Summer): 368–388.

——(1989). "Religion, Politics and Rationality." Paper presented at the 1989 meeting of the Southern Political Science Association, November, Memphis, Tenn.

Reventlow, Henning Graf (1984). *The Authority of the Bible and the Rise of the Modern World.* Trans. John Bowden. London: SCM Press.

Richards, Judith, Lottie Mulligan, and John K. Graham (1981). "'Property' and 'People': Political Usages of Locke and Some Contemporaries." *Journal of the History of Ideas* 42(January/March): 29–51.

Riley, Patrick (1974). "On Finding an Equilibrium between Consent and Natural Law in Locke's Political Philosophy." *Political Studies* 22(December): 432–452.

——(1976). "Locke on 'Voluntary Agreement' and Political Power." *Western Political Quarterly* 29(March): 136–145.

——(1982). *Will and Political Authority.* Cambridge, Mass.: Harvard University Press.

Robbins, Caroline (1959). *The Eighteenth-Century Commonwealthman.* Cambridge, Mass.: Harvard University Press.

Robinson, Ivary Thomas (1976). "The Difference between John Locke's Theory of Property and Karl Marx's Theory of Value." Ph.D. diss., Harvard University.

Rorty, Richard (1984). *Philosophy in History.* Ed. J. B. Schneewind and Quentin Skinner. Cambridge: Cambridge University Press.

Rossiter, Clinton (1953). *Seedtime of the Republic.* New York: Harcourt, Brace.

Roth, R. I. (1988). "Locke on Ideas and the Intuition of the Self." *International Philosophical Quarterly* 28(June): 163–169.

Rothbard, Murray (1978). *For a New Liberty.* Rev. ed. New York: Collier Books.

Russell, Paul (1986). "Locke on Express and Tacit Consent: Misinterpretations and Inconsistencies." *Political Theory* 14(May): 291–306.

Ryan, Alan (1965). "Locke and the Dictatorship of the Bourgeoisie." *Political Studies* 13(June): 219–230.

——(1984). *Property and Political Theory.* Oxford: Basil Blackwell.

Sabine, George (1961). *A History of Political Theory.* 3d ed. New York: Holt, Rinehart, and Winston.

Salvadori, Massimo (1960). "Why Locke?" In *Locke and Liberty: Selections from the Works of John Locke,* ix–xl. London: Pall Mall Press.

Sandel, Michael J. (1982). *Liberalism and the Limits of Justice.* Cambridge: Cambridge University Press.

——(1984). "The Procedural Republic and the Unencumbered Self." *Political Theory* 12:81–96.

——(1987). "The Political Theory of the Procedural Republic." In *The Rule of Law: Ideal or Ideology.* Ed. A. Hutchison and P. Monahan. Toronto: Carwell.

———(1988). "Democrats and Community." *New Republic*, 22 February, 20–23.

Sarkar, Husain (1982). "The Lockean Proviso." *Canadian Journal of Philosophy* 12(March): 47–59.

Schochet, Gordon J., comp. (1971). *Life, Liberty, and Property: Essays on Locke's Political Ideas*. Belmont, Calif.: Wadsworth.

———(1975). *Patriarchalism in Political Thought*. New York: Basic Books.

———(1988). "Toleration, Revolution, and Judgment in the Development of Locke's Political Thought." *Political Science* 40:84–96.

———(1989). "Radical Politics and Ashcraft's Treatise on Locke." *Journal of the History of Ideas* 50(July): 491–510.

Schouls, Peter (1988). "Locke and the Dogma of Infallible Reason." *Review of International Philosophy* 42:115–132.

Schwarzenbach, Sibyl (1988). "Locke's Two Conceptions of Property." *Social Theory and Practice* 14(Summer): 141–172.

Schwoerer, Lois G. (1990). "Locke, Lockean Ideas, and the Glorious Revolution." *Journal of the History of Ideas* 51(October/December): 531–548.

Seaman, John W. (1978). "Unlimited Acquisition and Equality of Right: A Reply to Professor Lewis." *Canadian Journal of Political Science* 11(June): 401–408.

Seliger, Martin (1963a). "Locke's Natural Law and the Foundation of Politics." *Journal of the History of Ideas* 24(July/September): 337–354.

———(1963b). "Locke's Theory of Revolutionary Action." *Western Political Quarterly* 16(September): 548–568.

———(1968). *The Liberal Politics of John Locke*. London: Allen & Unwin.

———(1971). "Locke and Marcuse—Intermittent and Millennial Revolutionism." In *Festschrift für Karl Loewenstein*. Ed. Henry Steele Commager et al., 427–457. Tübingen: J. C. B. Mohr.

Shalhope, Robert (1972). "Toward a Republican Synthesis: The Emergence of an Understanding of Republicanism in American Historiography." *William and Mary Quarterly*, 3d ser., 29:49–80.

———(1982). "Republicanism and Early American Historiography." *William and Mary Quarterly*, 3d ser., 39:334–356.

Shapiro, Barbara J. (1974). "Latitudinarianism and Science in Seventeenth-Century England." In *The Intellectual Revolution of the Seventeenth Century*. Ed. Charles Webster. London: Routledge and Kegan Paul.

Shapiro, Ian (1986). *The Evolution of Rights in Liberal Theory*. Cambridge: Cambridge University Press.

———(1990). "J. G. A. Pocock's Republicanism and Political Theory: A Critique and Reinterpretation." *Critical Review* 4(Summer): 433–472.

Shaw, Stewart Arnold (1967). "Locke's Concept of Power." Ph.D. diss., Columbia University.

Siebert, Frederick S. (1952). *Freedom of the Press in England, 1476–1776*. Urbana: University of Illinois Press.

Simmons, A. John (1976). "Tacit Consent and Political Obligation." *Philosophy and Public Affairs* 5(Spring): 274–291.

Simon, W. M. (1951). "John Locke, Philosophy and Political Theory." *American Political Science Review* 55(June): 386–399.

Simpson, John H. (1983). "Moral Issues and Status Politics." In *The New Christian Right*. Ed. R. Liebman and R. Wuthnow, 188–207. New York: Aldine.

Singh, Raghuveer (1961). "John Locke and the Theory of Natural Law." *Political Studies* 9(June): 105–118.

Skinner, Quentin (1978). *The Foundations of Modern Political Theory*. 2 vols. Cambridge: Cambridge University Press.

———(1988). *Meaning and Context: Quentin Skinner and His Critics*. Ed. James Tully. Princeton, N.J.: Princeton University Press.

Smith, Adam (1776/1981). *An Inquiry into the Origin and Causes of the Wealth of Nations*. 2 vols. Indianapolis: Liberty Classics.

Snare, Frank (1975). "Consent and Conventional Acts in John Locke." *Journal of the History of Philosophy* 13(January): 27–36.

Snow, Vernon F. (1962). "The Concept of Revolution in Seventeenth-Century England." *Historical Journal* 5:167–174.

Snyder, D. C. (1986). "Locke and Natural Law and Property Rights." *Canadian Journal of Philosophy* 16(December): 723–750.

———(1988). "John Locke and the Freedom of Belief." *Journal of Church and State* 30(Spring): 227–243.

Soles, D. E. (1987). "Intellectualism and Natural Law in Locke's *Second Treatise*." *History of Political Thought* 8(Spring): 63–81.

Sparks, A. W. (1973). "Trust and Teleology: Locke's Politics and His Doctrine of Creation." *Canadian Journal of Philosophy* 3(December): 263–273.

Speck, W. A. (1979). *Stability and Strife: England, 1714–1760*. Cambridge, Mass.: Harvard University Press.

Sperling, John G. (1962). *The South Sea Company: An Historical Essay and Bibliographical Finding List*. Boston: Baker Library, Harvard Graduate School of Business Administration.

Squadrito, Kathleen M. (1979). *John Locke*. Boston: Twayne Publishing Co.

Steinberg, Jules (1978). *Locke, Rousseau and the Idea of Consent: An Inquiry into the Liberal-Democratic Theory of Political Obligation*. "Contributions in Political Science," no. 6. Westport, Conn.: Greenwood Press.

Stephen, Leslie (1962). *History of English Thought in the Eighteenth Century*. Preface by Crane Brinton. New York: Harbinger Books.

Stewart, Carole (1986). "John Coleman, *John Locke's Moral Philosophy*." *Journal of the History of Philosophy* 24(January): 127–129.

Stewart, M. A. (1986). "John Dunn, *Locke*; R. S. Wollhouse, *Locke*; Neal Wood, *The Politics of Locke's Philosophy*." *Journal of the History of Philosophy* 24(April): 273–275.

Stillman, Peter G. (1974). "Hegel's Critique of Liberal Theories of Rights." *American Political Science Review* 68(September): 1086–1092.

Straka, G. (1962a). *The Anglican Reaction to the Revolution of 1688*. Madison: University of Wisconsin Press.

———(1962b). "The Final Phase of Divine Right Theory in England, 1688–1702." *English Historical Review* 77.

Strauss, Leo (1953). *Natural Right and History*. Chicago: University of Chicago Press.

———(1959). *What Is Political Philosophy?* New York: Free Press.

Suits, David B. (1977). "On Locke's Argument for Government." *Journal of Libertarian Studies* 1(Summer): 195–203.

Sullivan, William (1982). *Reconstructing Public Philosophy*. Berkeley: University of California Press.

Tarcov, Nathan (1981). "Locke's *Second Treatise* and 'The Best Fence against Rebellion.'" *Review of Politics* 43(April): 198–217.

———(1983). "A 'Non-Lockean' Locke and the Character of Liberalism." In *Liberalism Reconsidered*. Ed. D. MacLean and C. Mills. Totowa, N.J.: Rowman and Allanheld.

———(1984). *Locke's Education for Liberty*. Chicago: University of Chicago Press.

———(1988). "The Spirit of Liberty and Early American Foreign Policy." In *The Political Spirit*. Ed. Catherine H. Zuckert, 136–152. New Haven, Conn.: Yale University Press.

Tarlton, Charles D. (1978). "A Rope of Sand: Interpreting Locke's *First Treatise of Government*." *Historical Journal* 21(March): 43–73.

———(1981). "The Exclusion Controversy, Pamphleteering and Locke's *Two Treatises*." *Historical Journal* 24(March): 49–68.

———(1985). "'The Rulers Now on Earth': Locke's *Two Treatises* and the Revolution of 1688." *Historical Journal* 28(June): 279–298.

———(1988). "Ashcraft, Revolutionary Politics and Locke's *Two Treatises of Government*." *Political Theory* 16(May): 335–339.

Taylor, Charles (1985). "Atomism." In his *Philosophical Papers*. Vol. 2. Cambridge: Cambridge University Press.

Thompson, Martyn P. (1976). "The Reception of Locke's *Two Treatises of Government*, 1690-1705." *Political Studies* 24(June): 183–191.

———(1977a). "Hume's Critique of Locke and the 'Original Contract.'" *Pensiero Politico* 10, no. 2:189–201.

———(1977b). "The Idea of Conquest in Controversies over the 1688 Revolution." *Journal of the History of Ideas* 38(January–March): 33–46.

———(1980). "Reception and Influence: A Reply to Nelson on Locke's *Two Treatises of Government*." *Political Studies* 28(March): 100–108.

———(1987). *Ideas of Contract in English Political Thought in the Age of John Locke*. New York: Garland Publishing.

———(1988). "Significant Silences in Locke's *Two Treatises of Government*: Constitutional History, Contract and Law." *Historical Journal* 31(June): 275–294.

Tocqueville, Alexis de (1969). *Democracy in America*. Trans. George Lawrence, ed. J. P. Meyer. Garden City, N.Y.: Doubleday.

Trenchard, John, and Thomas Gordon (1969). *Cato's Letters; or, Essays on Liberty, Civil and Religious, and Other Important Subjects*. 4 volumes in 2; 3d ed., carefully corrected. London, 1733; facsimile edition. New York: Russell and Russell.

Tuck, Richard (1974). "'Power' and 'Authority' in Seventeenth-Century England." *Historical Journal* 17(March): 43–61.

———(1979). *Natural Rights Theories: Their Origin and Development*. Cambridge: Cambridge University Press.

Tully, James H. (1978). "John Locke's Writings on Property in the Seventeenth-Century Intellectual Context." Ph.D. diss., Cambridge University.

———(1979). "The Framework of Natural Rights in Locke's Analysis of Property: A Contextual Reconstruction." In *Theories of Property, Aristotle to the Present*. Ed. Anthony Parel and Thomas Hanagan, 115–138. Calgary Institute for the Humanities. Waterloo, Ontario: Wilfrid Laurier Press.

————(1980). *A Discourse on Property: John Locke and His Adversaries*. Cambridge: Cambridge University Press.

————(1981). "Current Thinking about Sixteenth- and Seventeenth-Century Political Theory." *Historical Journal* 24(June): 475–484.

Tuveson, Ernest Less (1968). *Redeemer Nation: The Idea of America's Millennial Role*. Chicago: University of Chicago Press.

————(1974). *The Imagination as a Means of Grace: Locke and the Aesthetics of Romanticism*. New York: Gordian Press.

Vaughn, Karen Marie Iversen (1971). "An Examination of the Economic Theories of John Locke." Ph.D. diss., Duke University.

————(1978). "John Locke and the Labor Theory of Value." *Journal of Libertarian Studies*, vol. 2, no. 4:311–326.

————(1980). *John Locke, Economist and Social Scientist*. Chicago: University of Chicago Press.

————(1982). Review of "*A Discourse on Property*." *History of Political Economy*, vol. 14, no. 39(Fall): 441–444.

Viner, Jacob (1963). "Possessive Individualism as Original Sin." *The Canadian Journal of Economics and Political Science*.

Waggoner, Jennings L., Jr. (1971). "The Dilemma of Civil Disobedience in a Lockean Perspective." *Journal of Thought* 6(January): 49–57.

Wainwright, William J. (1967). "Natural Rights." *American Philosophical Quarterly* 4(January): 79–84.

Waldmann, M. (1957). "A Note on John Locke's Theory of Consent." *Ethics* 68(October): 45–50.

Waldron, Jeremy J. (1981). "Locke's Account of Inheritance and Bequest." *Journal of the History of Philosophy* 19(January): 39–51.

————(1984). "Locke, Tully and the Regulation of Property." *Political Studies* 32(March): 98–106.

————(1989). "John Locke—Social Contract versus Political Anthropology." *Review of Politics*, vol. 51, no. 1(Winter): 3–28.

Wallace, John M. (1980). "The Date of Sir Robert Filmer's 'Patriarcha.'" *Historical Journal* 23(August): 1155–1165.

Walzer, Michael (1983). *Spheres of Justice*. New York: Basic Books.

————(1984). "Liberalism and the Act of Separation." *Political Theory* 12(August): 315–330.

Weale, Albert (1978). "Consent." *Political Studies* 26(March): 65–77.

Weber, Max (1946). *From Max Weber: Essays in Sociology*. Ed. H. H. Gerth and C. Wright Mills. New York: Oxford University Press.

————(1968). *Economy and Society*. New York: Bedminster Press.

Weston, Corinne Comstock, and Janelle Renfrow Greenburg (1981). *Subjects and Sovereigns: The Grand Controversy over Legal Sovereignty in Stuart England*. Cambridge: Cambridge University Press.

Weymark, John A. (1980). "Money and Locke's Theory of Property." *History of Political Economy* 12(Summer): 282–290.

White, Christopher Joseph (1980). "John Locke's Moral Justification for Economic Individualism." Ph.D. diss., Purdue University.

Wilson, Ian M. (1969). "The Influence of Hobbes and Locke in the Shaping of the Concept of Sovereignty in French Political Thought." Ph.D. diss., Oxford University.

————(1973). *The Influence of Hobbes and Locke in the Shaping of the Concept of Sovereignty in Eighteenth-Century France. Studies on Voltaire and the Eighteenth Century.* Vol. 101. Banbury, Oxon.: Voltaire Foundation.

Winch, Donald (1978). *Adam Smith's Politics: An Essay in Historiographical Revision.* Cambridge: Cambridge University Press.

Windstrup, George (1982). "Freedom and Authority: The Ancient Faith of Locke's *Letter on Toleration.*" *Review of Politics* 44(April): 242–265.

Winfrey, John C. (1981). "Charity versus Justice in Locke's Theory of Property." *Journal of the History of Ideas* 42(July/September): 423–438.

Wolff, Robert Paul (1977/1981). "Robert Nozick's Derivation of the Minimal State." *Arizona Law Review* 7 (1977). Reprinted in *Reading Nozick.* Ed. J. Paul. Totowa, N.J.: Rowman and Littlefield.

Wolin, Sheldon (1960). *Politics and Vision.* Boston: Little, Brown.

Wood, Gordon S. (1969). *The Creation of the American Republic, 1776–1787.* New York: W. W. Norton.

————(1991). "The Virtues and the Interests." *New Republic,* 11 February, 32–35.

Wood, Neal (1983). *The Politics of Locke's Philosophy: A Social Study of "An Essay Concerning Human Understanding."* Berkeley and Los Angeles: University of California Press.

————(1984). *John Locke and Agrarian Capitalism.* Berkeley and Los Angeles: University of California Press.

Woolhouse, R. S. (1983). *Locke.* Minneapolis: University of Minnesota Press.

Yolton, Jean S., and John W. Yolton (1985). *John Locke: A Reference Guide.* Boston: G. K. Hall.

Yolton, John W. (1956). *John Locke and the Way of Ideas.* Oxford: Clarendon Press.

————,ed. (1969). *John Locke: Problems and Perspectives: A Collection of New Essays.* Cambridge: Cambridge University Press.

————(1985a). *Locke: An Introduction.* Oxford: Basil Blackwell.

————(1985b). "Tarcov: Locke's Education for Liberty." *Political Theory* 13(November): 638–643.

————(1987). "French Materialist Disciples of Locke." *Journal of the History of Philosophy* 25(January): 83–104.

————(1988). "Locke and Materialism: The French Connection." *Review of International Philosophy* 42:229–253.

Zuckert, Michael P. (1974). "The Garden Died: An Interpretation of Locke's First Treatise." Ph.D. diss., University of Chicago.

————(1979). "An Introduction to Locke's *First Treatise.*" *Interpretation* 8(January): 58–74.

————(1986). "John Locke and the Problem of Civil Religion." In *The Moral Foundation of the American Republic.* Ed. Robert Horwitz. 3d (enlarged) ed. Charlottesville: University Press of Virginia.

Zvesper, John (1984). "The Utility of Consent in John Locke's Philosophy." *Political Studies* 32(March): 55–67.

About the Contributors

RICHARD ASHCRAFT is professor of political science at the University of California at Los Angeles. He has been a visiting professor at the University of Edinburgh, an academic visitor at the London School of Economics, and a visiting fellow of All Souls College, Oxford. Among his most recent contributions are *Locke's Two Treatises of Government* (1987) and *Revolutionary Politics and Locke's Two Treatises of Government* (1986). He is currently working on a study of John Stuart Mill and the Victorian working class.

ELDON EISENACH is chair and associate professor in the Political Science Department at the University of Tulsa. He has taught at Pennsylvania State University, Cornell University, and the University of Arkansas at Little Rock. He has been a Woodrow Wilson fellow, a National Endowment for the Humanities faculty fellow, and a visiting research fellow at the University of Exeter. He has published articles on English liberalism and is the author of *Two Worlds of Liberalism: Religion and Politics in Hobbes, Locke, and Mill* (1981). His current research focuses on American political thought and John Stuart Mill.

RONALD HAMOWY is professor of history at the University of Alberta and has taught at Brooklyn College, Stanford University, and Simon Fraser. He has published works on modern political and economic thought and on contemporary policy issues. He is currently working on an edition of *Cato's Letters* for Liberty Classics.

EDWARD J. HARPHAM is associate professor of government and political economy at the University of Texas at Dallas. He has been a fellow at the Institute for Humane Studies and has taught at the University of Houston. He has edited books on public policy issues, has coauthored a book on the history of political science, and has written articles on liberalism and the history of political economy and on the development of the welfare state in America. He is currently working on a study of the politics of Adam Smith.

STEPHEN NEWMAN is associate professor of political science at York University. He has also taught at Ripon College. He has written on the liberal tradition in Britain and America and is the author of *Liberalism at Wit's End: The Libertarian Revolt against the Modern State* (1984).

DAVID RESNICK is associate professor of political science at the University of Cincinnati. He has taught at Cornell University and has been a summer research fellow at the Institute for Humane Studies. He has published essays on John Locke, Karl Marx, and contemporary politics in America. He is currently working on a study of Locke's social and political thought.

KAREN IVERSEN VAUGHN is professor of economics at George Mason University and was chair of the Department of Economics for a number of years. She has taught at Queens College and the University of Tennessee at Knoxville. She is the author of *John Locke: Economist and Social Scientist* (1980). Her current research is in the history of economic thought and in the Modern Austrian School of Economics.

Index